A PROCESSION OF LANCASHIRE MARTYRS

AND CONFESSORS

A Procession of

Lancashire Martyrs

and Confessors

by

JOHN A. MYERSCOUGH, S.J.

Glasgow:
JOHN S. BURNS & SONS
195 Buccleuch Street, C.3

IMPRIMI POTEST: DESMOND BOYLE, S.J.,
PROVINCIALIS ANGLIAE.
DIE XXII APRILIS, MCMLVII.

IMPRIMATUR: † DONALDUS A. CAMPBELL,
ARCHIEPISCOPUS GLASGUENSIS.
DIE 12a MARTII, 1958.

First Published: April, 1958

Printed in Scotland

PREFACE

This little book is written for the Catholics of Lancashire who are unable to secure the larger and more scholarly works on the English Martyrs. Its main purpose is to edify by presenting a simple historical survey or panorama from the words of the martyrs themselves or from those of their contemporaries.

The chapters of this little pageant are stories in themselves and follow each other in chronological order. Many readers will be able to trace out for themselves the via dolorosa, along which the prisoners for the Faith wended their way to Lancaster Castle across the Ribble at Walton-le-Dale and on to the moors on the north bank. Through Preston they would pass near or possibly over the site of the present spacious church of the English Martyrs.

Many thanks are tendered to the Rev. Father T. Mulvany, S.J., of St. Wilfrid's, Preston, for correcting the first drafts of the MS. and for valuable information of local interest, and to the Rev. Father L. Cardwell, S.J., of St. Beuno's College, for securing for the writer books and documents otherwise inaccessible.

Occasion is also taken here to thank the Rev. Father L. O'Hea, S.J., the Rector of St. Beuno's College, for preparing the MS. for the press and reading the final proofs.

J. A. MYERSCOUGH, S.J.

ST. BEUNO'S COLLEGE,
ST. ASAPH,
FLINTS.
July 10, 1957.

CONTENTS

CHAPTER 1

THE GATHERING CLOUDS

I N the sixteenth century East Anglia and the north-eastern
counties, apart from the Midlands and the London
districts, were more thickly populated than those of the north-
west. Nevertheless, the Catholic resistance to the Tudor
Elizabethan religious settlement and the steadfast adherence
to the ancient Faith in Lancashire, present a striking and
thrilling chapter in the history of the English Martyrs.

This same steadfastness was manifested in the reign of
Henry VIII at the time of the suppression of the monasteries
and religious houses. The Pilgrimage of Grace, led by Robert
Aske, and the earlier Lincolnshire risings sufficiently testify
that the attack on these religious institutions was rightly
judged by the masses of the commoners to be an attack upon
themselves, as well as an attack upon their faith and convic-
tions. In their hundreds and thousands the commoners
suffered with the persecuted and expelled monks and nuns.
The suppression of the monasteries was the suppression of
the homesteads.

The commissioners appointed by Henry VIII to inquire
into the morality of the religious houses and monasteries by
royal command were placed under the direction of Thomas
Cromwell, himself no exemplar of Christian morals. Robert
Aske and his associates deemed it possible that the King
himself would be a better man if he could be rescued from
bad counsellors. In their initial visitations these commissioners were to deal gently at first and to try peaceful

persuasion, and, if that would not serve, gradually to apply pressure until the slaughter of abbots and selected monks and religious ensued.

By far the worst immorality rampant in any of the religious establishments at the time was the presence in them and forced upon them of Thomas Cromwell's commissioners. After billeting themselves on the monastic establishments at the cost of the community, the commissioners proceeded as follows:

" (1) The superior and his monks, the tenants, servants and neighbours were subjected to a minute and rigorous examination: each was exhorted, was commanded, to accuse the other; and every groundless tale, every malicious insinuation, was carefully collected and recorded.

" (2) The commissioners called for the accounts of the house, compared the expenditure with the receipts, scrutinized every article with an eye of suspicion and hostility, and required the production of all the money, plate and jewels.

" (3) They proceeded to search the library and private rooms for papers and books; and the discovery of any opinion or treatise in favour of the papal supremacy, or of the validity of Henry's first marriage (with Katharine of Aragon), was taken as a sufficient proof of adhesion to the king's enemies, and of disobedience to the statutes of the realm." (*History of England*, Dr. Lingard, Vol. V, p. 94.)

In the same reference Dr. Lingard adds a very significant footnote: The above " transactions are thus described by Catharine Bulkeley, Abbess of Godstow, in a letter to Cromwell: ' Dr. London has suddenly forced his way into my premises accompanied by a rout of followers, and threatens myself and the sisterhood, stating that he has the king's commission to suppress this house in spite of my teeth. When I made it plain to him that I would never surrender to his hand, being an old enemy, now he begins to entreat me, and inveigle my sisters one by one, in a manner otherwise than I have ever known any of the king's subjects to be so handled; and here he tarries and continues to tarry to my great cost and charge, and will not take my answer, that I will not surrender, till I know the king's gracious commandment, or your lordship's . . . And notwithstanding, that Dr. London, like an untrewe man, has informed your lordship that I am a spoiler and a waster, your lordship shall know that the contrary is true; for I have not alienated one halfpennyworth of the goods of this monastery movable or immovable.'

" Of this Dr. London, Fuller says, ' He was no great saint; for afterwards he was publicly convicted of perjury, and adjudged to ride with his face to the horse-tail at Windsor and Ockingham '(p. 314): to which may be added that he was also ' condemned to do public penance at Oxford for incontinency with two women, the mother and daughter ' (Strype, i. 377.)" (Ibid.)

Catharine Bulkeley was most likely Thomas Cromwell's appointment to replace an abbess who had resisted. Catharine conformed later and in view of this her complaints have all the more force. At any rate, they throw into stronger relief the determined resistance of the many religious superiors who remained steadfast at the time. Catharine Bulkeley, reconciled to the Holy See, retired to her home at Cheadle. She built the chancel of Cheadle church and glazed the window in 1556. There she lived a holy life, dying on 13th February, 1559, fortified with the rites of Holy Church. Lancashire examples of this steadfast fidelity were the Abbot of Whalley, John Paslew, two of his selected monks, William Haydock of Cottam and John Eastgate, and the Abbot of Sawley, William Trafford. These were all tried and condemned to death at Lancaster, and William Trafford, John Paslew and John Eastgate were executed apparently at Lancaster on the 10th

March, 1537, but the bodies of Paslew and Eastgate were taken back to Whalley and hanged outside the abbey on 12th March. There is a tradition that the two latter were actually executed at Whalley on that date. It is certain that William Haydock was executed the next day, 13th March, in a field nearby at Padiham Green. The rest of the monks were evicted for the most part and the tenants and dependants were driven from their homes to live like tinkers in the wilds of Pendle.

After the passing of the Act of Uniformity, 1559, in Elizabeth Tudor's first Parliament, when conformity to the State church along with the oath of supremacy was imposed by law, the Catholic hierarchy with one exception refused submission and suffered deprivation, imprisonment and exile. The State bishops appointed to the vacated sees were authorised and enjoined to make a visitation of their dioceses in order to report on the obedience of their subjects and subordinates to the new religious legislation. In connection with Lancashire, the reports of the " visitors " expressed almost complete dissatisfaction not only with priests and people but with those of the churchwardens who, although outwardly conformed, were aiding and abetting the recalcitrant Papists. Ralph Lynney, the old vicar of Blackburn who had retired on a pension before the death of Mary Tudor, had managed to secure through the churchwardens as far back as the reign of Edward VI, some legal security for his chalices and Mass vestments. He was typical of the recusant Lancashire clergy, and his immediate successor, James Hargreaves, who was " instituted " vicar of Blackburn, 24th October, 1555, was deprived for his resistance and was reported as being still in the district in 1575, as an " obstinate recusant." (Cf. Extracts from Abram's *History of Blackburn,* cited at end of the chapter.) Apparently both priests were harbouring " ousted " recusant priests from Durham who were opening schools for Catholic youth in the neighbourhood.

" The Catholics of Preston were staunch recusants in 1583, as appears from the State papers:

" ' Truly the Papists in these parts are lately grown so stubborn and contemptuous that in my opinion it were requisite their lordships did write a very earnest letter to my good lord, the Earl of Derby, myself, and the rest of her Majesty's Commissioners for Causes Ecclesiastical, to keep some sessions about Preston, Wigan and Prescott, where the people are most obstinate and contemptuous, and to deal severely and roundly with them, otherwise there can be no reformation (for the temporal magistrates will do nothing), neither can the country long continue in quiet and safety.' " (Extract from a letter of the State Bishop of Chester to the Privy Council. *Foley's Records, S.J.* Vol. 5, p. 392, footnote.)

At the accession of Elizabeth Tudor, the See of Canterbury was vacant by the death of Cardinal Pole, so that the Archbishop of York, Dr. Nicholas Heath, led the episcopal resistance to the State Protestant legislation. In this he was unswervingly supported by the last Benedictine Abbot of Westminster, the saintly John Feckenham. Such religious establishments as had been recalled from exile and restored during the short reign of Mary Tudor, resisted for the most part along with the hierarchy, with the result that the monks of Westminster Abbey, the Dominicans of Blackfriars, the Franciscans, the Brigittines and other religious institutes of men and women were deprived of their conventual residences and driven into exile, some years before the penal laws were well launched, and before the bulk of the people were wholly aware of what was happening. Many of these religious remained in the country and under a variety of disguises devoted themselves to the perilous apostolate of itinerary missionary labour.

No doubt the clergy as a whole did not present such a noble phalanx of resistance as their bishops. The official number of those who resisted is supplied by Camden, the Protestant historian, who gives about 192 out of a total of some 8,000 priests, the majority of whom according to these figures basely conformed. The proportion would not hold true in regard to the clergy of the northern counties, notably Durham, Richmondshire, Yorkshire and Lancashire. Also large numbers of priests were recusant and withdrew into voluntary exile to exercise their ministrations on the Continent. Among the remaining compliant clergy were doubtless included many Protestant ministers who had returned to England at the accession of Elizabeth Tudor and were appointed without much delay to the vacated parishes and cures.

The principal recusant leaders among the Catholic nobility were Sir John Southworth of Samlesbury Hall, John Towneley of Burnley, Alexander Barlow of Barlow Hall (Manchester), the Gerards of Bryn, the Blundells of Ince and their kinsfolk of Crosby, the Andertons of Lostock, the Worthingtons of Blainscough Hall, Warrington, the Seftons and Molineux of Liverpool, the Masseys of Merseyside and, in the Fylde districts, the Allens of Rossall, the Cliftons of Lytham, the Westbys of Mowbreak Hall, the Haydocks of Cottam, the Lathams of Mosborough, and many others. In reference to Sir John Southworth, " The following letter from the State Archbishop of Canterbury (Matthew Parker) to the Lords of the Privy Council gives the result of his examination of Sir John Southworth, who had been sent up from Lancashire as an obstinate recusant: ' It may please your honour to understand that this day being 13th July I have had Sir John Southworth here with me according to your Lordship's order. I offered him the form of submission prescribed by your honour, he refused to submit himself to any such subscription, his conscience cannot serve in most points of that order; he offered to promise not to receive or to sustain any such disordered persons as heretofore he has sustained and helped; he further seems to desire that he may be suffered to live according to his conscience and desires much to have leave to go over sea, the consideration of all such requests I refer to your honourable wisdom, which I beseech God to assist you to do what may please Him, and may be more in accordance to the safety of the Queen's Highness.' " (Cf. *Lydiate and its Associations,* by Rev. Thomas Ellison Gibson, part 2, pp. 210-211.)

It is manifest from the above letter that Matthew Parker was of a more clement disposition and endeavoured as far as he was able to secure leave for Sir John Southworth's requests. But Sir John was almost immediately transferred to the custody of the State bishop, Edmund Grindal, a bitter enemy of the Papists. His hostile attitude stiffened the resistance of Sir John Southworth, as it did that of Sir Thomas Fitzherbert of Swynnerton, whom Dr. Grindal reported to Secretary Cecil as " a very stiff man " who, as his gaolers stated, could not be induced to make even a semblance of conformity.

After the " Rising in the North," 1569, and during the subsequent decade, the missionary clergy trained in the Catholic seminaries abroad began to arrive in England. They were followed shortly by the English Jesuit missionaries and the violent persecution of Catholics made itself felt among the commoners of Lancashire. The State papers endorsed for the years 1582-1583 provide lists of Catholic recusants in Lancashire who were committed to Salford goal. A composite of two such lists is submitted as follows from *Foley's Records, S.J.,* Vol. 2, pages 135-159:

(1) *Priests in Salford gaol*: Revv. Thomas Williamson, Richard Hutton, James Bell (Martyr and Beatus), Ralph

Scott, Thomas Langton, Thomas Hoghton (died in prison), William Wilson, John Morren, Christopher Hankes, John Coppage (died in prison), Thomas Woods, John Alabaster, John Lough or Lowe, banished with Rev. George Ostcliffe.

(2) *Nobles and gentry*: Sir John Southworth of Samlesbury Hall, Sir John Towneley of Towneley, Burnley, Sir Alexander Barlow of Barlow Hall, Manchester, grandfather of the Blessed Ambrose Barlow, O.S.B. Messrs. Robert Hulme, Robert Holland, William Lough or Lowe, John Locknell or Hocknell, murdered by his gaoler (Cf. *Foley's Records, S.J.*, Vol. 3, p. 804), John Leigh, Ralph Worsley, Matthew Travers.

(3) *Schoolmasters*: John Burge, Humphrey Cartwright, Richard Aspinall.

(4) *Yeomen, Farmers, Husbandmen, Tradesmen*: Henry Jackson, tailor; John Finch, farmer (Martyr and Beatus); Oliver Platt, blacksmith and farmer; Thurstan Arrowsmith, farmer (the grandfather of the Blessed Edmund Arrowsmith); Thurstan Arrowsmith died of his sufferings for the Faith in prison; Thomas Hutton, farmer and husbandman; John Rushock; Henry Grimshaw.

(5) *Women indicted*: Elizabeth Dewhurst, widow; Lucy Sedgewick, wife; Catharine Marsh, wife; Mary Leigh, wife; Alice Hadcock, spinster (Aloysia Haydock), of Cottam Hall and sister of the Martyr, the Ven. Father George Haydock; she died in prison of her sufferings); Eleanor Challoner, spinster; Elizabeth Hawkinson, spinster.

(6) *Women searched for but not yet arrested for recusancy*: Dorothy Brereton, Lady, widow; Annie Massey, Lady, widow; Ann Sankey, wife of Thomas Sankey of Warrington; Anne Ashton, wife of Robert Ashton, Gent.; Jane Tarleton, wife of Robert Tarleton; Ellen Rigby, wife of Roger Rigby; Ann Moodie, spinster.

During the official visitation of Lancashire, Dr. Laurence Vaux, the Warden of Manchester College, having refused to deliver a report of recusant Fellows and students, fled to London. His colleague, Father John Coppage, refused to accept the new religious settlement, resigned and was cast into Salford gaol for his recusancy. For some time after, Father Laurence Vaux was harboured at Barlow Hall, where he concealed the documents and deeds of Manchester College. His further adventures for the Faith are taken from *Foley's Records,* Vol. 6, pp. 210 seq.: " A general and very close search for Catholics was made in various parts of London, by order of the Privy Council in the month of August, 1584. The following are extracts from certificates of the searchers returned to the Privy Council: —' Tower Hill. —Mr. Myddleton's house. Mr. Myddleton, gentleman, Mary, his wife, Margaret Myddleton, and four others. No guest, nor stranger, nor other suspected person, or other letter or writing found in the house; save only two Popish books, viz., Vaux's Catechism, and a *Refutation of Mr. Whitaker's Reprehension of the Late English Translation and Catholic Annotations of the New Testament.*' "

The Catechism referred to is Laurence Vaux's English adaptation of the famous Catechism of St. Peter Canisius, S.J., which had so successfully fostered the Faith in the minds and hearts of the people of central Europe. To the spread of this good work in England, Laurence Vaux had devoted his talents and energy with considerable success in the midst of terrible dangers and risks. A further interesting extract from the same State papers, in the same connection, is given in paraphrase as follows: " The author of this famous Catechism was Laurence Vaux, born at Blackrod, near Horwich and Chorley, county Lancashire; educated at Queen's College, Oxford, and sometime a member of Corpus Christi. About 1540, he applied himself to the study of

divinity, and received Holy Orders. In the reign of Queen
Mary, he passed his degree of B.A., and was made chaplain
to Dr. Brookes, Bishop of Gloucester, his personal friend,
who had given him every encouragement in his studious
enterprises. He was soon after chosen to be Warden of the
Collegiate Church of Manchester, but was deprived in the
beginning of Queen Elizabeth's reign for nonconformity, and,
going over to Ireland, was robbed of all his property and
narrowly escaped with his life. He then settled in the University of Louvain, and became a Canon Regular of St.
Augustine. He was sent from Rheims to England on 2nd
August, 1580, in company with Mr. Tichborne. (This was
Gilbert Tichborne of Hampshire, an outstanding confessor
of the Faith and a glorious example of fidelity throughout
the ninety-six years of his life.) Landing at Dover, they passed
safely through the scrutiny of the searchers, and were most
kindly treated by the authorities.

"Entering Rochester and not suspecting any danger, they
were recognised by two apostates, taken before the governor
and underwent a second and more severe search. The aged
monk, Father Vaux, was kept standing in his shirt for a long
time; at length his rosary beads and two prints were found
concealed in his clothes. The next day they were taken
before Lord Cobham and Mr. Vane, who addressed Mr.
Tichborne gruffly but behaved most civilly to the aged monk,
condoling with him upon his misfortune, which they attributed to the necessity of strictly guarding the ports in these
evil times to prevent the entrance of dangerous characters,
assured them that they had nothing to fear, but begged them
to wait for a little while, until they could communicate with
the Privy Council for further instructions. On the fifth day,
a long string of interrogations arrived from the Council, to
which, from the questioner's point of view, Father Vaux gave
such unsatisfactory answers that he was remitted with Mr.

Tichborne to Aylmer, the pseudo-bishop of London, before whom they appeared after a two days' journey. Aylmer addressed himself entirely to Father Vaux, sharply urging him and commanding him to acknowledge the supremacy of the Queen in matters ecclesiastical. To which the monk replied with a sedate countenance: 'The Holy Ghost has appointed Bishops as rulers over the Church of God.' Aylmer in reply said: 'Be obedient to your rulers.' Since that was precisely what Father Vaux had been doing all along, he said nothing but bowed politely. Aylmer then changed the conversation to other matters.

" 'What relation are you,' he asked, 'to that Vaux, who is the author of the *Papistical Catechism in English?*' Father Vaux having acknowledged himself to be the author, Aylmer said: 'But it contains heresy!' 'By no means,' replied Vaux, 'it was censored by the most learned and qualified Catholics before going to press, and they declared that it contained nothing contrary to the Catholic Faith.'

" The bishop then turned off to foreign affairs, and having received an answer the conversation ceased. Father Vaux then asked for his liberty, adding, 'For I trust you will not treat me more brutally than the English soldiers lately dealt with the monks and nuns of the various religious orders at Mechlin. The cruelty of the soldiers is incident to their profession, but you ought to show pity and mercy.'

" Aylmer replied: 'But I lately committed to prison two very wealthy men of noble families, Throckmorton and another whose income was £1,000 a year, on the grounds merely that they refused to go to the established church and attend public services; and can you, so notorious a Papist, hope to enjoy your liberty? '

" The good old man and his companion were thereupon committed to the Gatehouse prison, Westminster, which was then filled with many noble and loyal Catholics imprisoned for the Faith; among others were Mr. Towneley, Mrs. Heath and her daughter, of noble stock, besides aged priests and many pious laymen. Those who could afford to pay occupied the upper chambers or cells, but the rest were thrust down into the lower cells where the light of day did not penetrate. Owing to the constant increase of prisoners, the alms were insufficient to meet the needs of all; mutual conversation could be but rarely and timorously exchanged in the absence of the turnkeys. All these sufferings fell heavily on the aged monk, Laurence Vaux, and his sorrows were heightened by the fact that his two betrayers and the gaoler's wife were natives of Lancashire, as he himself was, and a third, more malicious if possible than the rest, was his own kinsman; so that he could with truth say: ' A man's enemies are those of his own household.' " (*Foley's Records, S.J.*, Vol. 6, pp. 713-714.)

Father Laurence Vaux died in this prison, a martyr for the Faith, in the year 1585, the year in which the cruel statute Eliz. 27 was passed, making it treason for a priest, ordained abroad, to enter England or to minister as such, and the death penalty was extended to all who should give shelter and harbourage to seminary priests and Jesuits, and the same liability upon all who should in any way " convey " or assist such priests in their ministrations. The same penalties were directed against those who became reconciled to the ancient Faith and those who assisted, instructed or received them.

While he was in prison, Father Laurence Vaux wrote a letter to his faithful friend and colleague, Father John Coppage, also a prisoner for the Faith, who was also destined to die of his prison-sufferings in gaol. This letter has likewise been preserved in the same series of State papers: " Laurence Vaux, late Warden of Manchester, to Mr. Coppage, endorsed: ' A letter of a priest sent out from some gaol here.'

" ' Good Mr. Coppage,

For my hearty commendations, I have received your kind letter, with a pair of gloves, for which I thank you most heartily. Thanks be to God for the greater liberty and freedom you have been granted. I am glad to learn that you have established a College of priests (a confraternity of priest-prisoners for the Faith). I pray God bless you all. Your prison rent-charges are small in comparison with ours, for I have to pay £16 a year for my room, and I have had to incur the extra expense of having a fireplace and chimney built in. I have engaged an artesan by the week to collect all the needful material, so that the chimney can be completed in seventeen days, and when it is finished I have to pay double the price for fagots and coal than I could buy them for were I a free man at liberty. Our prison-keeper knocks a great deal of profit out of us, not only for fuel but also for meat and drink. He keeps for himself the half of whatever we purchase, and because of this has reduced many of us to extreme want. But thanks be to God, as yet I have found no lack of friends here, who have influence and who hold me in great regard, especially since my Catechism has appeared in print. When I returned to England from the Continent, I entrusted the MS. of the Catechism to a friend in Cumberland to have copies published and printed. These only came out last year, and so many of them were sold at a shilling a copy that there is now not a single copy left for sale. A gentleman, residing within some sixteen miles from where you are, told me that he had 300 copies, which were circulated in the north, so there is no need there of a further supply; here, in these regions, the Jesuits and the seminary priests use the Catechism for the instruction of the people, and thanks be to God many are thus reclaimed to the Faith. I have done what you asked me to do in regard of Mr. Steward, who thanks you for your kindness; he still has his old lodging in the garrets of the house, and another old priest lives in the room next to his. In the chamber next to me is an old priest who knows you well, and wishes to be remembered to you; he was at one time clerk to the old lord Delawar, and kept his courts; he says he has seen you in company with our old Master, with my lord. He was at length ordained priest and beneficed in Queen Mary's time. Now he joins with me daily in Divine service. Do you know whether Mr. Worsley, a lawyer, was ever a student in the Middle Temple? Mr. Draybrooke (sic), one of my next fellow-prisoners, a man held in the highest esteem, a fellow-prisoner of mine for the Faith, wishes to know, and, if it is so, he begs cordially to be remembered to him; he was a student with him. I beg of you also to commend me to all the members of your pious association of priests. I pray God bless you all.

In haste, 21st August, 1583,

Yours only, L.

'You shall receive (along with this letter) several Spanish pistolets of gold, delivered by a carrier in Holme, a young man.'" (*Foley's Records, S.J.,* Ibid.)

The Father Thomas Houghton or Hoghton, who was a fellow-prisoner for the Faith with Father John Coppage, in Salford gaol, died therein of his sufferings. Father Hoghton was the son of the notable Mr. Thomas Hoghton, who built Hoghton Towers in 1562 but was not allowed to enjoy the fruits of his industry. Unwilling to conform, he was banished the realm and died in exile for his faith and conscience. He died in June, 1580, and he was buried at the Church of St. Gervase, Liege, where a handsome monument was erected to his memory. The inscription on this is as follows:

"Over against this spot lies buried the illustrious man, Mr. Thomas Hoghton, Englishman, who after ten years of voluntary exile, despoiled by the sectaries of his patrimony and all his goods for his confession of the Catholic Faith, died 2nd June, 1580, aged 63."

His son Thomas, exiled with him, became a missionary priest and died a martyr for his priesthood in Salford gaol, where he was incarcerated in 1582-1584.

The elderly well-to-do business-man and widower, John Anne, a cloth merchant of Wakefield and a member of the notable Catholic Yorkshire family, the Annes of Frickley, was a frequent visitor to Lancashire where, a devout Catholic himself, he had many Catholic friends of quality. John Anne at length divided his considerable estate among his grown-up children, and decided to become a priest. To carry out this project, he repaired to the Continent and from the College of Mignon, Paris, wrote letters to some of his Catholic friends in Lancashire. Two of these have been preserved in the volumes of the *Catholic Record Society*, Vol. 5, pp. 19-20: one addressed to John Talbot of Salesbury Hall; the other to Anne Southworth, of the neighbouring Samlesbury Hall.

A rough paraphrase of these letters is given as follows:

" Addressed to the Right Worshipful Mr. John Talbot, Esquire, (to be) delivered at Salesbury, Lancashire.
" Worshipful Sir,

My duty remembered; I have great pleasure in telling you that immediately after my arrival in Paris, I sent a letter to your servant, Richard Bowlton, in which I asked him to explain the matter which constitutes the subject of this present letter. Although I have a convenient messenger, I thought good to write direct to your Worship, lest peradventure my other letter came not to his hands. Sir, in regard of the gentleman of whom I spoke with you at home in your gallery, I have in two ways found the means of finding out how he fares, once a fortnight, for there are some every week to the place where I lodge; therefore, sir, your friend shall have no need to make any journey or incur any expense in this matter, for I will take care to let you know how his circumstances are, as occasion requires. I have also made arrangements that a friend of mine, who lives in the same place where the said gentleman dwells, shall immediately send me a messenger should the reason for it arise, and I have promised to defray all the expenses needful for his journey. Sir, in connection with any news, I cannot write of any, save that the situation between the Portuguese and King Philip still remains doubtful; whether they will accept him as their King or not. He has there a great expeditionary force both by sea and land, and great conferences and parleys are being held between both parties, that the affair might be ended without any bloodshed, which Almighty God grant so to be. As for any other matters, the bearer of this letter will be able to communicate to you better and more fully than I can write, for he is one whom you can trust. In conclusion, Sir, as my bounden duty is, I will not fail to commend you to God in my prayers, with my service and good will to Mr. George, Mr. Robert, their wives, to my old friend Myles, and the rest.

At Paris from Mignon College, this 8th of June, 1580.
Your Worship's most dutiful servant to the
best of his power,
Jo. Amyas, for so am I named at Paris."

The second letter is " addressed to Mistress Anne South-worth to be delivered to Samlesbury (Hall), in Lancashire." The style denotes an elderly and respected friend of the family writing to a younger member of it, who along with her brothers and sisters loved this kindly friend and guest, who always during his visits had a present for them all. Being rich and generous, John Anne was munificent in his gifts, but at the time of writing the letter in question, having given up everything for his vocation, he had perforce to acknowledge himself a poor man:

" Good Mistress Anne,

Your courtesy and gentleness towards me compel me to send you my greetings in a few lines, because words are of no great cost, even though well used and well chosen. Alas, in regard of gifts and presents I cannot send any because they cost money, and now I have none to spare; nevertheless, I am sending you an English piece of money as a little token, because it is not current coin in France, or perhaps I would have spent that too. I am especially writing to ask you to tender my humble respects and commendations to my good lady, your mother, of whom I would gladly have taken my leave when I came away, but since she was ill in bed at the time, I was unwilling to disturb her. My commendations also to Mistress Jane and to old Nanny. In fine, I entrust you to the Holy Spirit.

At Paris from the Mignon College, this 8th of June, 1580,

Always at your service to the best of his power,

John Amyas."

The bed-ridden lady was doubtlessly Lady Mary Southworth, the wife of Sir John Southworth, who was entered in the list of recusants, along with her husband, dated 1577. At the time of John Anne's final visit to Samlesbury Hall, Sir John was most likely in prison for the Faith, an outstanding example of devoted and uncompromising loyalty to the Catholic Church. The pious widower who did so much to console the family for the loss of such a father, became a priest and for some eight years laboured mostly in Lancashire as a missionary priest, until his arrest at the house of Mr. and Mrs. Murton, who were both committed to prison at York with the priest whom they had been harbouring. The Blessed John Anne or Amyas, along with his friend and colleague, the Blessed Robert Dalby, were both hanged, drawn and quartered for their priesthood at York on 16th March, 1589. Sir John Southworth survived his friend by some six years, dying in the year 1595.

It is only possible in this brief review to select a few examples of Lancashire recusancy and Catholic constancy, and William Crombleholme of Stidd, Ribchester, was a worthy member of the steadfast Catholic family of the Crombleholmes of Dutton and Ribchester. Every effort was made to induce William Crombleholme to conform, but the sufferings that had overwhelmed many found no weakness in his faith and constancy. From recusant lists, dated 8th March, 1585, he was a prisoner for the Faith in the Marshalsea along with Robert Holland of Clifton and John Williams of Ditton. William Crombleholme was moved about from one prison to another, until he was incarcerated in the Clink along with another recusant prisoner, William Higham, a member of an Essex family and a brother of the Catholic lady and martyr at Tyburn, the Blessed Ann Line.

Another Catholic nobleman of the times was Sir Richard Shireburn, who built but did not live to complete the palatial mansion of Stonyhurst. He had been granted a special exemption by the Queen herself without having to suffer any jeopardy either to his faith or conscience. He made full use of this by providing Mass-centres at Chipping, Chaigley, Bailey and elsewhere.

ABRAM'S " HISTORY OF BLACKBURN," p. 286.
Bk. 2, Ch. 1, under heading, " Annals of the Vicarage."

" Ralph Lynney, installed as Vicar about 1537, is before described in 1534 as receiver of the Rectory of Blackburn. He was witness to the will of John Talbot of Salesbury in 1552, and resigned upon a pension before 1554. His successor, James Hargreaves, presented by Philip & Mary, instituted 24th Oct., 1555, was deprived soon after the accession of the Protestant Queen Elizabeth for " papistry," and was yet in the district and reported for an obstinate recusant (Roman Catholic) in 1575."

p. 768.

APPENDIX III—CHURCH EFFECTS IN BLACKBURN, 1553.

" I am indebted to Mr. J. E. Bailey, F.S.A., for the appended transcript of an inventory of vestments, and other effects in Blackburn Church, made in 1553. temp. Ranulf Lynney, Vicar (see p. 286).

" ' This indenture made the xvth day of October, in the yere of the reigne of Edward the Sext by the grace of God King of England, france, and Ireland, defender of the feythe and on Earthe of the Churche of England and also of Ireland sup'me heade, betwixte Sir Thomas Holt Knighte Raffe Assheton Esquier & Jhon Bradill gentlema three of the comysssyon's upon the behalf of o'r souraigne Lord the King uppon the on p'tie and Ranulphe Lynney Veker off blagburne Jhon Issherwod & Giles bolton churche wardens of the same, thomas dale curate of Samesburye Gilbert Sharpuls & Willm. Warde churche wardens of the same, Richard Wodd curate of Harewodd James dobson and Jhon M'cer churchewardens of the same uppon the other p'tie, Witnesseth that wheare the said Sir Thomas holt Raffe Assheton and Jhon bradill have delivered at the tyme of the sealinge and delyvry of thes presents to the said Ranulphe Lynney Jhon Issherwod & giles bolton, on chales iiij vestments one coope three auterclothes two corporas fyve for whiche they aw xxvjli xijs. jd., to thomas france, thomas Winkeley & Edmund Leman on chalis on vestment on coope fower bells on of them being broken, to thomas Dale, Gilbart Sharpuls & Willm Ward two little bells on chalis p'cell gyld on vestment on albe & on amysse & other things belonging to a p'est to celebrate in wt. two old towels, to Ric Wodd, James Dobson & John M'crer three bells in the stepull on

vestment wt the apprt'n'nces thereto app'tening belonging to
the said churches and chapels savely to be kept to the use of
o'r sovraigne Lord the King, And the s'd Ranulphe, Jhon,
giles, thomas (Edmund), thomas, gilbert, Willm. Richard,
James and Jhon for them and their execut,rs do coven'nt and
graunt by thes pr'sents to & wt the said Sr thomas Raffe &
Jhon that the said chalices bells and other anoranments affore
rehersed shall not att any tyme hereafter be alienated
imbesilled or otherwise put away from o'r sovraigne lord the
King but shalbe awnswaraball & forthcuyng to the use of his
highnes at suche tyme and tymes as his ma'tie or his honera-
bull counsell shal demaund the same. In witness wheareof
the pties above named to thes presents interchaungeably have
sette ther seales and putte ther handes the day & yere above
wryten.

> p me Ranulphu Lynney vicariu.
> p me Thoma Ffrenche capelanu.
> p me Rich Wod caplu.
> p me Thoma Dale caplu.' "

The author is indebted to Father Ronald Hull, S.J., who
kindly contributed the above extracts.

CHAPTER 2

THE PRISON AND THE GALLOWS

THE preceding chapter concluded with a reference to an " oasis " of comparative peace for Catholics on the north bank of the Ribble, secured and maintained until the time of Oliver Cromwell by the Shireburns of Stonyhurst. Very different was the fate of Catholics on the south bank, from Burnley through the heart of Lancashire and on to Manchester. The Fylde districts were also infested with pursuivants during the first decades of the Elizabethan persecution.

Sir John Southworth and John Towneley were among the first batch of recusant prisoners taken to Salford gaol, and for some years until 1584 both noblemen were incarcerated in that prison. They proved a godsend to their fellow recusant prisoners, because they succeeded in forwarding outspoken complaints to the authorities in London in regard to the cruel treatment and robberies endured. John Southworth and John Towneley obtained leave to travel under escort to the metropolis, a leave conceded largely because two such redoubtable and fearless recusants were adjudged by the Protestant politicians of the time to be less dangerous in London than in their home county. An interesting account of these incidents is given in *Lydiate Hall and its Associations*, by the Rev. Thomas Ellison Gibson, pp. 210-229, passim.

In the same book a brief reference is made to Mr. John Towneley of Towneley, Burnley, who as far back as 1564-1565 was imprisoned for the Faith in Chester Castle, then in the Marshalsea, besides his incarceration in Salford gaol. He had also been imprisoned in York Castle, in the Blockhouses of Hull, and at length in the Gatehouse, Westminster, and other London prisons. For a time also he appears to have been a prisoner at Ely, probably at Wisbech Castle, and at Broughton, near Oxford, until at the age of seventy-three he was confined within the five-mile limit to his own home at Towneley. Besides this long term of imprisonment, the total amount of fines he had had to pay for his recusancy was about £5,200, a veritable fortune if expressed in present day monetary values. He died at the age of seventy-nine in the year 1607.

Another district of comparative tranquillity for Papists at this time was more or less in the Liverpool area, with its strongholds of the Faith supported by the Molyneux of Sefton, the Irelands of Lydiate, the Torbrocks of Childwall, and the Blundells of Crosby. A kinsman of this latter family, the Blessed Laurence Johnson, alias Richardson, priest, was the first Lancashire man to be martyred during the Elizabethan persecution. Through his parents, Richard and Margaret Johnson, the martyr was related to both the Blundells of Crosby and the Ince-Blundells. It was the martyr's sister, Helen Johnson, who was imprisoned for the Faith in the year 1582 at Salford gaol.

Mention is made here of a hallowed memorial on the Blundell estate at Little Crosby: "Within the park walls of Little Crosby is a spot of deep interest to the English Province, S.J., where repose the remains of many of its old members along with other priests." Baines, *History of Lancashire* writes: "A print is preserved in the British Museum of some . . . antiquities discovered in a certain place in 1611, called the Hardkirke within the lordship of Little Crosbie (sic), which place William Blundell, of the said Little Crosbie, Esq., inclosed from the residue of the said

Hardkirke for the burial of such Catholic recusants deceasing either of the said village or of the adjoining neighbourhood as should be denied burial at their parish church of Sephton.

"Hardkirke is within the walls of the park, and . . . Colonel Nicholas Blundell has erected a stone cross to mark the site. A few memorials of those who lie interred there still exist, but it has long been disused as a burial ground.

"From records of proceedings in the Star Chamber, it appears that the above act of charity on the part of Mr. Blundell in 1611 towards his fellow-Catholics did not escape the notice of the Government, but was the occasion of visiting upon him a heavy penalty, when some resistance to the authority of the sheriff brought him before the tribunal. 'And the defendant, Blundell, being a Popish recusant convict, and living in Little Crosby, Lancashire, inclosed a piece of ground and fenced it partly with a stone wall, and partly with a hedge and ditch, etc., kept and used the same for the space of ten years for the burial of Popish recusants, and Seminary priests, and for these offences two of the rioters were fined £500 a piece, and three others £100 a piece, and Blundell, for procurement of the riots and erecting the churchyard, £2,000. All committed to the Fleet prison, and the walls and mounds of the churchyard to be pulled down by the sheriff, and the ground laid waste by decree to be read at the assizes.' This infamous act, we are told, was performed by a posse of constables, amid the sound of trumpets." (F. Vol. 5, pp. 344-345.)

Of such a loyal family was the Blessed Laurence Johnson. As a boy he made his preliminary studies in Great Crosby at the local grammar-school. In due course he went to Brasenose College, Oxford. He was presented for his degree of B.A. on 25th November, 1572, having apparently been made a Fellow of Brasenose in 1569. The conditions demanded, however, stirred up a struggle within his conscience and ended in his leaving the University and proceeding to Douay, where he arrived in 1573. He was at length ordained priest at Cateau-Cambresis by the Bishop of Cambrai on 23rd March, 1577.

On 27th July of the same year, he began his missionary labours in England. He went to his native county and resided principally at Park Hall, the home of a Catholic Lancashire gentleman, Mr. Richard Hoghton. Here, under the guise of a schoolmaster, he conducted with success his priestly ministrations. In a letter now among the State papers, Mr. Christopher Hodgson wrote: " It is not as Mr. Johnson that I addressed you, but as my father, who brought me out of the land of Egypt and slavery . . ." This convert of the Blessed Laurence Johnson had gone to the English College, Rome, as a youth of eighteen in 1579, and was ordained priest in 1583, remaining on the Continent as a professor of theology and philosophy.

Laurence Johnson's reputation as a missionary of note among the Lancashire Catholic recusants, reconciling wanderers, strengthening the weak, giving the Sacraments to starved souls, soon put the pursuivants on his track, and his movements from place to place were traced. Not in Lancashire, however, was Laurence Johnson to be apprehended. It was an unfortunate slander and a palpable calumny which induced him to leave his native county for London, or at least occasioned him to accept a work of charity in the capital which led to his arrest.

During his abode with Mr. Hoghton, the Blessed Laurence met with a great trial, which prepared him for sufferings of even a graver nature. By a former wife, Mary, daughter of Ralph Rishton of Pontalgh, Richard Hoghton had three children, a son and two daughters, who, upon his marrying as his second wife, " a young gentlewoman, very virtuous and wise," dared to insinuate that the holy priest was unduly familiar with their step-mother . . . As soon as Laurence heard this, he comforted the gentlewoman by exhorting her to patience and continuance in virtue, and immediately departed from the house with the intention of going overseas. But before taking that journey in hand, he told his relative, Mr. Robert Blundell, of this decision to repair to the Continent. Mr. Blundell, then a very old and infirm man, had begun to regret the absence of his eldest son, who through the means of Father Laurence had gone to Rheims, probably to try his vocation. When the old man understood Father Laurence's purpose to go abroad, he gave him a commission to perform for him in London; for that purpose he gave the priest some money, no doubt to help the latter's expenses, and authorised him to collect a debt which a kinsman of his in London owed.

So Laurence departed and came to London, where he adopted the alias " Richardson." He did not stay long in London, but went to see a fellow country-man, with whom he had been long acquainted and whose name was Francis Goare, a tailor. Here he met by chance the kinsman with whom he had been commissioned to transact the business.

The priest said to this gentleman: " Sir, your cousin Blundell sent me to you to collect the sum of money you owe," and Laurence no doubt named the amount due.

In answer to this the gentleman said: " It is true I owe my cousin some money—but I pray, sir, was it not you yourself that conveyed my cousin, Richard Blundell, overseas?"

" Yes, indeed," replied Laurence, " it was I that took him over, and it is I, if God spare my life, that will bring him back again."

" Faith," said the gentleman, " I am very glad to hear you say so; therefore, I beg you to remain here awhile, and I'll presently return, and despatch your business "—and so departed.

Laurence supposed the gentleman had meant that he would have brought in the money at his return. But the event was contrary, for instead of money, he brought the pursuivants, who arrested Laurence Johnson and brought him before the magistrates, and being accused of being a priest, he was committed to prison. The good lady, who had been a victim of the calumny, lived on piously for many years, and the disparaging lie dissolved itself. She died a very happy death. On the contrary, the calumniators, the step-son and the two step-daughters, came to a disreputable end: the son was disinherited; one of the daughters had a child by her father's groom; the other lost her reputation, and married a " strolling fellow " and fled with him to Ireland. (Cf. *Lives of the English Martyrs,"* Dom. Bede Camm, O.S.B., Vol. 2, pp. 523-530.)

Similar calumnies were brought up against many of the martyrs, and sometimes in court, as in the case of the Blessed Thomas Cottam, but the spiteful calumny levelled against the Blessed Laurence Johnson, alias Richardson, made no appearance in the court charges, nor did Anthony Munday, the apostate witness against Johnson, make any reference to it.

On the fateful day at Tyburn, the Sheriff made one last effort. " Now, Richardson," he said, " if you will confess your faults and renounce the Pope, the Queen will extend her mercy towards you, and you shall be released."

The Blessed Laurence Johnson replied: " I thank Her Majesty for her mercy, but I must not confess an untruth, or renounce my faith."

One, Field, a preacher, surprised the Martyr by a sudden manifestation of his eagerness to have him executed at once, in a manner obviously incompatible with his profession. " Despatch him! despatch him! " he cried. The Blessed Thomas Cottam, who was present awaiting his own execution, smiled at the minister's eagerness, saying: " What! are you an executioner or a preacher? You ought to be ashamed of yourself."

After reciting the Pater, Ave and Credo, the Blessed Laurence Johnson, alias Richardson, was hanged, drawn and quartered for his faith and priesthood at Tyburn on 30th May, 1582.

Thomas Cottam was born in the year 1549 at Dilworth, Tarnacre, near Longridge, on the road to Chipping, some seven or eight miles north-east of Preston. His father, Laurence Cottam, was a wealthy man owning a considerable estate, and had married Anne, a daughter of a Mr. Brewer of Brindle. Both of them had conformed to preserve their estate, so that Thomas Cottam was brought up a Protestant. When he was old enough, his parents were able to send him to Oxford, where he took his degree of B.A. at about the age of twenty. On 14th July, 1572, he proceeded M.A. and then went to London, where he was appointed to direct a well-known grammar school of free education. In this post he was successful, and besides his own patrimony he was making good money on his own account, and began to lead in London a far from exemplary life. Apparently the Catholic Oxford movement of the time had exercised little or no influence on this wordly young man. The Rev. Arthur Pitts, afterwards his fellow-prisoner for the Faith and the priesthood in the Tower, speaks of Thomas Cottam's popularity while holding this post and states that he became " well known and beloved."

While leading a gay life in London, Cottam had the good fortune to meet with Thomas Pounde of Belmont, one of the greatest confessors of the Faith in those times and called by Thomas Cottam " the father of his soul, through whose help he had gained the priceless treasure of the Faith."

By the year 1575, Thomas Cottam had apparently given up his lucrative post and went to Douay to become a priest, and after a period of study there, having heard of the self-sacrificing labours of the Jesuit missionaries in India, he went to the Jesuit Noviciate at St. Andrea, Rome, to prepare himself for the Indian Mission. But after a few months there his health broke down, and for the time being his noviciate was suspended, while he was sent to Lyons to recuperate before returning to complete his term of probation. This was in the year 1579 when Thomas Cottam had already been ordained a deacon.

Apparently a short time before entering the noviciate at St. Andrea, he had paid a brief visit to England in January, 1578, and returned to the Continent on 14th May of the same year, with five students from Oxford, candidates no doubt for the priesthood. These, it is conjectured, were some of his old pupils of the Free Grammar School, London.

When Cottam left the Noviciate of St. Andrea, Rome, he was accompanied by the future martyr, Robert Johnson, a priest destined for the English mission. He was a native of Shropshire and was educated at the German College, Rome, and at Douay. The Blessed Robert Johnson was executed at Tyburn for the priesthood two days before the execution of his namesake, the Blessed Laurence Johnson, alias Richardson. Besides Robert Johnson, Thomas Cottam on leaving Rome was also accompanied by one Sledd, a secret spy of the English pursuivants, who was masquerading as a devout Catholic and candidate for the English mission, even to the extent of being a daily communicant, it is said.

He was not a sincere Protestant, but in reality a venomous apostate and a hater of the very name of Christianity. His particularly ignoble and paid duties were to get into touch with prospective Catholic missionaries destined for England and, after mentally photographing their features in his mind, send a minute description of them to the authorities at the various English ports and to the English embassies. Thomas Cottam and Robert Johnson arrived at Rheims on 11th April, 1580, doubtlessly from Lyons, where during his brief sojourn there Cottam had been completely taken in by Sledd. Sledd himself, on the occasion of the journey from Lyons to Rheims, managed to make a detour on his own part to Paris to give the English ambassador a detailed description of both Robert Johnson and Thomas Cottam.

Since the latter's health was unsatisfactory, it was decided to send him to England to recuperate, and accordingly on 25th May, 1580, Thomas Cottam was ordained priest. During his stay at Rheims, Cottam was thrilled with the arrival there of that notable party of missioners, whose landing in England a few weeks later was proclaimed by the enemies of the Church as an invasion. Some of the members of this notable party were Edmund Campion, Robert Persons, Ralph Sherwin, Luke Kirby, Alexander Briant and others. Thus Thomas Cottam was able to renew his friendship and acquaintance with those whose counsel on a very important matter was to set his conscience at rest for all time. Still hoping to complete his course of training as a Jesuit, and realising that his stay in England would be fraught with many dangers, Cottam called to mind those parting words of the Brother Porter when leaving St. Andrea: " Cave ne alius accipiat coronam tuam "—" Beware lest another receive thy crown."

On 5th June, Fathers Cottam and Robert Johnson set out for England with a party of missionaries conducted by Dr. Humphrey Ely. Dr. Humphrey Ely of Brasenose and afterwards St. John's College, Oxford, the same College where Thomas Cottam had later graduated, on declaring himself a Catholic was obliged to leave Oxford, and betook himself in 1570 to Douay. Here he devoted himself to the study of law, in which he graduated and obtained a professorship. He also took a convenient house, where he boarded English students in the University, of whom there were a good many besides those at the English College. (Cf. *Douay Diaries*, March, 1577.)

From March, 1577, he became a member of the College at Douay and followed its fortunes to Rheims. After the committal of his friend, the Blessed Thomas Cottam, Dr. Ely retired to Spain, but returned again immediately to Rheims and became a priest. He received the three sacred orders in March and April, 1582, and said his first Mass on St. George's Day. He became Professor of Civil and Canon Law at Pont-a-Mousson in 1586, and died there in 1604. (Cf. *Lives of the English Martyrs*, Vol. 2, p. 543, footnote, Dom. Bede Camm.)

Therefore, Dr. Humphrey Ely was not in orders when in the year 1580, disguised in military costume, he conducted his party to England and in due course landed at Dover. Sledd's minute description, however, of Father Thomas Cottam with whom he had feigned an intimate friendship, was already in the hands of the port authorities. A contemporary description of Sledd himself reads as follows: " This most perfidious and detestable man attached himself to some at Rome, and having gained their familiarity and completed his business there, he accompanied them back to England."

From Sledd's descriptions, the Mayor of Dover and one Stephens, a searcher, recognised Father Cottam almost immediately. Owing to the good services of Dr. Humphrey Ely, Father Cottam was allowed bail, and since the Mayor

of Dover and his colleagues took the Doctor to be a gentleman of military rank, they committed Father Cottam to his
custody as a prisoner. Hence, Dr. Humphrey Ely was commissioned to take the priest in question to London and to
hand him over to Lord Cobham, the Ports' Authority. The
Mayor of Dover also entrusted to the Doctor a letter of
introduction and explanation addressed to Lord Cobham. Dr.
Ely readily undertook to fulfil the commission and played
the rôle imposed upon him to perfection. He took Father
Cottam to London and there released him.

It would seem that Father Cottam could easily have made
his way back to his native county, where it was possible that
he might have found safer harbourage. Since his superiors
had sent him to England, not to labour on the mission but
for the purpose of recovering his health, it would seem that
they also desired him to go to a place where his recovery
would be better assured.

He remained, however, in London for reasons of conscience, knowing as he did that the failure of his friend the
Doctor to deliver him up to Lord Cobham along with the
letter of explanation would soon be discovered, and that his
friend would most assuredly be arrested and condemned to
death for treasonable disobedience; not only this, but also
that Dr. Humphrey Ely would be questioned on his recusancy
and be presented with the oath of supremacy. Father
Cottam, therefore, had no wish to secure his own life and
liberty, at the cost of his friend and benefactor. He went,
therefore, to seek the advice of a Catholic prisoner for the
Faith, probably a priest, with whom he had been acquainted
overseas, or, as may be thought, Thomas Pounde of Belmont.
Whoever this confessor was, he agreed with Father Cottam
that he was bound in conscience to deliver himself up in order
to save the life of Dr. Ely. At once, Father Cottam sought
out Dr. Ely and explained to him the duty that lay before

him. The good priest asked for the letter addressed to Lord Cobham, so that he could deliver both himself and the explanatory letter to that official.

Dr. Humphrey Ely, however, was adamant and refused decisively either to deliver Father Cottam to Lord Cobham or to hand the Father the letter in question: " You shall not have the letter," said Dr. Ely, " nor can you in conscience yield yourself up to such an adversary and persecutor, having now such an opportunity of escaping his cruelty."

Father Cottam, being far from satisfied with the result of that conversation, brought up the matter at a conference of some of his fellow-priests in London. The conclusion arrived at by his consultors on this occasion was that he could avail himself of his liberty, and do as Dr. Ely had recommended. These same priests, however, at a later conference, agreed that the case was difficult, and one that called for further consultation. It was then that Father Cottam approached Father Persons, the Jesuit Superior in England, and Father Edmund Campion. To these he stated the case in his own words, " Was it his bounden duty, in order to avert the great danger from his keeper and friend, to give himself up to the Privy Council?"

The Jesuit Fathers fully appreciated the difficulties of the case and although they were competent to decide the matter for themselves, preferred to refer the case to the judgment of the missionary clergy at their next conference. For greater safety this was held in a small house on the south bank of the river in Southwark.

In this latter conference, it was decided that Father Cottam was right, and that he should give himself up in such a way that his benefactor would suffer no hurt. Eventually Dr. Ely agreed to that decision and, taking the matter into his own hands, went himself to the Mayor of Dover and explained the situation that had arisen and returned to him the letter he had addressed to Lord Cobham. Dr. Ely also assured the Mayor of Dover that Father Cottam could be in no wise induced to give himself up, if by so doing any harm to Dr. Ely would result. The Mayor of Dover in reply assured Dr. Ely that, provided Father Cottam was delivered into the custody of Lord Cobham, no further action could or would be taken against himself. An arrangement was then made between these two gentlemen which liberated Dr. Ely from having to effect the delivery himself. It was to be arranged through the Mayor of Dover, that a deputy of Lord Cobham should call upon Father Cottam and take him into custody. The place of this meeting was specified, and then Dr. Ely returned to London and saw Father Cottam. He explained to him in detail how he could satisfy his conscience and yet save the lives and liberties of others involved in the case.

" Now God be praised," exclaimed Father Cottam, " I should never while I lived have been without scruple, if I had escaped from them. There is nothing to prevent me from going to the place appointed, except some business which I have to do."

" Why, it is but ten o'clock yet, and you have until four o'clock to finish your business," said Dr. Ely, " and then you can go to them."

" And where must I go?" asked Father Cottam.

" To the ' Sign of the Star,' " answered Dr. Ely, " in new Fish Street, and there you must inquire for one Mr. Andrews, my Lord Cobham's deputy; to him you must surrender yourself."

" I will," replied Father Cottam. The two friends then parted and never saw one another afterwards. True to his word, Father Cottam went to the place specified and at the appointed time without the company of anyone. He yielded himself up as a prisoner and for some days was incarcerated in the Marshalsea. This terminates the abbreviated account of the longer and fuller narrative given by Foley (Vol. 2, pp. 149-156).

After some time, he was taken to the Tower, where on account of his outstanding defence of the Catholic Faith he was singled out along with the Blessed Luke Kirby to undergo the new and excruciatingly cruel torture of the " Scavenger's Daughter." Since as a notable schoolmaster in London he had been well known, every effort was made to induce him to save his life by conforming to the State church.

Although the martyr himself never for a moment wavered, his calm and gentle bearing was eagerly accepted as a sign of submission, both in the court-room and at the very scaffold, where he was twice taken down from the cart, as one who had yielded. The anxiety of the officials in Father Cottam's case was lest so many of his erstwhile pupils who loved and revered him, should be converted by his death. On each of these occasions the Blessed Thomas Cottam gently and persistently corrected the misunderstanding so unmistakably, that he was placed back into the cart. Father Cottam's main plea was that, being a Jesuit in preparation for the Jesuit Indian Missions, he had returned for a brief space to his native country to recuperate, and that on regaining his health and strength, he would return to the Continent to complete his course. The witness, who took notes of what the prisoner said in court, apparently grasped the gist of this plea and recorded it with fairness, albeit a Protestant, and in spite of some biased glosses. He reported Father Cottam's statement, of which the following is a paraphrase: " It was neither my purpose nor my commission to come into England (for missionary purposes); neither would I have come, had not God otherwise driven me; for my missionary destination was an appointment to the Indian mission-field: and there I would have gone had the state of my health been satisfactory. But in the meantime, it pleased God to visit me with sickness, and being counselled by the physicians to come to England for the sake of my health—for otherwise, as they said, if I failed to follow their advice, I should never recover it—and for that reason and no other, I came into this realm."

The Blessed Edmund Campion, also a prisoner in court at the time, interposed on Father Cottam's behalf: " Indeed, the physicians in Rome hold it for certain, that if an Englishman falls sick amongst them, there is no better way, nor scarcely any other alternative for his health's sake, than to return to England and there take his natural air, which agrees best with his constitution." (*Lives of the English Martyrs*, Vol. 2, p. 552, Dom Bede Camm., O.S.B.)

At Tyburn the martyr was continually pestered with efforts to induce him to stage a kind of semblance of conformity. As a last resort, he was forcibly made to watch the dismemberment of his fellow-martyr, the Blessed Laurence Johnson. But instead of the expected revulsion, Father Cottam was heard to be praying and quite audibly uttered the words: " Good Laurence! thy soul pray for me." As it had been during his trial, so then at Tyburn, the unswerving strength of his faith was made manifest to all. He in his turn was hanged, drawn and quartered on 30th May, 1582, after two years' imprisonment which for a time he had the privilege of sharing with his fellow-Jesuits, the Blessed Edmund Campion and the Blessed Alexander Briant.

Later kinsfolk of the Blessed Thomas Cottam became Catholics and were entered in the State records as recusants. " It is uncertain whether it was in the Blessed Thomas Cottam's lifetime or at what period, but his brother John, who succeeded to the estates, and his wife Catharine, became Catholics and frequently appear on the recusant rolls. Their only child was a girl, Priscilla; but in the register of the

English Catholics non-jurors in 1715, appears a Lawrence Cottam of Dilworth, Gent . . .''

Father Arthur Pitts, a fellow-prisoner of Thomas Cottam in the Tower, stated that when on 29th May, a day within the octave of the Ascension, the Lieutenant of the Tower delivered a message to Father Cottam that he was to die the next day. "He came to the window over against my door, saying with a joy of heart and voice: ' Give God thanks with me, for to-morrow is my day. And now I hope I shall not escape the happy hour, which I have earnestly so long desired, because I find my name first in the roll of the four assigned to die to-morrow.' "

CHAPTER 3

THE VENERABLE GEORGE HAYDOCK AND THE BLESSED JOHN NUTTER, PRIESTS

GEORGE HAYDOCK was born at Cottam Hall, near Preston, and was the youngest child of Vivian or Evan Haydock and Helen, his wife, formerly a Miss Westby of the Catholic family of Westby, Mowbreck Hall in the Fylde. This good lady's father was Mr. John Westby, who had married a daughter of Sir John Southworth of Samlesbury Hall. Another daughter of John Westby of Mowbreck Hall, Elizabeth, married the heir and afterwards the owner of Rossall Hall, George Allen, the elder brother of Cardinal William Allen. George Haydock, therefore, was born, as far as family and connections were concerned, in the strongest and most steadfast Catholic traditions.

Helen Haydock, née Westby, died at Cottam Hall in the year 1558, when George Haydock her youngest child was but an infant in arms. As she lay dying, her husband, Vivian Haydock, was so inconsolably broken-hearted that the dying lady made a last effort to comfort him in his great grief. She took the infant George in her arms, and then raising herself on one elbow, she pointed to the Latin words embroidered on a piece of cloth covering a table near the bedside: " Tristitia vestra in gaudium vertetur "—" Your sorrow shall be turned into joy." From thenceforth those words became the Haydock family motto. After this good mother's death, the widowed husband with an elder son Richard went to Douay in 1573, and father and son were subsequently both ordained priests in the year 1577.

Their example was followed later by the young George Haydock. As a priest, the father, Vivian Haydock, became Procurator General for Douay in England, and filled that office with great success but not without grave personal risks and dangers to himself. Later, during his trial, the Venerable George Haydock was closely questioned concerning his father:

The Commissioners: " What are you?"

George Haydock: " A priest."

Commissioners: " Where is your father?"

George Haydock: " He is dead."

Commissioners: " You lie."

George Haydock: " I do not lie . . ."

Commissioners: " Is not your father gatherer (Procurator) for the Seminary at Rheims?"

Answer: " Yes."

Commissioners: " We know it well, and if we could catch him, double traitor that he is, he shall smart for it."

(Cf. *Catholic Record Society*, Vol. V, p. 58.)

The elderly priest, Vivian Haydock, was hunted from place to place, and at length his constitution gave way. It was whilst staying at Mowbreck Hall that he received the shock which speedily laid him in his grave. On the Eve of All Souls' Day, some time before the arrest of his son George Haydock, Vivian Haydock stood, robed in his vestments, at the foot of the Altar in the domestic chapel at Mowbreck awaiting the clock to strike twelve. As the bell tolled the hour of midnight, the old priest, a fugitive in hiding, suddenly beheld the decapitated head of his favourite son George, slowly rising above the Altar, whose bloodstained lips seemed to repeat those memorable words, "Tristitia vestra in gaudium vertetur "—" Your sorrow shall be turned into joy." In one sense it was a horrible apparition and at the sight of it the old man fell down in a swoon. He was carried at once to his secret chamber (probably a hiding-place). (Cf. *Haydock Papers,* pp. 21-25 passim.)

There was but time for the old priest to describe the vision before he breathed his last. His body was borne to its last resting-place, and was laid beneath the chapel at Cottam Hall by his son, Dr. Richard Haydock. The latter had taken the degree of Doctor of Divinity and became a professor of theology at Douay.

George Haydock himself studied for four years at Douay, and then went to the English College, Rome, where he was ordained deacon. The climate of Rome disagreeing with him, he returned to Rheims where he completed his course and was ordained priest in 1581. Unfortunately there is no space here to insert the beautiful Latin letter which George Haydock wrote to Father Agazzari, S.J., the Rector of the English College, Rome, at the conclusion of which he commends the soul of his father to the prayers of the good Rector. He also mentions that his father, recently dead, had some claim to those prayers, since Vivian Haydock had always made a point of praying for the good estate of the English College at Rome. (Cf. *Catholic Record Society,* Vol. V, pp. 21-23.)

In 1581, almost immediately after his ordination, George Haydock was sent on to the English mission. "He landed in London at nightfall, and having sought in vain for a lodging in Holborn, apparently found one in the neighbourhood of St. Paul's churchyard. The next day, he made it his business to see Mr. John Towneley, who was at the time a prisoner for the Faith in the Gatehouse. After that, he paid a visit to his cousin, Mr. William Hesketh, of Poulton-le-Fylde, who was also a prisoner for the Faith in the Fleet. Shortly afterwards, he paid a third visit, which was the immediate cause of his arrest; this was to the house of a certain Hawkinson, who had been formerly in the service of the Haydocks of Cottam Hall and who had then been of great assistance to George Haydock by his good counsels and directions, when the young man was preparing to set out for Flanders to become a priest. At that time, Hawkinson was a devout Catholic but had unhappily apostatised. His sister, Elizabeth Hawkinson, was of finer mould and was among those who had been arrested in Lancashire for recusancy and committed to Salford gaol. Meanwhile, George Haydock, utterly unaware of the state of things, made haste to pay Hawkinson a visit as an old friend whom he wished to thank for the services he had rendered, and also to tell him all that had happened since they had last met. The priest was well received by his former friend, who apparently said nothing about his own defection, but after George Haydock had left him, he at once arranged with two apostates and pursuivants, Norton and Sledd, to arrest the priest as he was leaving the house. Hawkinson had taken care that the arrest should not be made in his house. The date of the arrest was either on Sunday, 4th February, or on Tuesday, 6th February, 1581-2." (Cf. *Lives of the English Martyrs*, Burton and Pollen, pp. 38-39.)

According to the Annual Letters of the English College, Rome, for the year 1581, there is a notice of eight priests having been sent to England about that time, " three of whom, Pitts, Haydock and Bishop, have been arrested . . . and have given illustrious proof of their constancy in the Faith." (*Foley's Records, S.J.*, Vol. 6, pp. 74, 77.)

The details of the actual arrest appear to have been as follows: George Haydock, on passing through St. Paul's churchyard, entered an adjacent bookseller's shop and was arrested there by the apostate pursuivants and dragged into a church nearby, where certain ministers of the State church endeavoured to induce him to abandon his Faith, all to no

purpose. Haydock was then duly arraigned and brought
before Cecil himself. After that, he was sent a prisoner to
the Tower, where he was closely confined while suffering
from a most painful and lingering disease which he had contracted abroad. In his cell, a Protestant minister came to
dispute with him, and finding that after a lengthy disquisition
he had made no headway, angrily asked George Haydock
point blank, whether or not the Queen was the head of the
Church.

"By what authority," asked Haydock, "do you ask me
this question?"

The minister replied: "Were you a true servant of Christ,
you would surely not inquire as to my authority but would
make open profession of your belief before everybody."

"Do you, heretic as you are, reproach me with cowardice
in the cause of God?" said Haydock. "I believe that the
Queen neither is nor can be the head of the English Church."

"Who, then?" asked the minister.

"The Roman Pontiff," replied Haydock.

"Traitor!" exclaimed the minister, "you dare to say as
much, because there are no fit witnesses to convict you of
your statement."

"Not so," rejoined Haydock, "I am making a confession
of my faith."

"If so," challenged the minister, "put down in writing
what you have said just now."

"I have neither pen nor paper," replied Haydock, "yet
will I gratify you to the best of my power," and taking up
a piece of charcoal the priest wrote as follows on the door
of his cell, "Gregory XIII is the Head of the English and
the Universal Church, to whom the whole world must be
subject, if it would be saved." (Ibid., p. 106.)

On 7th February, 1583, the Feast of St. Dorothy, Virgin
and Martyr, to whom there is a traditional devotion among

the Catholics of Lancashire, George Haydock was summoned to trial and remained adamant in the profession of his Faith, refusing again every proffer of liberty and reward, if he would but conform. At this trial he received sentence of death for having been ordained priest by the Pope's authority. The good priest regarded the date of his trial and condemnation as so happy an event that he attributed it as a blessing obtained for him by the intercession of St. Dorothy, and marked the date on the calendar of his breviary which he gave to his distinguished fellow-prisoner for the Faith, Dr. Creagh, the Archbishop of Armagh. The story told of St. Dorothy is that one of her executioners, Theophilus by name, denied her firm belief that her execution was an instantaneous journey to Heaven and perhaps half jokingly asked her to bring him a rose from Heaven's gardens, as soon as she arrived there. Immediately after her execution, the story relates, St. Dorothy appeared to Theophilus and presented him with the rose he had asked for. What is certain in this episode is that Theophilus became a Christian and died a martyr.

The Venerable George Haydock, priest, with his mind and heart full of the sacred words quoted by his dying mother, " Your sorrow shall be turned into joy," endured his own martyrdom at Tyburn where he was hanged, drawn and quartered on 12th February, 1584. He was the fourth Lancastrian to suffer martyrdom in the Elizabethan persecution. The fifth native of Lancashire to die for the Faith in the same persecution was the Blessed John Nutter, priest, who was executed at Tyburn on the same day and on the same occasion as the Venerable George Haydock.

The Nutters were a Catholic family of some position, owning an estate at Reedley Hallows, Burnley, which included farmland in the Pendle Forest district. Here two brothers, Robert Nutter, the older of the two, and John

Nutter were born, and both were destined to suffer martyr-
dom for the Faith. They were apparently brought up
Catholics and were educated along with a young friend,
Robert Woodroffe, later a priest, at a Catholic grammar
school in Blackburn, kept by a Catholic schoolmaster, Mr.
Yates. In due course, Robert Nutter went to Oxford and
John Nutter to St. John's, Cambridge but, for reasons of
conscience, both brothers left their respective Universities and
together went overseas, both arriving at the English College,
Rheims, on 29th August, 1579.

For a time John Nutter acted as tutor to eleven young
men whom he at length conducted as a party from Rheims
on 3rd October, 1581, to the Jesuit College at Verdun, where
he handed them over and then returned immediately to
Rheims to complete his own course. John was eventually
ordained sub-deacon at Soissons on 10th June, 1582, by the
local Bishop, Charles de Rouci-Sissonne, and finally deacon
and priest at Laon on 22nd September of the same year by
the Bishop, Monsignor Valentine Douglas, O.S.B. He said
his first Mass on 1st October, 1582, and left Rheims on 24th
November for the English mission, in the company of his
friends, Robert Woodroffe and Samuel Conyers.

At Rouen, Robert Woodroffe had to stay behind for
reasons of health, and the two others continued their journey
to Havre, where they had to remain so long waiting for
favourable weather, that their funds ran out and they contracted debts. On this account, John Nutter undertook the
return journey to Rouen to get money for his companions
and himself to enable them to pay their debts and continue
their journey to England. In the meantime, it was agreed
that Samuel Conyers was not to wait for Nutter's return if
Robert Woodroffe arrived and a suitable ship was found, but
to embark at once and sail over. On reaching Rouen, John
Nutter found some others who were intent upon sailing to

England. One of these was Peter Lawson of Brough, Yorkshire, who later, as a prisoner in England, is described in
the prison-list as a priest. For a short time John Nutter had
to rest, since his constitution had been almost ruined by
disease. Eventually he was able to return to Havre, and in
a few days all business having been settled, the party of four
were able to embark on a ship bound for Scarborough. The
four in question were the three priests, John Nutter, Samuel
Conyers and one unnamed, who was apparently not Robert
Woodroffe who had evidently been unable through sickness
to follow on to Havre. The fourth companion, Peter Lawson,
may or may not have been in holy orders.

During the voyage a violent storm arose and the ship
foundered on the coast at Norfolk, and John Nutter, having
become perilously ill, was put ashore at a port called Dunwich,
now wholly submerged by the encroaching sea. Although the
ship was lost, the crew and passengers were all saved. Among
the wreckage washed ashore later was a bag containing
several Catholic books, copies of Dr. Vaux's Catechisms, New
Testaments in Latin, Primers, and books of devotion. This
bag was discovered by two ministers who guessed that it
belonged to the sick man who had been put ashore. When
questioned, John Nutter, supporting the disguise on which his
life rested, described himself as a merchant from York and
formerly an apprentice of one Mr. Bannister of Preston in
Amounderness, Lancashire, who was a draper; and then
employed in York, as a factor, a capacity in which John
Nutter stated that he had taken a consignment of broadcloth
to Rouen, and that after a period of illness there, he was
returning with some books to deliver to the agent of
" Monsieur " (the Duke of Anjou). (The full account may
be read in Vol. V, pp. 38-39, *C.R.S.*)

Realising that his interrogators knew more about him than
he had at first thought, John Nutter relinquished this story

and openly confessed his Faith and his priesthood, nor did he ever falter in that profession.

Sick man though he was, John Nutter was manacled in irons and taken a prisoner. The date of his arrest appears to have been 15th January, 1582-3, and he was incarcerated first of all in the Marshalsea, where his health recovered and he at once expended his newly won strength in a singularly fruitful missionary apostolate among the prisoners, causing many of them to return to the unity of the Catholic Church. At length, the day of his martyrdom came when he was led to Tyburn on 12th February, 1584, where he was hanged, drawn and quartered for his priesthood, and he is now honoured as the Blessed John Nutter.

Peter Lawson remained a prisoner for the Faith, loyal and steadfast to it, in the Marshalsea, and at length died in the same prison in the September of 1586.

CHAPTER 4

THE LADIES OF ROSSALL HALL

T H E Earl of Derby was commissioned to deal with the determined recusancy of the influential families of the county and the equally determined resistance of the people. In this the Earl was eagerly supported by the State Bishop of Chester, Dr. Chatterton, a bitter hater of Papists, and the lamentable apostate, Sir Edmund Trafford. For his known hatred, the politicians in the Council had selected him to be the Sheriff of the County of Lancashire. " It might be said he was merely waiting for this opportunity systematically to pursue with insults and to despoil of their property all who remained steadfast to the ancient Faith. He was almost a freakish interruption in the splendid Catholic traditions of the Lancashire Trafford family, so nobly manifested by the martyred Abbot of Sawley, William Trafford.

" In the next generation, however, this breakage was repaired when Sir Cecil Trafford, knighted at Hoghton Towers, returned to the Faith of his ancestors." (Cf. *Haydock Papers*, p. 31.)

It was in no way religious zeal for the Protestant cause which actuated Sir Edmund Trafford; the rewards and plunder to be had from successful and active pursuivancy were almost irresistibly alluring to those whose Christianity was of secondary import. Edmund Trafford, for interests of his own, saw to it that the Privy Council were duly furnished with lists of convicted recusants incarcerated in Salford gaol.

This Sheriff's raids on the various Catholic homesteads were widespread and his spies or minions, for a share in the spoils, were ever ready to direct his attentions to the same.

One example of this style of looting is seen in the case of the notable Catholic family of the Allens of Rossall Grange in the Fylde. After the death of George Allen, the elder brother of Cardinal William Allen and heir of the notable home where William Allen was born, the extensive estates excited the greed of a covetous neighbour, the apostate, Edmund Fleetwood, who designed to rob the widow, and her family of three daughters, of the Rossall estates. He lost no time in notifying Edmund Trafford of the lady of Rossall who was harbouring missionary priests. On more than one occasion, the Cardinal himself had visited his home to consult on Catholic affairs with his recusant elder brother, George. If there was one person in the whole world whom the politicians of the Privy Council, and notably Cecil himself, wished to capture, it was Cardinal William Allen. The possible prize to be won was too great to be ignored, and kindly neighbours warned the widow, Elizabeth Allen, who at the time, 1580-2, was harbouring nearly a dozen priests, that the pursuivants under Sir Edmund Trafford were, in their systematic raids on Catholic households, drawing nearer to Rossall Hall.

The actual Hall or Grange no longer exists, since the land it once occupied near the shore between Blackpool and Fleetwood has been washed away, and the old buildings with it, by the encroaching sea. An old tower connected with Rossall Hall is still in existence.

Elizabeth Allen was formerly a Miss Westby of the Catholic Westby family of Yorkshire and Mowbreak Hall, not many miles from Rossall. Her sister, Helen Westby, had married Vivian Haydock and was the mother of the Martyr, the Venerable George Haydock. During the years 1562-1565,

William, afterwards Cardinal, Allen, stayed with his kinsfolk and other Catholic friends, and then William Westby, the father of Mrs. Elizabeth Allen, was in residence at Mowbreck Hall. His son and daughters, John, Helen and Elizabeth, were outstanding examples of Catholic loyalty. " In 1582, the Council received the following information (Dom. Eliz. cli, No. 74, 1581), ' Richard Haydock, priest, is either residing with his brother at Cottam Hall, two miles from Preston in Lancashire, or with his uncle, three miles from his brother's house. His uncle's name is John Westby and the house where he lives is called Mowbreck Hall, in Lancashire.' " (*Haydock Papers,* p. 36.)

The ladies concerned in this record of heroic suffering for the Faith were Elizabeth Allen (née Westby), the widow and mistress of Rossall Hall, her three daughters, Helen, Catharine and Mary, who later married Thomas Worthington, the eldest of the boy confessors whose story is told in the subsequent chapter. There were also two other relatives in residence at Rossall Hall: Isabella Allen, a sister of Cardinal Allen, who had married into the Catholic Conyers family of Hinton, Yorkshire, and Aloysia or Alice Haydock, the sister of the martyr, the Venerable George Haydock. At the time she was seriously ill and was being tenderly nursed at Rossall Hall by her aunt, Elizabeth Allen. There was also a young son, John, who was at the time of the raid on Rossall Hall at college on the Continent. The suspicions, therefore, that Cardinal Allen might be in hiding at Rossall were not groundless.

Since the tenantry and dependants together with the household staff were devoted to the good lady of Rossall Hall, the raid had to be directed by the pursuivants with some caution. In the first place, Sir Edmund Trafford, the Sheriff, sent there a spy who masqueraded as a friendly and devout Catholic but, although well received, deceived no one. At nightfall on the Eve of the Epiphany, 1583, a man came to the door, who pretended to be the bearer of a message from some Catholic friends of the family. He was kindly received and given lodgings for the night; but in reality he was the Sheriff's spy and repaid the hospitality shown him by stealing out of bed and searching every corner of the house during the course of the night, in the hope of finding the hiding-place of Mrs. Allen.

The actual raid occurred early on the following morning, the Feast of the Epiphany, when at the time there was only one priest in the house. The raiders, helped by a band of ruffians out for loot, were firmly resisted by the household staff demanding their warrant. After some trouble, the raiders managed to break through the barrier of servants and began their search of the house for the priest, Mrs. Allen, and her sister-in-law, Mrs. Isabella Conyers. The search failed and the household staff refused individually, in spite of every kind of inducement, to take an oath to answer every question put to them by the pursuivants. In order to give these servants a lead, the false guest proceeded to swear that his hostess was hidden somewhere in the house. He also stated on oath that he had been locked up all night in his bedroom to prevent him from discovering her hiding place. But he had reckoned without the faithful steward, William Anyon, who had shared the same room with him during the night and who stepped forward at once and proved him before his face to be a perjurer.

In order to exhaust her larder and so shorten the stay of the unwelcome raiders, Mrs. Allen invited bands of villagers and labourers on the farms and land to come and take their meals at the Hall. Thus for a time the raiders themselves were almost prisoners until the arrival of reinforcements by whose assistance they were able to evict these formidable guests who, however, left behind them a dozen men to act as a bodyguard for Mrs. Allen's three daughters. Eventually a warrant was issued for the arrest and imprisonment of these men and they were taken away under escort to be tried in court.

On the way, a notice was given by a spy to the officers of the escort that Mrs. Allen was hiding in the house of her steward, William Anyon, at Chirkbridge. The house of this good man was searched thoroughly from floor to ceiling. They found, however, no trace of Mrs. Allen, who had previously entrusted to his safe-keeping a sum of money reserved for her three daughters, lest that too should fall into the hands of the sequestrators and despoilers. The searchers found this money, a sum of £500, hidden in a bin full of flour. In spite of William Anyon's vigorous resistance, this money was taken. He was himself robbed of £3 and the flour in the bin was deliberately spilled on to the floor and rendered useless by being trodden underfoot. In the meantime, Mrs. Allen was extremely anxious about the safety of her daughters, exposed to grave dangers from the raiders in occupation of the Hall. Miss Aloysia Haydock, an invalid and known to be the sister of the martyr, the Venerable George Haydock, was cross-examined and urged to betray her kind hostess, and she was pressed to conform and to take the unlawful oath. On firmly refusing to comply with these requests, she was arrested and sent to prison, the effects of which hastened her death.

The three Allen girls, Helen, Catharine and Mary, prisoners in their own home, succeeded in hiding the keys by means of which they could be securely locked up and, although the officer in charge had given orders that the three young ladies were to be taken to the house of the Sheriff, the guards left at Rossall Hall delayed carrying out that order. So, on a suitably dark night by pre-arrangement, the three girls were able to slip out of the Hall and reach the banks of the River Wyre, where a boat awaiting took them across to the further bank, and for a fortnight or so they were wandering about, hardly daring to seek shelter in any house for fear of re-arrest.

At length, the three daughters reached Warrington, and were sheltered by an uncle during a critical time when that town was being searched for the priest and martyr to be, James Bell. Search was also being made for another active priest, Thomas Worthington, and his brother, Mr. Richard Worthington. At this kinsman's house they were happily joined by their mother, Elizabeth Allen. She endeavoured to invoke the law of the land for the protection of her property against the unjust claims of Edmund Fleetwood, but, being a recusant, she was treated as an outlaw. However, Edmund Fleetwood did not secure the property in its entirety, for Cecil, the Lord Treasurer, took the lion's share, and was generous enough to leave a few scraps for the jackals.

A fuller and more detailed account of this truly heroic adventure for the sake of Faith and conscience is contained in the *Haydock Papers* and in Dom Bede Camm's *In the Brave Old Days,* pages 117-136.

Mary, third daughter of Mrs. Allen, eventually married Thomas, the eldest son of Mr. Richard Worthington of Blainscough Hall, the same Thomas who, while no more than a boy, proved himself to be a heroic champion of the Faith.

Robbed of all her property, Mrs. Elizabeth Allen sought the Continent along with her daughters Helen and Catharine, and the three ladies had to travel by night, hiding in woods and outbuildings to avoid arrest. The journey took them more than two months until they eventually arrived at Rheims on 19th September, 1584. On 17th March, 1590, they went to live in Flanders, and Helen and Catharine became nuns at the Convent of St. Monica, Louvain. Helen died in the year 1603 and Catharine in 1612.

In the meantime their heroic mother went to live at Namur, generously helped in her poverty and distress by Cardinal William Allen, who secured for her a pension from King Philip II of Spain. In order to insure the regular payment of this grant to the impoverished widow, Cardinal Allen was insistent in writing to the Governor of the Low Countries, Count Mansfield. In the end she appears to have retired to Louvain where she spent her last happy years with her daughter Mary and her son-in-law, Thomas Worthington.

Chapter 5

THE YOUTHS OF BLAINSCOUGH HALL

BLAINSCOUGH HALL, the home of the Catholic Worthington family, had been subjected to more than one raid by the pursuivants during the same period, and in one of these the Blessed Edmund Campion was nearly captured. At the time, Father Campion was walking in the park at Blainscough Hall, not far from the house and near a pond. He was disguised in the rich apparel of a courtly knight, and was totally unaware of a troop of pursuivants, mounted on their horses and riding up the drive towards the house. With great presence of mind, one of the maid-servants darted from the house and with a vigorous push precipitated Father Edmund into the muddy pond. The incident attracted the attention of the cavalcade and the scene caused much merriment, but the " staging " of it proved to be the perfect disguise it was meant to be, and the pursuivants rode on to the Hall.

It is thought that the principal quarry of these pursuivants was Father Thomas Worthington, with Father James Bell, the martyr, and the recusant gentleman of Blainscough Hall, Mr. Richard Worthington, the younger brother of Father Thomas Worthington, D.D., who later became the President of Douay College and finally a Jesuit. On this occasion the pursuivants failed to make their anticipated capture, and all three made their escape. Sir Edmund Trafford, however, did not give up the search, for an infamous spy in the Sheriff's employ handed in a report that Thomas Worthington the priest, together with his four nephews, Thomas, Robert,

Richard and John, the four sons of Mr. Richard Worthington, were staying at the house of Mr. Sankey, of Great Sankey, Warrington.

At the time, a strenuous search was being made for Father James Bell and, on receiving the pursuivant's report, the Sheriff gave orders for a troop of some twenty soldiers led by the under-Sheriff, to make a raid on Sankey House. This took place on 12th February, 1584, at three o'clock a.m. The raiders broke into the house and first seized the four boys. They strove at once to extract information from them with terrorising threats and questions. Had they intended to go to any Papist seminary abroad? What arrangements had their father and uncle made for them? Where were their father and uncle at the time? Where had they last seen them? Had they attended Mass? Along with the boys they arrested George Hothersall, a relative whom they suspected of being about to go to a pontifical seminary overseas. They also arrested a William Cromwell, whom they suspected of being either Father Bell or Father Worthington.

They then searched every corner of Sankey House for Father Worthington, with no result. So eager were they to arrest him that, leaving a guard at Sankey House, they hastened to the house of Mr. Harvard of Earlstown, two miles distant, and diligently searched there and every other house and lodging in Warrington. They set a watch both upon Warrington bridge and the banks of the Mersey, and on other points to prevent any escape. This storm raged for two or three days, but they failed to find Father Worthington who, totally unaware of the search being made for him, was actually in Warrington itself, at the house of a sick gentleman to whom he was administering the Sacraments. The three nieces of Cardinal Allen were in Warrington at the time under the care of an uncle, and luckily escaped the search.

In the meantime, unable to shake the constancy of these youthful prisoners, they left the two younger Worthingtons, Richard and John, in charge of Mr. Sankey and took the two elder ones, with the two gentlemen whom they had also captured, to Wigan, where the prisoners were examined by the Earl of Derby and Chatterton, the Bishop of Chester. No headway could be made with any of these four prisoners. The elders boys were taken to Preston for further interrogation and here they were held in custody until the younger brothers, Richard and John, had been brought from Mr. Sankey's house to join them.

It was thought that the two younger boys could be induced with less effort to divulge the information wanted. The youngest, John, was selected and was kept fasting for some time to weaken his resistance. He was at length brought before the commissioners, a small boy not quite twelve years old. After being deprived of food for a whole day, the little prisoner was offered wine in too large a quantity, which he drank as requested but, against all expectation, the boy retained a clear head and refused either to conform or to give the information for which they asked. The boy in his own way added with simple sincerity that he had been given the wine to make him drunk so that they could induce him to say what they wanted but, by the grace of God, he continued, his head was quite clear and he was, as he said, " compos mentis." They then began to press him for information about his father and his uncle the priest. By this time the child was suffering pains because of the quantity of wine he had had to drink on an empty stomach, and the more they plied him with questions, the more the boy complained of his pains. At length, he won a boy's victory; he became violently sick in the court room and had to be taken out immediately. The scene had been so disgraceful and palpable an exhibition of brutal bullying that the Earl and

Dr. Chatterton and the other officials present, in order to deflect the shame of it all from themselves, tried to blame the attendants.

They then called in the eldest, Thomas Worthington, a boy of sixteen. The Earl of Derby began very gently by promising him and his brothers great rewards if he himself would attend and persuade his brothers to attend a service in the State church, " to which," he added, " it is not necessary that you should attach any faith, but only to be present, and to influence your brothers by your example." Thomas Worthington, however, was not to be bought in that way. Eventually Dr. Chatterton took up the cudgels and commenced by adopting a kind and suasive manner, but finding this of no avail, he began to use the weight of his authority. He ordered the youth in the name of his allegiance and observance due to the Queen's Majesty to answer on oath to all the questions put to him. The boy declined to do this, stating that he could not swear to matters he did not fully understand.

" But if," said Chatterton, " you wish to speak the truth, I think you may safely swear to it." Thomas Worthington, however, had his answer: " You may be sure that what I shall say will be the truth, but it is my religious duty not to mention anything which might be injurious to myself and my dearest friends; an oath so taken to the injury of others and of the one who takes it is not binding." Dr. Chatterton then resorted to an illustration. He held up his handkerchief, saying, " What if you stated that on oath which can injure no one; for instance, that the handkerchief which I am holding up in my hand is a handkerchief?" " I could not accept that," replied Thomas, " there being not sufficient cause to justify an oath."

After this failure to win any victory over the eldest boy, the next eldest, Robert, was summoned for interrogation and he also showed that his Faith was proof against any of their wiles. A short time later, a clever and wordy specialist in the art of controversy, a man called Fox, was requisitioned to argue the points out with the four boys. They resisted the temptations put before them of most desirable rewards, if they would but make a show of conformity and disclose the required information. They were reminded of the misery and the wretchedness of the life before them if they refused.

" The youths, on the contrary, declared that they would rather live by begging within the pale of the Catholic Church than stained with the crime of schism (as it appeared to them to be at the time) superabound in all the delights of the court of the Earl of Derby, or the palace of the pseudo-Bishop." (Cf. *Foley's Records, S.J.,* Vol. 2, pp. 116-133, from which the above and the following abbreviated account of the " Worthington Boys " is taken.)

The four boys were then taken to Manchester to be placed not in prison with other recusants but in a house of correction. Here threats of punishment were employed and one of the interrogating zealots, a Mr. Ashton of Chatterton, when he heard of their resistance, exclaimed: " What is this! Such little boys refusing to join in our religious services and prayers? If this little germ increases, and their elders are allowed to join it, it will come to pass that we shall never succeed in extinguishing the papistical religion in our England."

From then onwards, the treatment of the four young prisoners became more cruel and heartless. They were stinted in food and general comfort, and Dr. Chatterton himself made use of the threat that unless they conformed they would be arraigned at the next assizes and charged with treason. The boys were all legally under age for such a charge and its penalties, but even in those days there were diabolic experts in the art of psychological torture. When all these disgusting

means failed to move the four boys, the bishop, Dr.
Chatterton, became excessively angry and this gave an
opening to one of the principal attendants, presumably at
the house of correction, a rough, hard and brutal man called
"Bull." He offered his services to Dr. Chatterton, and
asserted that, if authorised to do so, he would undertake by
the rod and birchings to induce them in a few days to obey
the Queen's demands. The angry State bishop nodded and
said, "Certainly; undertake the task, friend Bull, and try all
you can and don't spare them unless they conform and show
themselves complying."

The next morning the brute entered the boys' room armed
with four or five canes, long and thin, and addressing
Thomas, the eldest, said, "What are you going to say
now, Thomas? Will you go to our churches and places of
prayer?"

"You had a sufficiently decided answer from me, yesterday," said Thomas.

"But I expect another answer from you now which will
be more in accordance with what you are asked to do,"
replied Mr. Bull, who gave Thomas no more time to reply,
for he had decided to make an example of him in the presence
of his three younger brothers. He seized him savagely,
dragged him out of bed on to the floor and gave him a
severe flogging, saying, "I'll make you set a good example
to your brothers." In spite of this suffering, Thomas refused
and declared boldly that nothing would induce him to say
or do anything against his Faith and conscience. Bull then
seized Robert, the second eldest, dragged him out of bed
on to the floor and inflicted the same flogging upon him,
but was unable to induce any promise of conformity. Robert
was as loyal and uncompromising as his eldest brother.

The man then turned his attention to the two younger
boys, Richard and John, and, asking if they would now

consent to join the State church, notwithstanding the terror
of the rods met with a determined refusal. He then dragged
the pair on to the floor and adjusted their clothes. He paused,
however, for Thomas, then sixteen years old, was, according
to the law as it then stood, liable to a fine of sixty gold
crowns per month for recusancy, but was exempt from the
penalty of scourging. It is not unlikely that an intelligent
youth like Thomas Worthington was well aware of this and
intimated as much to Mr. Bull. The latter, therefore,
refrained from beating Richard and John and told them that
there would be another occasion and opportunity some time
later for inflicting the beating.

He then told the gaoler to shut the two elder boys in
separate rooms. He ordered the younger boys to get dressed
and he took them away with him to Dr. Chatterton who
had authorised him to inflict the illegal floggings. The law
being proverbially two-edged, the good bishop was at some
pains to extricate himself from possible commitments. He
now had the two younger boys on his hands, and for a time
was in a quandary to know what to do with them. At length
a rigid Dutch Puritan expressed himself pleased and willing
to take Richard and lodge him in his own house. He treated
Richard kindly and endeavoured to educate him gently but
without force in the Protestant faith. In this matter, Richard
was well able to defend himself, and the kindly Dutchman
did not endeavour to constrain the youth to attend the
services in any State church. Like many other non-political
Protestants at the time and later, he had little or no sympathy
with political and legal coercion in matters of religious observance and his own tendency was towards non-conformity, as
far as the State church was concerned.

John Worthington was taken by the bishop to his palace
and for some four days was treated well, allowed to take
his meals at the episcopal table. But this period of peace

did not last long, for John refused to break the laws of abstinence.

"Why is it, John," asked the bishop, "that you refuse good and wholesome food? Why from a scruple of conscience do you observe this abstinence, when as yet you know so little? Do you not see me eat flesh meat?" "Yes, I do," said John, "for you eat whatever comes first." John was sent forthwith to take his meals at the second table with the servants, where neither flesh nor fish over-abounded.

Meanwhile Dr. Chatterton became ill and his wife, Catharine, began to treat John to a series of readings from Fox's *Book of Martyrs*. John's comment on all this was blunt and definite: "If any other Catholic prince whatever should obtain the reins of government, he would treat my Lord Bishop in the same manner, and burn him for heresy." Since Catharine had been reading in the presence of the sick bishop, the latter heard John's downright remark and said, "That would by no means happen, for he would obey those in power. I should not be so refractory and contumacious against the Popish prince, should any such by chance rule over us, as Papists now are, for then, as good subjects, we should observe the laws." The boy John, having for one so young suffered horribly at the hands of the enemies of his Faith, had a reasonable answer for "trimmers." "But yet," he added, "that sort of obedience would not free you from the punishment of the laws, for whether you seemed to be converted or not, you would be consumed in the avenging flames." In other words, there was a Hell! After this interview, Dr. Chatterton made arrangements for John to be sent back to the house of correction in Manchester, where his two elder brothers, Thomas and Robert, were still detained.

After the disposal of Richard and John, the bishop of Chester's emissary, Bull, returned to Manchester commissioned to deal with Thomas and Robert Worthington. These latter were sent to attend a course of studies at a school where lectures on Protestantism were given by selected experts. Prior to this, Bull had made known to them that in accordance with Dr. Chatterton's orders they were both of them to be fettered arms and legs with heavy irons unless they conformed.

"Come, then," said the man Bull, "for although the commands of the Lord Bishop are otherwise, this time you shall not be chained, but to school you must go, and I will carry the fetters under my cloak." The schoolmaster, who was something of a savage, failed to induce the two boys to attend the required religious services and prayer-meetings and, although the other scholars were encouraged to mock them, many of them became edified by their faith and steadfastness to the point of conversion, all the more so because the two Worthingtons ably defended and expounded the Faith and led their preceptors into making silly answers which exposed their ignorance, much to the amusement of the rest of the youths. The "host" or keeper of the two boys was often drawn into nonsensical answers, and, on this being pointed out to him, would fall into a rage. He determined, therefore, to lay a trap for them and on returning from a religious service on one occasion, he said, "I wish you had been present at this service, since in the sermon it was proved that a woman was once consecrated Pope." Robert Worthington replied, "Whoever it was that dared to assert this, he clearly and impudently lied."

"But the preacher," said the keeper, "was our bishop."

"What of that?" replied Robert, "I don't except him from the rest, and he has committed a sin in publicly preaching this and you also in listening to it." The enraged keeper drove Robert from the table and from his house. Infuriated, he reported the affair to Dr. Chatterton, who directed him to be sworn on oath in regard of his accusation.

He himself took a more lenient view of the matter, and when Robert was called upon to repeat his statement, the boy did so, recalling to mind that the angry keeper himself had declared that he had heard the bishop make the asseveration in his sermon. Dr. Chatterton stated that he could not remember having made such a statement in his sermon; he therefore passed over the affair in silence and ordered that Robert Worthington should be entrusted to the care of a less irritable keeper.

The third brother, Richard Worthington, had given serious offence to Dr. Chatterton by omitting to raise his hat when that prelate passed him on the road. The result was that his Dutch host dismissed the boy from his house, and Richard was placed in the custody of a cruel and surly constable. Learning of this, the kind-hearted Dutchman intervened and took the boy back. Never once did that Protestant gentleman ever use any kind of constraint, but endeavoured to explain to Richard the advantages that would accrue to him if he conformed. He would, for example, inherit almost immediately his father's rich patrimony, forfeited by his two recusant elder brothers. Many had fallen from the Faith through like temptation, but not Richard Worthington.

The three other brothers, Thomas, Robert and John, in custody at Manchester, were informed one day that they were to be dragged to the service in a State church by a party of constables unless they went there willingly. Under guard, therefore, and to avoid violence, the three boys, much against their will, were paraded to the service in question. Although the boys had been compelled, their action was speedily noised abroad as an act of conformity to the Establishment. Thomas, however, wrote a report contradicting that rumour and clearly stated that they had been compelled to attend against their wills. He stated further that in order to kill such a rumour and to remedy the evil, he and his brothers would never again enter such churches unless dragged there by violence, and that they were ready to be thrust into gaols or to live in the house of correction . . . and by the help of God's grace they would never give assent either in word or deed to any such religious services. On reading this report, Dr. Chatterton said to Thomas, " I myself will take care that you shall be corrected and chastised, and if I only live, I will bring it to pass that you shall follow our ecclesiastical rites."

Many friends, some of whom had conformed, proffered bail for the three brothers on the condition that, if released, they would not go abroad. This they rejected, and they refused for one moment to accept the truth of a report that their parents had conformed and desired the four sons to do likewise.

Thomas and his younger brother John made their escape from custody in Manchester. The remaining prisoner, Robert, could not be induced to give any information, under threats of severe chastisement, of the details of his two brothers' escape from the house of correction, nor as to where they had gone. So he was ordered to be removed from Manchester and to be imprisoned in the bishop's palace at Chester. As a last resort, Robert was urged to conform to save his own father from much suffering.

All this had no effect upon the resolution and faith of Robert Worthington. Two of his close friends had taken care to ascertain the day on which he was to be taken to Chester Castle, and they contrived a plan to liberate him from his captors. On the day itself, they went early to Manchester and waited at an inn nearby for the departure of Robert and his custodians. They had also arranged for two horsemen to ride out to the village of Budworth, a short distance on the way, and to stay at the inn to reconnoitre and learn the strength of Robert's escort. Apparently only one unmounted constable was to be the youth's guard. Hence, when Robert and the latter were on their way to Chester, a horseman rode up and overtook them. He reined his horse and, looking at the boy, observed that he was tired. He then offered to mount the boy behind him, and for some nine miles they all travelled together at a walking pace, until they reached an inn and refreshed themselves. Continuing the journey after, the constable gladly agreed to his prisoner's mounting again behind the stranger, who then turned to thank the constable, saying, " Good-bye, good sir, I will ease you of this charge. Tell your master that I am going direct to London! " Having spoken thus, the horseman with his passenger, applying his heels to the horse, galloped away.

" Bad luck to me! " said the constable, who began a useless chase. At length, a second horseman kindly joined in the search, and as the number of searchers grew, he led them anywhere but in the right direction, for he also was a friend of Robert Worthington and likewise in the plot.

There was a happy reunion in the hospitable house of a Catholic gentleman in Stafford, where the three boys, Thomas, Robert and John, met their father, Mr. Richard Worthington, and the uncle—the much hunted priest—Dr. Thomas Worthington. While they were happily united in this Catholic household, there was a midnight raid of the pursuivants and the three boys and their father had to spend the rest of the night in the open air. Later, all four were arrested and taken back into the house. The father, however, and his three sons were not the persons for whom the raiders were searching; their quarry was the priest, Father Worthington, and the good lady of the house, who had taken the pursuivants under her control, saw to it that they did not capture him. Indeed, she arranged matters so well that Mr. Richard Worthington was permitted to go home and, when the coast was clear, Father Worthington and his three nephews proceeded towards London. Unfortunately a false friend, masquerading as a Catholic, accompanied them, and when the party, including other priests and recusants, reached Islington, near London, the apostate betrayed them all to the notorious Topcliffe, who on their arrest claimed for himself all their horses as his special perquisite, for they were excellent animals.

Father Thomas Worthington was imprisoned in the Tower, and the two other priests with him were put in the Clink. The youth, Thomas Worthington, was imprisoned in the Gatehouse, Westminster. But Robert and John Worthington, along with two other companions, managed to effect their escape.

Later, on 21st January, 1585, sentence of banishment was passed on twenty priests and one recusant layman. Among the priests were Thomas Worthington, Arthur Pitts, and the notable Jesuit superior in London, Jasper Heywood, who led the protest of all of them against the injustice of the sentence of banishment. In spite of their protests, they were taken to the Thames embankment and shipped to Normandy.

Meanwhile, Richard Worthington, the third of the four heroic brothers, attempted to escape from the custody of his Dutch keeper by explaining in a letter to his mother how this could be done with the help of a colleague when returning from school. The letter, however, fell into the Dutchman's hands, who himself wrote to Mrs. Worthington agreeing to free her son from his custody on payment for his keep, and provided the boy would not be sent abroad. He then made arrangements for Richard to be taken away by a friend. Richard, nevertheless, hastened to London, where he joined Robert and John and, after many risks and dangers, the three youths succeeded in crossing the Channel and reaching Rheims. The youngest brother, Laurence, who was an infant at the time of these occurrences, later made his way to the

Continent and became a priest and a Jesuit, as also did his brother John. Robert did not survive long after his sufferings, and died on 18th January, 1585, at the age of seventeen.

Four years later, on 8th June, 1589, Richard also died at the age of sixteen. Their noble father, Mr. Richard Worthington, died a prisoner for the Faith, on 25th September, 1590.

Thomas, the eldest of the Worthington boys, finally succeeded in reaching the Continent and eventually married Mary Allen, the daughter of the valiant lady and widow of Rossall Hall, Elizabeth Allen, who spent her last years in happiness and peace in the household of her son-in-law, Thomas Worthington; and the present chapter ends in conjunction with the conclusion of the preceding chapter. Thomas Worthington died at Louvain in the year 1619.

Chapter 6

Part 1—RENEWAL OF EXECUTIONS AT LANCASTER CASTLE

SOME forty-seven years had passed since the execution at Lancaster Castle of the Abbot of Sawley, William Trafford, who with his Cistercian companions died for the Faith and for conscience. Executions for loyalty to the Faith were resumed in the year 1584, and the two martyred victims were a priest, the Blessed James Bell, and a farmer, the Blessed John Finch.

James Bell was born at Warrington in 1520 and after graduating at Oxford was ordained priest in the reign of Mary Tudor. When the new ecclesiastical settlement, totally at variance with the ancient Faith, was made statutory by Elizabeth Tudor's first Parliament in 1559, James Bell was not among the priests who resisted. Although he never seriously believed in the Protestant Reformation, he apparently found it easier to conform and to follow the trend of the times. He was never happy in the new ministry, and it is thought that because of a conscientious reluctance to exercise in it the cure of souls, he was never appointed to a benefice or a parish. In consequence of this, he was reduced to very great poverty and eked out a scanty livelihood by supplying here and there as a curate.

At the age of sixty years, his circumstances were so straitened that he returned to his native Lancashire, where he thought he would have a better chance of securing a chaplaincy of some kind without the cure of souls. He little minded how small the stipend should be, provided it

enabled him to live in comparative ease and comfort suitable to his age. Something had to be done quickly, apparently, before the infirmities of old age overtook him when
helpless and destitute. He was, however, fortunate in his
quest and found the kind of chaplaincy he required, which
was at the disposal of a gentleman whose wife was a Catholic.
James Bell, therefore, applied to this good lady and through
her services received the post. She had taken pity on the
unhappy elderly man, whom she knew to be a priest. Her
compassion was all the greater because of his miserable state
of sin, and she commenced to exhort him to give up his
apostasy and service contrary to the sacred functions for
which he had been ordained. She did not hesitate to remind
him that he had been ordained priest to celebrate Mass and
to administer the Sacraments according to the Catholic practice in the unity of the Catholic Church. These he had not
only neglected for some twenty or more years, to the great
danger of his own soul, but had also exercised the " contrary
abominable devices of the heretics." With many good words,
she besought him to have a better care of his own soul, and
reminded him of the good which he might yet do to others,
by his example and labour, in part satisfaction for his former
evil life. (*C.R.S.*, Vol. 5, pp. 74-75.)

Although James Bell did not immediately respond to that
sound advice, the words of this good woman made a deep
and lasting impression upon him and, when he became
dangerously ill and the good lady visited him in his sickness,
he submitted himself to her good counsels and consented to
her charitable suggestion that she should bring to him " a
grave and virtuous priest." She waited, however, until he
himself asked to see the priest in question of his own accord,
actuated by divine graces.

Her good services were rewarded, for James Bell eventually asked her to bring the priest, and having made a devout

confession he was absolved and formally reconciled to the Church in the year 1581. For a year or so, he devoted himself to penance and spiritual exercises, applying himself to the study of the Breviary, the ceremonies of the Holy Mass, the Sacraments and the other duties of his priesthood.

Simultaneously with his recovery of the state of grace, James Bell in a wonderful manner recovered the health of his body. When the term of his period of penance and pre- paration was concluded, he received all the needful faculties and for two years was the apostolic and intrepid Papist missionary whose labours were so fruitful in Lancashire that the Earl of Derby and the Sheriff of the county with their pursuivants spared no pains to capture Father James Bell.

In those two years the extent of his missionary journeys included nearly all the Catholic houses and Mass-centres in Lancashire. The accident of his final arrest is described in paraphrase from an ancient account preserved in the same Records, as follows:

" When he had thus truly fed the poor flock of Christ by word and example for the space of two years and more, in the month of January, 1584, as he was travelling alone and on foot from one Catholic house to another, he met one of the common pursuivant spies.

" Mr. Bell, thinking him to be an honest man, asked him the way to a certain town. This wretched fellow, suspecting forthwith that the good old man was a priest, began to question him whence he had come and whither he was going. Mr. Bell, pausing in his answer to these questions, was at once subjected to another; he was asked what he was, and Mr. Bell answered freely and without fear that he was a priest. ' Well,' replied the busybody, ' you shall have to come along with me.' Father Bell, old and infirm, made no useless resistance. The spy brought the old priest to a Justice of the Peace before whom he again openly confessed to be a priest, but that for many years he had not lived according to his priestly calling and functions, and moreover stated that now he was reconciled and was desirous to celebrate Mass, if he could find a suitable place and all the other things needful for that purpose. He told the Justice also that recently he had received authority to hear confessions and to absolve, and that the same authority came from the Pope."

Father Bell had long made up his mind to profess his Faith boldly, anywhere and at all times, when those times came. " When the Justice and his colleagues begged him to return to the State church or go to a service therein, he utterly refused and repeated again that he was still grieved and still begged God's mercy and pardon that he had ever functioned at or attended their schismatical service. And so he was sent to Manchester and there imprisoned (in the Salford gaol), sometimes in the loathsome dungeon, and sometimes with other priests in another place." (*C.R.S.*, Vol. 5, pp. 75-76.)

Two other priests were arrested about the same time by Sir Edmund Trafford, the High Sheriff of the county: Father Thomas Williamson and Father Richard Hutton. After some time spent in Salford gaol, these two priests, along with Father James Bell and a recusant farmer of Eccleston, near Prescot, named John Finch, were selected for arraignment at the Lenten assizes at Lancaster Castle. During the journey to Lancaster, Father Bell was singled out for special ignominy, his hands being tied behind his back and his legs tied under the horse he was riding, by no means a comfortable position for an old and infirm man who had a long and slow journey to make. In the old document cited above, strong words are used in reference to his treatment, and the manner of his conveyance is described as " very rude and barbarous." At the subsequent trial in Lancaster Castle, the judge had received instructions not to condemn to death more than two of these four prisoners, with the result that the jury, finding all four guilty of repeatedly denying the Queen's supremacy in matters ecclesiastical and of affirming that of the Pope, Fathers Thomas Williamson and Richard Hutton were condemned to perpetual imprisonment, and Father James Bell and Mr. John Finch were condemned to death. On receiving the death-sentence, the Blessed James Bell with a radiant countenance turned to the judge and said, " I beg Your Lordship would add to the sentence, that my lips and the tips of my fingers may be cut off for having sworn and subscribed to the articles of heretics, contrary both to my conscience and to God's truth."

He had been captured in the way described, at Golborne, between Wigan and Warrington. On 20th April, the Blessed James Bell was hanged, drawn and quartered at Lancaster Castle for the priesthood and the Faith.

His companion, John Finch, was born of a wealthy family at Eccleston, near Prescot, and appears to have been brought up a Protestant or to have conformed on his own account. Though his parents had the means of enabling him to go to a university, John Finch gave up schooling and went to London to seek his fortune with some relatives who were in the legal profession, without success, and he was forced to take service in a household. He was a young man of some twenty years when he left Lancashire, and, finding no prospects in London, he returned home and married a virtuous girl who owned a farm, which John Finch managed profitably. Becoming dissatisfied with the State religion, he spent some time in considering the merits of that church and those of the Ancient Faith. He was eventually reconciled to the Faith, and, after exercising a devoted and diligent apostolate as a catechist and an instructor of lapsed Catholics, he became an active " conveyor," assisting the missionary priests and finding them harbourage.

His final arrest was the outcome of a despicable trick planted on him by that worst of all enemies, the apostate Catholic masquerading as a devout one, who had won the respect and friendship of John Finch. In reality, that wretch had married a concubine of the Earl of Derby, and for suitable payment readily accepted the ignominious task of a pursuivants' spy. Knowing that John Finch could summon hunted priests to any place where their services were needed, he intimated to him that several Catholics, including women, were anxious to have the ministrations of more than one priest, and John Finch, trusting the man, arranged to provide one who came to him at his bidding. The priest in question was Father George Ostcliffe and, when the planned raid was carried out, both John Finch and the priest were arrested and, after some time in the custody of the Earl of Derby, were committed to Salford gaol—where John Finch met the steadfast Catholics Thurstan Arrowsmith, Ralph Worsley, John Burge, a schoolmaster and other prisoners for the Faith.

Thurstan Arrowsmith, strongly objecting to the reading of the Protestant Scriptures by a " reformed reader " while the Catholic prisoners were taking their meals, interrupted so vehemently that the reader could not continue and in this Arrowsmith was strongly supported by John Burge. At length, Ralph Worsley undertook the reading, but even so the matter had to be referred to one of the priest-prisoners, who allayed their scruples by reminding them that their purpose at table was to take their meal, and not to attend to any reading. Whatever the nature of the reading might be, it could not deprive them of their natural and just rights. But this comparatively comfortable state of things in the new Fleet prison at Manchester could only last so long as the prisoners were able to pay their prison fees.

When the Catholic prisoners became destitute, as they invariably did, they were transferred to the "House of

Rogues," or "house of correction," and met death from starvation and exposure. Thither the above-named Catholic martyrs for the Faith were transferred. Not the least of John Finch's sufferings was the false rumour noised abroad that he had co-operated in the betrayal of Father George Ostcliffe. However, the lie was soon dispelled by his steadfast profession of the Faith at the examinations before the Earl of Derby, in the presence of Dr. Chatterton, and later during his final trial at Lancaster, and by his violent resistance to forced attendance at a State church service.

Most of this account is taken, abbreviated, from an old document, detailing the life of John Finch and his martyrdom. The same source tells of the violence used to drag Catholic recusants to the State church services from the "House of Rogues." "From thence, they caused some of the prisoners to be dragged by force by parties of strong men to the State church service; a proceeding which was not accomplished without exhausting struggles and bloodshed, which not only the prisoners suffered, but those who were using force upon them.

"In all this turmoil and wrestling, John Finch, being of great strength and very unwilling to be brought to a place which he loathed above all others, kept a posse of several men busy with him, who might have been more usefully employed in some more profitable work and with less pain to themselves. What spurred them on was their spite against John Finch, because of his manifest loathing of their religious services and proceedings. They dragged him to church with such fury and barbarous cruelty as though they were drawing a beast to the slaughter; dragging him by the heels through the streets upon the cobbles in such a manner, that his head was very bruised and wounded and left a trail of cobblestones besprinkled with his blood. It was a pitiful spectacle to all who beheld it and was bemoaned by the people. To this affliction, instead of bandages for his wounded head, they added other cruelties. Immediately after this struggle, they thrust him into a deep, dark, cold and malodorous dungeon, which was built on the middle of a bridge. There he could rest his weary bones upon the cold and damp earth, and refresh his lungs with the unwholesome and dank air." (*C.R.S.*, Vol. 5, pp. 82-3.)

While incarcerated there, he sent word to Dr. Chatterton asking that he might speak with him alone. The State bishop of Chester refused the request, though John Finch asserted that he would do him no bodily harm. " Let me be bound to a post, and thus speak with you," the martyr had urged, but Dr. Chatterton may have been afraid of what John Finch had to say to him. From this bridge-prison, Finch was again constrained to attend a State church service, and, witnessing all the preparations for the anticipated struggle, John Finch went there quietly, although none the less forced and against his own will.

He was afterwards so grieved at what he considered to have been a grave fault and for the scandal it might cause to other Catholics, that he sought to perform a public penance as a public expression of contrition for the lapse. On being taken one day from the dungeon on the bridge for an " airing," he asked that he might ride on horseback because of the pains of bodily soreness. This request was granted and John Finch, once mounted, jumped out of the saddle and precipitated himself into the water. Instead of swimming away, he stood up in the shallows with his head above the water and remained motionless.

The old document states that although the enemies of the Faith regarded the incident as attempted suicide, Catholics both at large and in prison clearly understood it to have been a penitential act and a signal to them that John Finch had not conformed or betrayed the Faith. He was at length taken for trial to Lancaster Castle along with his fellow-martyr, the Blessed James Bell, where both were condemned to death for the Faith. To a minister sent to reason with him in the condemned cell, the Blessed John Finch expressed the desire that he should not trouble him, " For I am not of your religion, neither will I be, for anything you can say. God give you grace to amend." (Ibid., p. 87.) This ancient narrative is endorsed by Father Persons, S.J.

On 20th April, 1584, the Blessed James Bell and the Blessed John Finch were both hanged, drawn and quartered at Lancaster Castle.

Part 2—THE ISLE OF WIGHT MARTYRS

In the year 1586, two missionary priests, Robert Anderton and William Marsden, both natives of Lancashire, having embarked for England were caught in a violent storm in mid-Channel. The storm was so overpowering that the crew on board gave themselves up for lost. Not so the two priests who, kneeling down on deck, prayed for the safety of all on board and for themselves that they might not be deprived of the chance of martyrdom. The storm abated and both passengers and crew were safely landed on the Isle of Wight. The islanders, hostile to Papists, had the two priests arrested almost immediately and committed to prison. From here they were taken to Winchester to be examined by the State bishop, who thought to amuse himself on controversial points with two young Papist priests whom he judged to be somewhat raw and simple. The brilliance, however, of Robert Anderton astounded the bishop, and since the audience showed a disposition to be amused at his discomfiture, he lost his temper and resorted to abuse. He made a clumsy slip of which Robert Anderton was not slow to take advantage. The bishop taunted the two priests with " the Pope Joan " myth, and harangued long and tediously on that subject.

" Although it is easy to refute this fable," replied Anderton, " being the foul fabrication of heretics long since exploded, yet if it were true, my Lord, it was not for you to propound so absurd an insult! "

" Why?" asked the bishop.

" Because," replied Anderton, " the basis of your faith, the citadel of your religion, is that you profess a woman to be the head of your Church. Surely, whether we call her Pope Joan or Queen Elizabeth matters little. With what face, then, can you object that to us as an infamy, which is your special glory? How can you taunt the Roman See with what you proudly regard as the bulwark of your religion?"

There was no reply to that, and the two priests were arraigned for trial before Judge Anderson. Although he adjudged them guilty of treason, he deferred execution of the death sentence without the direct authorisation of the Queen. So on 10th March, 1586, they were sent to London and placed in the Marshalsea to be tried by two specially appointed members of the Privy Council. These interrogators had little difficulty in extracting from the priests what they regarded as treasonable matter and what their victims knew to be essential in the determined profession of their Faith.

It would seem that some attempt had been made to save the lives of these two young priests, who were already under death sentence. The Privy Councillors deputed in London to adjudge whether the death sentence should be ratified, expressed an assumption that for the future the two prisoners would adhere to their promise never to try to persuade anyone in the matter of religion. In that case, it may be inferred, that the two priests would have been reprieved and sent into exile.

But neither would buy his life by such repudiation of their apostolate. Both denied ever having made such a promise, and Marsden declared that to persuade the people of the truth of Catholicism was the sole object for which he had come back into England. The deputies could do no more, and " the Queen," the proclamation said, " could only let the law take its course." The Blessed Robert Anderton and the Blessed William Marsden were sent back to the Isle of Wight with full authorisation that the sentence should be duly carried out. These two Blessed martyrs were hanged, drawn and quartered for their priesthood in the Isle of Wight on 25th April, 1586.

Both martyrs were Lancashire men. It is thought that the Blessed Robert Anderton was a son of Hugh Anderton of Euxton Hall, near Chorley, and that his mother was the second wife of Hugh Anderton. She was Alice, the daughter of Alexander Standish of Standish Hall. The Blessed William Marsden was born at Chipping, and was the son of a recusant yeoman of Thornley, a short distance north-east of Longridge, named Richard Marsden.

About the year 1578, both the martyrs had been at Oxford. Robert Anderton was at Brasenose College and William Marsden at St. Mary's Hall. (Cf. *Lives of the English Martyrs*, Vol. 1, Burton and Pollen, pp. 202-203.)

In spite of their Catholic environment, these two martyrs had either been brought up Protestants or had conformed, possibly to fulfil the conditions for matriculation or graduation at Oxford. They returned to the ancient Faith and went to Douay, where they were received into the Church by a Jesuit, doubtless Father John Cullam, B.A., and they arrived together with six companions at the English College, Rheims, on 10th July, 1580. Both received minor orders in Rheims Cathedral, on 25th March, 1581, at the hands of Monsignor Cosme Clausse de Marchaumont, bishop of Châlons-sur-Marne. Anderton was ordained sub-deacon on 24th September, 1584, and priest on 21st March, 1584-5, in Rheims Cathedral, by Cardinal de Guise. Even before he was admitted to major orders, Anderton was regarded as an excellent preacher, and in April, 1583, he was selected out of the whole College to deliver an oration in the presence of the chief authorities of Rheims, ecclesiastical and civil.

William Marsden was ordained sub-deacon in December, 1584, and deacon on 16th March, 1585. It is not recorded when he was ordained priest. Although not so brilliant as Anderton, he appears to have made his mark in the College. Of both these martyrs, a contemporary friend, later Father Warford, a Jesuit, who was with them at Oxford, Douay and Rheims, has given a precious description: " Anderton was of moderate height, but somewhat less than Marsden. The latter had always a pale complexion. Anderton had a more manly countenance, but had evidently suffered from sickness as a child. Both had black eyes, beards slight, which would have been brown when fully grown. Both of them were most unassuming, but full of life and spirits, and they were remarkable for their piety and zeal for sacred things." (Ibid., pp. 203, 204, 210.)

Part 3—A MARTYR FROM BLACKBURN

Five days before the execution of the Blessed Robert Anderton and the Blessed William Marsden, another Lancashire man was martyred at Tyburn. This was the Venerable William Thomson, priest, who, while labouring in the London region had adopted the alias " Blackburn," the name of the town in Lancashire where he was born and brought up. Little is known of his early years but, since Blackburn had never surrendered its right to have a Catholic school, it appears reasonable to infer that William Thomson, blessed with good Catholic parents, had always been a Catholic and, since more than one of the houses of the Catholic gentry in the vicinity made provision at great risk and cost for the free board, lodging and preliminary education for promising Catholic youths aspiring to the priesthood, it seems likely that William Thomson had availed himself of these opportunities. Such minor colleges were provided by the Cliftons of the Fylde and later at Lytham House by the Tyldesleys of Marley Hall, near Leigh, by the Towneleys of Burnley, and elsewhere in the county.

In due course, William Thomson went to Rheims and was eventually ordained priest in the year 1584. He was sent almost immediately into England and was soon catalogued on the list of the notorious apostate and spy, the wretched George Elliot, as one of the priests at large in London " of gentlemanly demeanour."

For two precarious years he ministered in the city and was harboured for the most part in the house of the blessed and noble Anne Line. Before her marriage to Roger Line, a steadfast Catholic and recusant, she was a Miss Higham of a distinguished Essex family. Unhappily, her father had conformed and had expelled Anne and her brother William from their home because they would not follow his example. The young William Higham after different periods in prison for assisting priests and for recusancy, at length made his way to Spain, where he became a Jesuit lay-brother.

After her marriage the valiant lady, Anne Line, devoted herself to the perilous work of harbouring priests, instructing converts and helping her fellow-Catholics in every work of

mercy. She had even arranged that a hunted priest who died
in her house should be buried therein with the full approved
rites, lest the body should be taken by the pursuivants and
thrown unceremoniously into a common pit. Father Thomson
is reported also to have been harboured by Sir John Arundell
of Lanherne, who at the time was confined to a house which
he had rented at Ely Place.

For some time, Father William Thomson was the confessor
of Anne Line, and, when the good priest was under threat of
execution for his priesthood, he promised her that if God
should make him worthy of that glorious end, he would pray
that she might obtain the like happiness. Some time later,
after the martyrdom at Tyburn of William Thomson, the
Blessed Anne Line told another priest of the promise made
to her by her martyred confessor and spiritual director.

It is thought that he was actually arrested at the house
of Roger Line, the husband of Anne Line, situated in
Bishopsgate Street, while celebrating Holy Mass. Roger Line
and Mrs. Line's brother, William Higham, both under
nineteen years of age, were serving the Mass at the time, and
were arrested and imprisoned along with the priest. (Cf.
Lives of the English Martyrs, Vol. 1, Burton and Pollen,
p. 201.)

In due course, " In the Sessions of Oier and Terminer at
the Justice Hall, Old Bailey, the 18th of April, 1586, William
Thompson, alias Blackburn, made priest at Rheims in
France by the authority of the Bishop of Rome and remaining within this realm after the term aforesaid was condemned
there for treason." Thus, the official notice, and everything
in official order. So the Venerable martyr, William Thomson,
was hanged, drawn and quartered for the priesthood at
Tyburn on 20th April, 1586. The Blessed Anne Line, some
fifteen years later, was hanged at Tyburn for harbouring
priests, 27th February, 1601.

The proclamation cited above in the case of Father Thomson and his companion martyrs was one of the many public expressions of the Statute 27, Eliz., of 1585, imposing the death penalty on all missionary priests who, being ordained abroad, remained in England.

CHAPTER 7

LANCASTRIANS MARTYRED IN OTHER PLACES, 1590 - 1600

A PERIOD of sixteen years was to pass before there were any further martyrdoms for the Faith at Lancaster Castle. Most people in North Lancashire whether Papist or otherwise were edified by the constancy of the martyrs or shocked by the cruelty of their death. There was therefore need of caution on the part of the officials during this period. One of the reasons may be cited in the words of a spy: " Also they in Lancashire and those parts, recusants, stand not in fear by reason of their great numbers. Likewise I have heard it reported publicly amongst them that they of that county have beaten divers pursuivants, and made them vow and swear that they would never meddle with any recusants more. And one pursuivant in particular was made to eat his warrant and vow never to trouble them nor any recusants more." (*Foley's Records, S.J.*, Vol. 2, pp. 140-141.)

Perhaps for the same reasons there were no public executions of Catholics for the Faith in Manchester. Nevertheless the town was " a great centre of persecution under William Chatterton, the bishop of Chester. The clergy of the collegiate church were his agents. Hollingworth on page 14 tells us, ' The Queen and her Council appointed Manchester to be the place wherein to imprison and confine such Papists as they thought fit, and to train up their children in the Protestant religion.' " (*Foley's Records, S.J.*, Vol. 7, p. 482.)

The consequence of this latter measure resulted in the population of towns like Rochdale and other south-eastern

Lancashire municipalities, including Manchester itself, becoming largely Protestant.

During this period there were Lancashire men who won the martyr's crown elsewhere, and the first of these was Miles Gerard, born at Brynn, near Wigan, a member of the notable Catholic family of the same name. Little appears to be available concerning his early years, but later he devoted his talents and energy to the dangerous task of teaching Catholic youths, and labouring, as so many other Catholic men and women were doing at the time, to save and screen the young from heretical proselytism. For some time he was engaged upon this work as a tutor at Morleys Hall, Leigh, a house owned by the Catholic family of the Tyldesleys, who had considerable estates in Lancashire, including Myerscough Lodge, near Brock and Claughton, and Fox Hall, Blackpool.

Most likely, pursuivancy drove him from Leigh to the Continent on an errand of charity, it is said, to discover for a Catholic lady, whose husband had been long in exile, whether the latter was alive or dead. Having received no communication for a long time, she was again contemplating matrimony and wished to know whether she was free. Miles Gerard tried hard to fulfil this commission to the best of his ability, and went to Rheims, where he was eventually ordained priest in 1583. He remained on the Continent until 1589, when he was sent on to the English mission in company with the priest who was to be his fellow-martyr, the Blessed Francis Dickenson, who had been ordained in the same year, 1583. The latter was a convert, born at Otley in Yorkshire, and appears to have been a young man of some twenty-four years old, whereas his travelling companion and missionary priest, Miles Gerard, was about forty years old. For some years after his ordination Miles Gerard had been employed in teaching and for a time had stayed at Abbeville and Treport, no doubt in quest of the exiled George Williams, who was reported to have been at Rouen and Paris, places which Miles Gerard had been unable to reach because of the unheavals at the time in France. (*C.R.S.*, Vol. 5, pp. 169-173.) It seems unlikely that he obtained the information required by the lady in question.

The two missionaries, apparently meeting each other for the first time, embarked at Calais. Their ship ran into a violent storm and was wrecked on the coast of Kent, but the two priests and the crew were rescued. Some members of the crew, knowing the two passengers to be priests, reported them to the port authorities. They were promptly arrested and cast into prison at Rochester, where they were arraigned and tried. Both were condemned to death for their open profession of the Faith and their priesthood, and the Blessed Miles Gerard and the Blessed Francis Dickenson were hanged, drawn and quartered at Rochester on 30th April, 1590.

Some years before that date, the martyr's kinsman, Mr. Nicholas Gerard of Brynn, when an old and infirm man, gave a splendid manifestation of his faith and constancy in the event narrated as follows. His own brother, Sir Thomas Gerard, had unhappily conformed and used every persuasive effort to induce his brother Nicholas to do likewise. At length he resorted to force, and had the old man carried protesting to a service in the State church. Although at the time, Mr. Nicholas Gerard was enduring a violent attack of sickness and pain, he was carried in the church right up to the place where the minister was conducting the service. Instead of joining in the service with the congregation, Mr. Nicholas Gerard commenced to sing the Psalms in Latin with such a loud and powerful voice that the minister could not be heard, and he constrained the persons who had carried him in to take him out of the church in order that the service could continue.

Incidentally, it was the daughter of Mr. Nicholas Gerard who married Robert Arrowsmith, the son of Thurstan Arrowsmith. This Catholic couple were the parents of the Blessed Edmund Arrowsmith, and they had the farm at Haydock in the parish of Winwick, where the martyr was born. This Catholic household had also been subjected to a cruel raid by those paid home-wreckers the pursuivants, and the homestead was roughly searched by the raiders for hidden priests. They tried every bed and hole with their swords in search for any evidence of Papist practices. In the end, Robert Arrowsmith, his wife Margery, formerly Miss Gerard, and other retainers were tied two and two and taken prisoners to Lancaster Castle. The four young children of Mr. and Mrs. Arrowsmith, of whom one was the future martyr, Edmund Arrowsmith, having been routed out of their beds by the raiders, were left destitute standing in the cold, clothed only in their nightdresses, for no other member of the household had been allowed to dress them. At length, some kindly neighbours came to the rescue of the four little ones and for the time being took care of them.

Great pressure was brought to bear upon Robert Arrowsmith and his brother, Peter Arrowsmith, to make them conform and, since neither was allowed freedom to manage the farm at Winwick except on the fulfilment of conditions against their faith and conscience, they succeeded in escaping to the Continent. Peter Arrowsmith eventually died of wounds received in the wars and was honourably buried at Brussels. Robert, the father of the martyr, after many adventures and hardships, paid a visit to his brother, Dr. Edmund Arrowsmith, then a professor at Douay. The latter was a man of great holiness and learning, and his exiled brother spent some time with him.

Eventually Robert Arrowsmith, as soon as the venture seemed possible, returned to England broken in health. He did not long survive and, foretelling the time of his death, he made a pious and edifying end. In the meantime, the valiant widow, Margery Arrowsmith, managed the farm and continued the heroic struggle of supporting her four children. That she was related to the Blessed Miles Gerard is taken for granted, but the degree of kinship is not available.

Another Lancashire man martyred about the same time was the Venerable George Beesley, who was born at " The Mount," Goosnargh, some five miles north-east of Preston. " The Mount " at the present time appears to be spoken of locally as " The Hill," a name used to designate the present Catholic chapel of St. Francis, served by the Benedictine Fathers.

Little appears to be known concerning George Beesley's early years, but since Goosnargh, Whittingham, Haighton and Fernyhalgh have always been traditionally strong Catholic centres of recusancy, it was very probable that he was born of good Catholic parents and was brought up a devout Catholic.

George Beesley, as soon as he was ready, went overseas to prepare himself for the priesthood and was ordained at Rheims in 1587. He left Douay for England in company with the martyr, the Blessed Christopher Bales, on 2nd November, 1588. The journey across the Channel was undertaken with two more priests, both Jesuits—the Blessed Edward Oldcorne and Father John Gerard. The latter has described part of the sea voyage as follows: " We four priests embarked, a lucky load if I exclude myself, for my unworthiness robbed me of the crown of martyrdom. The other three all met a martyr's death for the Faith. The two priests from Rheims were quickly captured, *consummati in brevi, impleverunt tempora multa.* Their names were Christopher Bales and George Beesley. But my companion, Father Oldcorne, worked and toiled for almost eighteen years in the Lord's vineyard before he too watered it with his blood.

" After crossing the sea, we sailed up the English coast. On the third day, my companion and I saw what seemed a good place to put ashore in the ship's boat. As we thought it would be dangerous for all of us to land together, we asked God's guidance in prayer. Then we consulted our companions and ordered the ship to cast anchor off the point till nightfall. At the first watch of the night, we were taken ashore in the boat and dropped there. The ship spread its canvas and sailed on." (*John Gerard, An Autobiography of an Elizabethan*, Philip Caraman, c. 2, pp. 8-9.)

Since Oldcorne and Gerard effected this landing at a spot on the coast roughly halfway between Great Yarmouth and Cromer, Christopher Bales and George Beesley most likely landed on the Yorkshire coast near Flamborough Head. Apparently George Beesley was in Yorkshire for some time and was harboured at the houses of a Mr. and Mrs. Dalton, and of a Mr. and Mrs. John Wells, and these four kindly persons were arrested for sheltering the seminary priest George Beesley. (Cf. Christopher Grene's MS. " F," cited in *Foley's Records, S.J.,* Vol. 3, p. 750.)

An intrepid recusant prisoner, Richard Webster, a Catholic schoolmaster, who had been incarcerated for twelve years, chiefly in the Marshalsea, on being questioned concerning " one Bisley," a Catholic agent, who had constantly tricked the arch-spy Phelippes and his minions, " ingenuously " confessed his dealings with George Beesley. For that reason, the Attorney-General gave it as his opinion that such an admission was sufficient to justify arraignment for treason and a trial involving the death-sentence. (*C.R.S.,* Vol. 5, p. 214.)

During the short period while he was at large, Beesley was a notably active apostle. According to the description of a spy, Father Beesley was a powerfully built man with very dark hair and a full and well-grown beard. Apparently he had worked his way southwards and for a time was harboured by that noble Catholic couple, Mr. John Gage and his wife, of Haling, Croydon, Surrey, doubtlessly at their London house, St. John's Street, Clerkenwell, Middlesex. Mr. and Mrs. John Gage were arrested and condemned to death for harbouring George Beesley and, although pardoned, suffered several years' imprisonment. (*C.R.S.*, Vol. 11, Part 2, p. 571.) The priest was probably arrested with them, and his associate, Richard Webster, remained in prison until the accession of James I.

For some time George Beesley was submitted to Topcliffe and his assistant torturers, but the greater the torture the more downright and unqualified were the martyr's expressions of the Faith. Before his execution he was confined in the Tower, and to this day in the Martin Tower may be seen the martyr's elaborate inscription signed with his name, George Beisley, as he spelt it, and to which he added the word " priest." The whole is well carved out with the I.H.S. and the Cross Keys of the Holy See, and also the passage in Latin from the Psalm: " As the hart panteth after the fountains of water, so does my soul after Thee, O God." When along with the Venerable Montford Scott he was brought to the gallows in Fleet Street, the former, who was stripped to his shirt, had knees hardened with kneeling in prayer. A Protestant observer audibly said: " I would be glad to see any of our ministers with knees as much hardened with prayer." The sight, too, of Father George Beesley evoked exclamations of surprise, for this once stalwart man was a mere skeleton and a sight so shocking that some one cried out: " I came to see traitors and have seen saints." The two priests were slaughtered in Fleet Street on 1st or 2nd July, 1591. (Cf. *Catholic London*, Douglas Newton, p. 257.)

Another Lancashire martyr suffered at Tyburn a year or so later. He was a Catholic gentleman named Roger Ashton, who was born at Croston near Ormskirk. Having desired to marry a Catholic lady who was his second cousin, he had applied through the usual channels to the Holy See for the needful dispensation from the impediment of consanguinity. This was no doubt granted, but in the eyes of the authorities in England at the time, such communications were regarded as infringements of the Statute of Premunire and therefore treasonable.

According to reports cited in *Foley's Records,* Volume 1, pages 41-42, Roger Ashton was an agent for pensions due to the King of Scotland, and had lived for some time in Scotland, only coming to England, it is presumed, on business in the service of the Scottish King. The English authorities, however, sent a communication to Scotland demanding the execution of Roger Ashton for alleged breaches of the Statute of Premunire, or that he should be handed over to the Queen's authority, where he would be even more severely dealt with. This appears to explain the reference of Father Christopher Grene in his M.S. " F," cited in *Foley's Records,* Volume 3, page 745, and dated 27th February, 1591, which states that Roger Ashton made good his escape to Tyneside, and along with another Lancashire gentleman, Oliver Cotton, and a Mr. Robert Musgrave, succeeded in embarking upon a ship bound for the Continent.

Unfortunately, the vessel ran into a storm shortly after leaving the estuary of the Tyne, which was so violent that the ship had to return to port in the Tyne, where the three fugitives disembarked at South Shields. Here they soon found shelter in the house of a notable harbourer of priests, Ursula Taylor. The pursuivants, however, lost no time and, having raided this house, arrested Ursula Taylor and her guests, who were all sent to prison in Durham. From here they were transferred to different prisons in York and, after a brief time, Roger Ashton and Oliver Cotton were sent to London. On payment of a large sum of money or bond, Oliver Cotton was released and allowed to return home to his father's house in Lancashire, but Roger Ashton was detained. (*Foley's Records, S.J.,* Vol. 3, p. 754.) He was arraigned and tried, being condemned for the Faith and for his devoted obedience to the Church. He was hanged, drawn and quartered at Tyburn on 23rd June, 1592.

On the main road between Preston and Blackburn, a mile or so east of Samlesbury Hall, is the rural district of Osbaldeston, the name of the Catholic family to whom the estate originally belonged and whose members were the lords of the manor. Of this family was born Edward Osbaldeston, destined to be crowned a martyr. Little is available concerning his early years, and the beginning of his glorious record commences with his ordination to the priesthood at Rheims in 1585. After that, he remained on the Continent until he was sent on to the English mission, 27th April, 1589. The sphere of his four years of apostolic labour was the North Riding, Yorkshire, and in the State papers endorsed for the year 1593, among a number of active missionary priests labouring in the north-eastern districts the names of Richard Holtby, a Jesuit, and Edward Osbaldeston are included. These two priests were personal friends, and the success of their ministrations was noted by spies and the reports made about their activities sufficiently testify to the fruitfulness of their labours in a most dangerous mission field.

When after four years Edward Osbaldeston was arrested and committed to York Castle, he wrote an account of the circumstances of his arrest in a communication which he managed to have delivered to Father Richard Holtby, his Jesuit friend, from whom he sought counsel. Richard Holtby took care to preserve this communication, and in main substance it reads as follows: " I was arrested at Tollerton by Mr. Clarke, an apostate priest, on the Feast of St. Jerome, at night time, a circumstance much more to my comfort than at any other time, because in him I had such a special patron to whom I could commend myself, and such a great champion under Christ to whom in all my troubles and tribulations I could fly as to a special friend of God. Besides, it pleased God, much to my consolation, to show that sign of His love for me, that my arrest took place on that day instead of any other. The reason is, that God in His Divine goodness, called me to the priesthood, and that upon the Feast of St. Jerome I said my first Mass and for the first time consecrated the Blessed Body and Blood of my Lord and Saviour, Jesus Christ, and received Him with great reverence and devotion, and so I have ever since held St. Jerome in great devotion.

" The morning before I was taken away from the house into custody I said prayers to St. Jerome, and in his merits I offered myself a sacrifice to God, and dedicated my journey as a prisoner to Him, directing myself to His good will and pleasure, that I might walk aright in my vocation, and to follow St. Jerome as long as God should see it expedient for His Church and most conducive to His honour and glory; and that if it pleased Him to preserve me still as He had done before, I would never refuse to labour, nor murmur at any pain or inconvenience. If on the other hand, it should please His Divine Majesty to suffer me to fall into the hands of the persecutors, then it would please His Divine goodness to direct me and keep me straight to the very end, which I hope that He will, after having bestowed upon me all my life so many blessings and gifts without number and quite inexplicable. Because of this, my present hope and trust are much strengthened that He will be certain and sure in my regard, now that I am concerned in the weightiest affair that has ever been placed upon my shoulders.

"Hence, considering all this and an infinite number of other similar incidents, I now find great consolation and fully trust in Him and His Divine goodness and distrust only myself. But I can do all things in Him that strengthens me. And this actual narration about myself on that fateful morning and all that has happened since, is in itself a source of strength and consolation to me, and helps me in the contemplation of Heavenly truths of every kind. As I have in the past felt the help of His graces in many lesser and lighter crises, when He was not so near as He is now, so now when He is nearer have I the greater reason to hope and trust. Therefore I have not the slightest doubt that through His graces I shall finish that which has been begun by Him and for Him, and this work I pray God that I may accomplish worthily, when His good will and pleasure call for it and not before, and that I may desire nothing else in this life but that which may best please Him and honour Him and our Blessed Lady His Mother, and all the court of Heaven. I also desire that which will be most edifying in the sight of the people, so that they may be strengthened in the way of Jesus, the King of Bliss.

"The details of my arrest are as follows: Francis Sayer and myself arrived at the inn at Tollerton some time before Mr. Clarke, who eventually came before nightfall. At first I did not recognise him, because I was under the impression that he was still in the south of England. However, at supper I managed to take a closer look at him and came to the conclusion that, as I thought, he was Mr. Clarke. For the moment I felt certain that he had not recognised me, and that if he had, he would do nothing about it and would not betray me. I was, however, mistaken in this, and things happened otherwise than I had thought; God forgive him for it. When it was time to retire for the night, Mr. Clarke rose up and went out, only to return with the constable and the local curate, and we were placed in custody and imprisoned for that night in the inn.

" The following morning, in company with Mr. Clarke, we were taken as prisoners to York, and Mr. Clarke stood near by while I was being examined and questioned before the Council, but he made no statement at that time. I was again examined in the afternoon and Mr. Clarke was again present but did not speak. On that occasion, nothing was said to me. What will follow God alone knows; however, I will not be too hopeful of any chance of acquittal, but prepare myself for death or whatever else may happen to me.

" I hope Mr. Clarke still has my horse, for he rode on it in my company to York, and his attitude towards me all the time we were together was silent and unfriendly until we reached Skelton, and then he and another rode on ahead. Besides my horse they have taken from me a whole set of vestments and other articles of my ministry.

" And now I beg of you for the sake of God to let me know what you hear and learn and what is the best course for me to take in all circumstances. Tell me also as far as you can, how my martyred brethren who have gone before me behaved, so that I may imitate them; for now I desire no privileges, no exemptions, but merely to live in discipline and order as is characteristic of the common life. This I yearn for, that what I have or shall have, will only be that which all have in common. Therefore I beg of you to direct me in all things, both in regard of my apparel and diet and in everything, so that as my brethren have gone before, claiming no exemptions or anything extra, so do I desire to follow their example in the humble and lowly way."

On the copy of this communication the following is written in Father Richard Holtby's own hand: " He had a desire and voice to enter into the Society." (*Foley's Records, S.J.*, Vol. 3, pp. 10-11.)

No time was allowed Father Edward Osbaldeston to carry out that purpose, for he had been arrested at Tollerton on 3rd September, 1594, and after his trial and condemnation to death at York, he was hanged, drawn and quartered for his priesthood on 16th November, 1594.

The words of Edward Osbaldeston just cited express with crystal and refreshing clarity the mind of the martyrs, and for other reasons besides that, the letter of the Venerable Edward Osbaldeston has been given in full.

A comparatively short bus-ride from either Preston or Blackburn brings one to Balderstone, Osbaldeston and Oxendale, the estate of the Catholic family of the Osbaldestons, the members of which were wealthy and prosperous in the fifteenth and sixteenth centuries. This family never relinquished the Faith during any of the crises of penal times or later. In the seventeenth century Sir Edward Osbaldeston, called after his glorious kinsman, the Venerable Edward Osbaldeston, was a noble example of Christian chivalry, perfect manners and scholarship. At Osbaldeston Hall, being proficient in a variety of subjects, he devoted his spare time to scientific experiments and mathematics which he had studied successfully at the Catholic colleges abroad and in which he excelled. His life as a devout Catholic and an exemplary knight well merited the epitaph which may be read to this day on his tomb in the church grounds at Blackburn where he was buried in 1636. " Here lyeth the body of Sir Edward Osbaldeston, a charitable, courteous and valiant knight."

Like most of the distinguished Catholic families, the Osbaldestons became impoverished through cruel financial persecution, but kept the ancient faith. The last of the family to occupy the Hall was Alexander Osbaldeston, who in the eighteenth century had first to mortgage his estate and then dispose of all his personal possessions. By the year 1714 Osbaldeston Hall had become little more than a ruin.

CHAPTER 8

Part 1—THE BLESSED JOHN RIGBY

JOHN RIGBY was born at Harrock Hall, not far from Croston, Mawdesley and Parbold. He was the younger son of Nicholas Rigby of Harrock in the parish of Eccleston, and at the time of the martyr's birth the family was in very reduced circumstances owing to the usual fines and sequestrations imposed by the penal laws for recusancy. Although through constraint the family had conformed to the State religion, young John Rigby, in spite of having been brought up a Protestant, was only a nominal one. It seems evident that his parents had instilled Catholic truths and principles into the young boy with much care and diligence, so that John Rigby had always been a Catholic at heart.

While still living with his parents in Lancashire, the straitened circumstances and jeopardy in which the family found itself forced John Rigby, though a gentleman born, to take service in the London household of Sir Edmund Huddlestone. While in London and able to visit many Catholic prisoners for the Faith, he had the good fortune to meet the then future martyr, Father John Jones, alias Buckley, a Franciscan. The latter was at the time in prison, but was apparently allowed a certain amount of freedom in visiting other Catholic prisoners, of which the good priest made the fullest apostolic use. John Rigby confessed to him that he had always been a Catholic at heart, but had sometimes attended the services in the State church. After a brief period of instruction and preparation, the young man was formally reconciled by this saintly Franciscan, who was eventually hanged, drawn and quartered for the Faith and the priesthood at Thomas' Waterings, Southwark, on 12th July, 1598. He is now honoured as the Blessed John Jones.

Among other friends, John Rigby had the esteem and affection of Father Henry Garnet, martyr, and Jesuit Superior in London. In a letter to the General of the Jesuits at Rome, Father Garnet, referring to the execution of the Blessed John Rigby, wrote: " He died under such torments and with such constancy, that I consider his case to be without parallel at the present time." (*Foley's Records, S.J.,* Vol. 7, p. 965.)

While in London, John Rigby had become acquainted with a priest-prisoner for the Faith, John Pibush. The Blessed John Pibush was martyred at Thomas' Waterings, Southwark, a few months after the execution in the same place of the Blessed John Rigby. In a letter Father Pibush wrote to Father Henry Garnet, martyr himself and the true friend of all martyrs, he stated that he was ever and anon asking the gaoler to tell him all he could about John Rigby.

The details of the Blessed John Rigby's trial and execution, so graphically related in Bishop Challoner's *Memoirs of the Missionary Priests,* pages 238-245, were also collected and preserved by a contemporary Lancashire man and admirer, Dr. Thomas Worthington, the President of Douay College at the time.

The circumstances which led to the arrest of John Rigby while in London were in connection with a delicate work of charity he was asked to undertake by his employer, Sir Edmund Huddlestone. This gentleman's daughter, Mrs. Fortescue, a widow, had been summoned to appear before the court at the Old Bailey on matters of religion, most likely recusancy and an alleged harbouring of Papist priests. She had in fact been harbouring the priest and Jesuit, Father

Gilbert Gerard of the Lancashire family of that name. At the time, his two brothers, Thomas and Alexander Gerard, were prisoners for the Faith at Wisbech Castle. Alexander was living there on 29th April, 1598, but his brother Thomas had died there before at the age of twenty-eight. Alexander Gerard was a missionary priest and Thomas was apparently about to be ordained when he was sent to England on sick-leave and there arrested. In a list drawn up by a spy in London, Father Gilbert Gerard is mentioned as being harboured by Mrs. Fortescue, the widow of Sir Edmund Fortescue. (Cf. *Foley's Records, S.J.*, Vol. 7, p. 293.)

At the time of this summons, Mrs. Fortescue was ill and not able to appear. Sir Edmond Huddlestone, her father, sent John Rigby to the Old Bailey to testify that his daughter was unable to appear in answer to the summons. This service would have been managed easily enough had not a certain Sir Richard Martin been one of the commissioners. He knew John Rigby and for some reason had conceived a grudge against him. He began to interrogate him about his own religion, and John Rigby professed himself to be a Catholic, refusing either to attend a service in a Protestant church or to take the oath of supremacy tendered to him. For this, he was sent a prisoner to the Newgate, committed there by the Lord Mayor. The Lord Chief Justice requested the prisoner to sign his name to the profession he had made—namely that he had always been a Catholic at heart, and that sometimes he had gone to the Protestant church; but, being convinced in his own conscience that this way of acting was not consistent with his conscience, he had been reconciled by Mr. Buckley, in the Clink, and for two or three years had not gone to church. The keeper at Newgate had been ordered to put him in iron chains, and, when this was done, John Rigby said, " I would not change my chain for my Lord Mayor's great chain." With those words he gave a tip to the man for the trouble he had in fastening on those fetters. The date of John Rigby's arrest was 14th February, 1599-1600 and, after a time in the common gaol, he was removed to the prison called the White Lion, in Southwark.

On Wednesday, 3rd March, he was arraigned for trial. His case was not called up that morning, but at lunch time a number of judges sent for him to question him about the statement he had made and signed with his own hand at the first examination. A certain Justice Gaudy showed him the document and asked him if the signature was his. John Rigby affirmed that it was and, in spite of every well meant effort to win him to conformity and to induce him to save his life, the staunch Lancashire Catholic said, " No, my Lord, whoever informed Your Lordship that ever I did yield in any point of my profession of Faith was not my friend, nor ever had my approval of what such an informant implied. I assure you, my Lord, I am a true subject and obedient to Her Majesty and her laws in anything which may not hurt my conscience; but to say I will go to church (a State church service), I never will. Yes, rather than Your Lordships should suspect me however slightly of having such a mind to consent, take my first answer as it is; there is my hand, here is my whole body, and most ready I am and willing to seal it with my blood."

One of the judges stated that they had been told that Mr. Rigby was a simple young man and willing to recant, but they now saw that he was a resolute and wilful fellow, and that the law must take its course. " Let me have the law, in the name of Jesus," said John Rigby, " and God's will be done." The next day, being Thursday, the trial was resumed and effort was made to induce John Rigby to conform. In reply to every argument, the martyr repeated the story of his reconciliation to the Church and proclaimed courageously his firm faith in what they had called the Romish religion, a faith he had always at heart from the beginning.

The treasonable charge they then brought against him was that he had allowed himself to be converted by a Romish priest. Since the priest in question was the martyred Franciscan, the Blessed John Jones, who before his execution on 12th July, 1598, had been allowed the freedom of the prison to minister to the prisoners, John Rigby claimed that his own reconciliation by the same priest could not be treason. Nevertheless, the jury gave a verdict of guilty. This seriously grieved the presiding judge, Gaudy, who had a great regard for the young man. " My good Rigby," he said, " do realise that I am not seeking your death. Will you attend a service (in the State church)?"

" No, my Lord," replied Rigby. Very reluctantly the judge then passed the death sentence. Judge Gaudy, however, procured him a reprieve and John Rigby continued in prison until the next assizes. At the subsequent trial, the presiding judge, Kingsmel, was less friendly and when Rigby in answer to the opening interrogation said, " I am the same man that I was before; it is not lawful for me to go to your church; I will not go to it," the judge asked why there were no iron fetters on his legs. These were brought, and after making the sign of the Cross, the martyr kissed them. They were then riveted firmly on to his legs and apparently remained fast. The next day of the trial, the shackles in an unaccountable way slipped from his legs, although they had been strongly and firmly riveted on. John Rigby smiled at the incident and asked the gaoler to have them fastened on tighter. Shortly after this had been done, the irons slipped off again. The martyr himself called upon his keeper to have them replaced in a firmer way, " for I esteem them," he said, " as jewels of too great a value to be lost." The keeper's man who had already put them on twice before, refused to do so a third time, so that the gaoler had to send for another man to fix them on again. As this was being done, John Rigby called to mind that a Catholic maid had told him that very morning, that during the night before she had dreamed that his irons had fallen from his legs. He told this to the keeper or gaoler and said: "You see, the girl's dream has proved itself true."

On this occasion, John Rigby was sentenced and condemned to death by Judge Kingsmel, and Judge Gaudy, who was present, was seen by some to burst into tears. The martyr was then asked what he thought of the strange falling off of his fetters, which most people thought to have been miraculous. John Rigby answered simply enough: He hoped it was a sign that the bonds of his mortality would soon be loosened.

On Saturday, the 21st of June, word was brought to him that he was to die that day. The place of the execution was to be Thomas' Waterings, in Southwark, and on his way there, lying on the hurdle, he attracted the notice of the Earl of Rutland and a Captain Whitlock, both on horseback. They stopped the procession. Seeing so fine a young man laid on the hurdle, the two gentlemen asked him his name, his age, and why he had been condemned to death. They were genuinely sorry that such a fine specimen of a man with so palpably sincere and honest a demeanour should be in such a predicament. John Rigby answered them, saying: "My name is John Rigby, a poor gentleman of the house of Harrock in Lancashire; my age about thirty years; my judgment and condemnation to this death is only and merely because I answered the judge that I was reconciled, and had refused to go to the State church services." The captain urged him to do as the Queen demanded and conform, and turning to the Sheriff he conferred with him about the matter.

For a space the two gentlemen accompanied the hurdle, until the captain, calling a halt, asked Mr. Rigby whether he was a married man or a bachelor. " Sir," replied Rigby, " I am a bachelor; and more than that, I have never had any intercourse with a woman." The captain added that it was indeed an achievement for a man of his years; that it must have involved a great effort of self-restraint.

" I should hate to speak anything contrary to the truth; but I assure you," said the martyr, " that it is a fact, and that is more than I need have said." The captain accepted his word and agreed in conclusion that he had worthily deserved a virgin's crown. " I pray," he concluded, " God send you to the Kingdom of Heaven, and I want you to pray for me." (The vivid story of the subsequent conversion of the Earl of Rutland and of Captain Whitlock is told in *Tudor Sunset,* by Mrs. Wilfrid Ward.)

On reaching the scaffold, the Blessed John Rigby knelt down and said the Pater, Ave, Credo and Confiteor. When the executioner helped him to mount the ladder, he gave him his last gold crown. As soon as the martyr was suspended, he was cut down from the rope and, landing on his feet, stood upright and motionless, as one momentarily stunned. The butchers, however, floored him and the terrible drawing began. " God forgive you," the martyr cried out in a loud voice, " and Jesus receive my soul."

A rough brute of a fellow, who was not one of the official executioners, in order to silence the martyr, set his foot on John Rigby's throat, while the others held firm his legs and arms. He was, however, still so strong that even when they were in the act of pulling out his heart, he complained bitterly of the barbarity with which the execution had been carried out, and there was much weeping at the loss of such a fine man. The Blessed John Rigby was martyred at Thomas' Waterings, Southwark, 21st June, 1600.

A month later, on 26th July, the Dominican brother of the Blessed John Nutter, Robert Nutter, was hanged, drawn and

quartered for the priesthood at Lancaster Castle. He was
born at Reedley Hallows, near Burnley, and like his brother
was brought up a Papist. For a time both appear to have
conformed, probably with a view to graduation at the universities. Robert, the elder, went to Brasenose College, Oxford,
whereas his brother John went to St. John's College, Cambridge. In both universities there were as yet strong Catholic
influences which ultimately led to the conversion and reconciliation to the ancient Faith of Robert and John Nutter.
They both went to Rheims and Robert was ordained priest
a year before the Blessed John Nutter's ordination in 1582,
and most likely Robert went to England a year before John,
who was martyred at Tyburn in 1584.

Robert Nutter laboured as a missionary in England over a
period of eighteen years, but a considerable portion of that
time was spent in exile for the Faith and in and out of prisons
for the same reason. He was in fact arrested and imprisoned
in the Tower at the same time as Dr. Thomas Worthington,
1583-1584. There he was placed in a dungeon and loaded
with iron chains for some twenty-seven days from February
onwards, and was only removed from his cell so that he
could be tortured.

It appears that Father Robert Nutter was subjected to a
long period of agony in the torture chamber, for it was
apparently only in the following November that he was taken
back to his original dungeon in the Tower and remained there
for two months and fourteen days. He was at length condemned to banishment with the party of some twenty priests
and a recusant layman. It will be remembered that Father
Jasper Heywood, the superior of the Jesuits in England, and
Father Thomas Worthington were among these exiles. "A
new expedient was now entertained by the authorities of
banishing the priests they held in chains, either because they
felt that they gained nothing by their death and slaughter at

home, or else that they reckoned upon gaining great praise by publishing abroad in many places this special act of coloured clemency." (Cited in *Foley's Records, S.J.*, Vol. 1, p. 401.)

The banished priests in question protested against the injustice of this condemnation, as well as did the Catholic layman. They were all servants of God, who coveted the crown of martyrdom and deliberately raised the point, so that they would be able to prove to their own authorities overseas that they had been forcibly expelled from their missions and that they were not running away from them. While sailing across the Channel, the exiles asked of their guards to see the warrant and text of their condemnation to banishment in order to have certain proof. They were eventually landed and disembarked at Boulogne and released to go their ways. Father Robert Nutter, as well as the others, made little delay in availing themselves of the opportunity as soon as one presented itself of returning to England. Having done so, Robert Nutter was arrested again and committed to the Marshalsea, where he was a fellow-prisoner of the Blessed Ralph Crockett.

Part 2—ADVENTURES IN LANCASHIRE

From the Marshalsea Robert Nutter was transferred to Wisbech Castle and was among the number of priests who at that time made their escape from that prison of cruelty and death. Some of his associates in the escape were the five martyrs, Thomas Sprott, Thomas Benstead, alias Hunt, Thurstan Hunt, alias Greenlow, the Jesuit, Robert Middleton, and Edward Thwing. The latter priest, although not known here with certainty to have been a refugee from Wisbech Castle, was a colleague of Robert Nutter in Lancashire. Father Henry Garnet, the Jesuit superior in London and

kindly friend and benefactor of all missionary priests, mentioned in a letter to the General of the Jesuits these escapes
from Wisbech: " Upwards of four years ago, a very virtuous
priest named Sprott, together with nine persons . . . escaped
one night from prison . . . I provided him with a room and
all the necessaries in London, and sent him to some friends
of mine in the country. Last year, another very excellent
priest named Thomas Benstead, having effected his escape
from Wisbech Castle, I received and equipped and recommended him to the same friends. But both these good
priests, going together to introduce each other to my friend
in Lincolnshire, were apprehended and martyred." (*Foley's
Records, S.J.*, Vol. 7, p. 1347, footnote.)

The Venerables Thomas Sprott and Thomas Benstead alias
Hunt were hanged, drawn and quartered for the priesthood
at Lincoln, 11th July, 1600. The four notable priests, who
came to Lancashire and whose zeal made so great an impression on Lancashire recusants, also aroused the county pursuivants to bestir themselves. These priests were Robert
Nutter, a Dominican; Edward Thwing, formerly a professor at
Douay; the intrepid Thurstan Hunt, a member of the notable
Catholic Yorkshire family of Carlton Hall, near Leeds; and
a Jesuit, Robert Middleton.

The Venerable Robert Middleton was the son of Thomas
Middleton of York, the brother, it is thought, of the Blessed
Margaret Clitherow. It was some time after her marriage
that she became a Catholic, and her glorious example no
doubt influenced her kinsman to become not only a Catholic
but also a missionary priest and a Jesuit. He was likewise
destined to share with her the glory of martyrdom. Like her
contemporary, the Northumbrian martyr, George Errington,
the Blessed Margaret Clitherow had her devoted associates of
women helpers who risked everything to help the hunted
priests and oppressed Catholics. Many of these lost their

lives in terrible prisons. One of these associates in York at the time appears to have been a Lancashire lady, Bridget Maskew. She and another associate of the Blessed Margaret Clitherow, named Anne Tesh or Tesse, were recusant prisoners for the Faith before the Bench at York Castle during the trial of the Venerable George Errington and his companions in 1596. These two ladies were also condemned to death on that occasion but reprieved and released after the death of Elizabeth Tudor. These seems to have been, besides the bonds of the Faith, an obvious co-operative link between the Catholic apostolic activities of the Venerable George Errington with his associates and those of the Blessed Margaret Clitherow and her associates.

Anne Tesh for a time was a fellow-prisoner at York Castle with Margaret Clitherow, committed there for the same reasons. " On 12th March, 1586, Anne Tesh was imprisoned with Margaret Clitherow on the testimony of a Flemish boy. The two spent the time until Monday, 14th March, in prayer and abstinence with so much joy that Margaret said several times: ' Sister, we are so merry together that, unless we are parted, I fear we shall lose the merit of our imprisonment.' " (*Lives of the English Martyrs*, Edwin H. Burton, D.D., and J. H. Pollen, S.J., p. 194.) Thus Father Robert Middleton, S.J., brought into Lancashire something of the lustre of " The Pearl of York."

The advent of these four priests into Lancashire was, reasonably enough from their point of view, regarded by the local anti-Catholic authorities as a campaign to be vigorously opposed. The fiery leaders of it were Robert Nutter and Thurstan Hunt. Bishop Challoner gives a description of the character of Robert Nutter from a statement of a contemporary, Dr. Champney: " That he was a man of a strong body, but of a stronger soul, who rather despised than conquered death, and went before his companion (Mr. Thwing) to the gallows with as much cheerfulness and joy as if he was going to a feast, to the astonishment of the spectators." (*Memoirs*, p. 248.)

Robert Nutter and Edward Thwing were the first of the four to be arrested and committed to Lancaster Castle, where they were tried, condemned to death for their priesthood and hanged, drawn and quartered on 26th July, 1600. Shortly after the execution, a kinswoman of the Venerable Edward Thwing, heart-broken at the loss of a revered relative, went to Father Robert Middleton to " lament the loss of a good man. To whom Mr. Middleton answered, ' Madam, I would I might this day ride a good way and out of my way, to have so good a chance as he had.' And so his desire was fulfilled, for that same day he was apprehended." (*C.R.S.*, Vol. 5, p. 388.)

Robert Middleton was born at York in 1571 and brought up a Protestant, and remained in that faith until the age of eighteen when he became a Catholic. He went to Douay and was there for three years, and after that he appears to have gone to the English College at Seville. From there, he proceeded to Rome and entered the English College at the age of twenty-six on 14th April, 1597, where he received the minor orders later in the same year and was probably ordained priest at the same time. In the following year he went on to the English mission, on 20th April, 1598. In London, he was well known to Father Henry Garnet, who wrote of him in a letter to the General of the Jesuits as " little Mr. Robert Middleton," whose application to become a Jesuit was accepted. While a prisoner for the Faith, Father Robert Middleton was notified by Father Henry Garnet of his admission. (Cf. *Foley's Records, S.J.*, Vol. 7, pp. 962-963.)

Father Thurstan Hunt, the son of Mr. Hunt of Carlton Hall, near Leeds, went to Rheims on 19th September, 1583, and returned to England as a priest in 1584. He was a man of unusual courage and boldness and had adopted as an alias the name " Greenlow." (*C.R.S.*, Vol. 5, p. 385.)

An interesting letter was found on Thurstan Hunt's person when he was finally arrested near Preston. It was addressed to the Queen and its main purport was to disprove that Catholics had anything to do with a Puritan rebellion led by the Earl of Essex and to protest against the bad habit of the enemies of the ancient Faith of " foisting every manner of plot and rising upon Catholics to their cost in cruel sufferings and penalties." It would seem not improbable that Thurstan Hunt was the author of the letter. (*C.R.S.*, Vol. 5, pp. 381-384.)

For a period both priests were prisoners in London and from there were transferred to Lancashire. On the way there they managed to break away from their escort and made their own way into that county. Robert Middleton, however, was re-arrested again a few miles north of Preston by Sir Richard Houghton, who sent the following notice of the fact to Secretary Cecil: " Yesterday, I apprehended a seminary priest on a road that leads into a part of Lancashire called the Fylde.* The priest was well-horsed and armed with a pistol; there was with him one other man (Thurstan Hunt, alias Greenlow), who escaped from me, and as yet I cannot find him although I have caused diligent search and pursuit to be made after him. The priest that is apprehended called himself Robert Middleton. He had no letters nor any other thing of importance found upon him, saving only a Popish prayer book. He had in his purse only forty shillings or thereabouts, which I suffered him to keep for his maintenance in prison, and have already sent him to Lancaster Castle, there to be safely kept in the common gaol until the assizes

---

* At a spot on the Garstang Road between Barton and Myerscough.

. . . From Preston, this 1st day of October, 1600." (*Foley's Records, S.J.*, Vol. 7, p. 1367.)

A desperate attempt was made to rescue Father Middleton under escort on his way to Lancaster from Preston. The leader of this escort was a certain Henry Breres of Preston in Amounderness, a draper, who gave the details of the attempt, shortly after, during an examination before Henry Hodgkinson, Mayor of Preston. Henry Breres stated " that he was commanded by the Mayor and others to convey to the common gaol of the county Robert Middleton, delivered to the Mayor by Sir Richard Houghton and Thomas Hesketh. As he and his troop of guards were going, they were over-taken five miles off by four horsemen and one who was on foot. This latter asked whether the prisoner was a priest, and Breres replied that the answer to that was of no importance and no business of theirs. However, they invited the priest to go with them, a proposal to which he consented. But to prevent him from escaping, Breres struck the priest from his horse, and thereupon the four horsemen with their weapons drawn violently, attempted to rescue the priest from them. Perceiving this, Breres drew his own sword upon them and prevented the priest from escaping. The other three horse-men outrageously attacked Breres' troopers, who also drew their weapons. After a desperate struggle, the rescuers were defeated, and one of them named Greenlow was caught after a long chase and wounding one of his pursuers, and was taken to Preston." (Ibid.) Greenlow was without doubt Thurstan Hunt, and his arrest put an end to the noble apos-tolic adventures of four great priests in Lancashire. Sir Richard Houghton and Thomas Hesketh, Attorney of the Court of Wards and Liveries, lost little time in notifying the London authorities of the zeal and efficiency of pursuivancy in Lancashire.

A specimen of their noble and unqualified profession of their faith and priesthood at the trial is supplied in Father Robert Middleton's statements. These were made during his examination on 30th September, 1600, before Sir Richard Houghton and Thomas Hesketh, Esq., Attorney of the Court of Wards and Liveries, and are cited in paraphrase as follows:

" He says that his name is Robert Middleton, and that he was born in the county of York, and was the son of one Thomas Middleton of the said city (York), and is now of the age of thirty-one years. His education was in the city of York until the age of eighteen, during which time he thinks that he did go to the State church as a matter of custom, but after that time he refused, and on being asked who had persuaded him to become recusant, he stated that he was only at liberty to give as reasons for the step he had taken his own conscience and the reading of books. He stated also that for six or seven years after, he had lived partly in London and partly in Kingston-upon-Hull, and on being asked at what places in regard of London, he would not answer, and in regard of Kingston-upon-Hull, he stated that he had been many times the guest of Mr. Richardson, a merchant and alderman of that town. Afterwards, having a mind to go to one of the seminaries at Douay or at Rome, he went on board ship at Hull and landed at Calais. Being asked what ship, he says it was a ship from Newcastle, as he thinks, laden with coal for Calais. From thence he went to Douay and continued there for a space of three years, during which time one Dr. Barrett was the President there, who is now dead, and, being asked what Englishmen lived at that time in the College, he refuses to answer that question because he is resolved to answer no more than questions concerning himself only.

" He states that after that, he was summoned by the Pope to Rome, or else his superior directed him along with many others to do so. He says he promised before his departure from Douay to become a priest. He says moreover that he lived in the College at Rome for one year and was there directed by his superior to take the order of the priesthood, which he did accordingly in Rome and received his letters of ordination from the Bishop living in Rome, but what the latter's name was he does not disclose; nevertheless, he admits that he did receive the order of priesthood by authority from the Bishop of Rome. He also says that before he came to England, he had an audience with the Pope, and from him or by his appointment he received his expenses for the journey and the Papal Benediction, and so was despatched to England with all speed in the company of divers others whom he refused to name. He embarked for England at Flushing in a Dutch ship and was landed at a port on the south coast of England, but the place he refused to name; neither will he declare in what places in England he stayed, nor how he travelled into Lancashire, nor what place there he received harbourage, nor whither he was bound for this night when he was apprehended. Neither will he declare the name of that person who was in his company when Sir Richard Houghton placed him under arrest; and being asked whether he had said Mass, christened children, officiated at the marriage of any person, or reconciled any to the Church of Rome, he affirmed that he had, and indeed any other function and duty proper to the office of a priest. He states also that such as he has reconciled he carefully instructs in the Catholic Faith. Being required to declare whether or not he had in the course of such instructions and reconciliations used any kind of persuasion, that if the Pope should invade the realm of England for the alteration of religion by force, whether those that are reconciled to the Catholic Roman

Church should take any part with the Queen's Majesty against the forces of the Pope coming for such a purpose; to this question he says that he makes no answer, because of his doubts concerning it. Being asked finally whether he considers the Queen's Majesty to be the lawful Queen of England, he replies that in temporal matters he does so consider and has always done, and moreover that he will pray that God would make her a good Catholic. Then being asked likewise whether Her Majesty ought to be Queen of England, notwithstanding the Pope's excommunication; to this question, he says he will not answer, nor reply to any more questions.

(Signed) Richard Houghton.
Thomas Hesketh."
(*Foley's Records, S.J.,* Vol. 7, ibid.)

The martyrdom took place at Lancaster Castle at the end of March, 1601, when the Venerable Thurstan Hunt and the Venerable Robert Middleton were hanged, drawn and quartered for the priesthood and for the Faith.

Although the verses are rough, " The Songe of four Priests that suffered death at Lancaster," written, it is thought, by a contemporary member of the Anderton family of Lostock, Father Laurence Anderton, a Jesuit, gives vivid expression of the reverence and devotion contemporary Lancashire Catholics had for these four great priest-martyrs.

" Amongst these gracious troups, that follow Christ His train,
To cause the Devil's stoops, four priests were lately slain,
Nutter's bold constancy with his sweet fellow Thwing,
Of whose most meek modesty Angels and Saints may sing.

Hunt's dauntless courage stout, with Godly zeal so true,
Mild Middleton, O what tongue can half thy virtue shew?
At Lancaster lovingly these martyrs took their end,
In glorious victory, true faith for to defend."

(Cf. C.R.S., Vol. 5, p. 385.)

Although he never laboured in his home county, Thomas Laithwaite, born in Wigan, 1576, became a missionary with most edifying and thrilling adventures from the day of his landing at Plymouth, 1604-5 until the day of his death from sufferings for the Faith, in London on 10th June, 1655. His parents, Henry and Jane Laithwaite, née Bolton, were staunch and devout Catholics, and well-to-do townsfolk of Wigan, where throughout the most violent periods of persecution, the Catholics managed the miracle of providing suitable schools for Catholic youths and children. These noble parents, therefore, were able to give their surviving children, six sons and two daughters, a sound Catholic education, with the result that four of the sons, Thomas, Edward, Francis and John, became priests and Jesuits, and one daughter a nun. For a time the second eldest, Edward, became a zealous Protestant, but with no mind for pursuivancy. When he heard that his elder brother, Father Thomas Laithwaite, had been arrested and cast into the common gaol at Exeter, he journeyed there for the purpose of effecting his release by persuading him to conform. Love and sympathy for his brother's awful plight actuated Edward, besides his zeal for the Protestant cause, for the saintly priest had been cast into a terrible prison den packed with some eighty prisoners of both sexes who were criminals and felons, the men being chained to the walls. For four months this good priest endured an indescribable martyrdom, until he managed to secure a cell to himself. The result of the brotherly interview was that Edward was converted and became a devout priest. (Cf. *Foley's Records, S.J.*, Vol. 7, p. 429.)

CHAPTER 9

IN THE REIGN OF JAMES I

ALMOST immediately after the accession of James I in the year 1603, an Act was passed confirming the existing penal statutes against Catholics. Persecution continued, but this was not caused simply by religious hatred; it was the consequence of the King's personal avarice. The new monarch had in fact a mind to suspend all executions on grounds of faith and conscience. But he must reward his favourites while saving his own purse. So he empowered them to collect and retain for themselves all recusancy dues wherever they could find them. The untold tortures which this wicked policy inflicted on the more well-to-do Papists did not stir his conscience for he made claim to all the despotic powers and attributes of his predecessor. In spite of the royal wishes, however, six public executions of steadfast and loyal Catholics occurred during the year 1604-1605, for no other reason than their fidelity to the Holy See, their faith and conscience. Among these martyrs was a Lancashire layman, the Venerable Laurence Bailey. Little is known of him beyond his name, his faith and the cause for which he surrendered his life at Lancaster Castle.

" Laurence Bailey was a Catholic layman, who was apprehended in Lancashire for having aided and assisted a priest who had fallen into the hands of the pursuivants and escaped from them. For this supposed offence he was cast into prison where, as we are told by Molanus in his catalogue, page 77, he suffered much with great patience and constancy; and being brought upon his trial was condemned to die . . . as a felon, by the statute of the 27th Elizabeth. He was executed at Lancaster, Dr. Worthington says some time in August; but Molanus says it was on the 16th of November, 1604." (*Memoirs of Missionary Priests*, p. 280.)

Parliament's haste to enforce the Statutes against Papists displeased the King, and on his initiative many of them were released from prison, and it is likely that Father Christopher Southworth was among these. He was the son of that redoubtable confessor of the Faith, Sir John Southworth, and was preparing for the priesthood at Rheims during the period of his father's imprisonment. When the English College was opened at Rome, Christopher Southworth was among the first company of students to arrive there in 1580. He was ordained priest at Rome by Dr. Goldwell, bishop of St. Asaph, in the month of October, 1583, and was ministering in Lancashire for two or three years in the neighbourhood of his own home, Samlesbury Hall, Pendle, and Barton, near Broughton: " At Barton Hall, so long the seat of the territorial lords of the name, resided the widow of Richard Barton, who died in 1569, Anne, daughter of Sir Thomas Southworth of Samlesbury Hall, and sister of Sir John Southworth, and she constantly appears in the records of recusants. In 1584, she is reported as harbouring ' an olde priest,' that is, a Marian priest, and Mr. Haydock, a seminary priest, was often there. This would be Vivian or Evan Haydock, mentioned elsewhere. One of her nephews, the Rev. John or Christopher Southworth, was reported as resident in those parts in 1585, and no doubt often said Mass at Barton." (*C.R.S.*, Vol. 15, p. 312.)

While at the English College, Rome, Christopher Southworth was one of the fifty or so students who signed and forwarded a petition for the retention of the Jesuit administration of the College. Among these petitioners was the martyr, the Blessed John Cornelius.

In the year 1587, Christopher Southworth is entered in the State papers as having been arrested and incarcerated in the Compter Prison, Wood Street, London, where he was a companion in suffering of Thomas Pounde of Belmont, with whom he was eventually transferred to Wisbech Castle. (Cf. *Foley's Records, S.J.,* Vol. 3, pp. 436, 615, and Vol. 6, pp. 143, 507.)

In the apostate Gee's list, dated for the year 1624, among the number of priests and recusants at large during the years preceding that date, the names of two secular priests are included, both Southworths. One of them was Christopher Southworth, and the other a kinsman, possibly a nephew, John Southworth, who was in London about the year 1619, and is the martyr now beatified. Apparently Christopher Southworth is believed to have been the intrepid missioner who ministered for some years during the early part of the reign of James I to dispersed Catholics in the wilder regions of Pendle Hill. On horseback with the usual pedlar's box containing the necessary articles for his priestly ministrations, he continued to serve his own people until the hue and cry after him forced him to leave Lancashire. The tale of these last thrilling adventures is told in that most interesting and gripping book, *Mist Over Pendle,* by Robert Neill.

After the Gunpowder Plot, 1606, there followed a violent period of persecution during which a notable Lancashire man, the Blessed John Almond, was crowned a martyr. He was born at Allerton, near Liverpool, and as a boy was educated at a school in Woolton. Later, according to the Diary of the English College, Rome, he was admitted there as a student at the age of nineteen. Being ordained sub-deacon and deacon in the March and April of 1598, he was raised to the priesthood on 21st April of the same year and sent to England on 16th September, 1602.

Incidentally, there was an elder brother, Oliver Almond, a priest, who had been a missionary in England some years before John Almond. It was noted in the State papers that Oliver Almond was an active missionary priest in Berkshire: " Oliver Almond is a priest and is harboured by Mr. Winchcombe in Berkshire, near Newbery (sic), the name is Henwicke. If he is not in the house, there is a great tree wherein he is hiding. He is a little man." (Cited in *Foley's Records, S.J.*, Vol. 1, p. 381.) In a report made to Cecil by one who appears to have been a dupe of the apostate and spy, Anthony Munday, there is the following reference to Oliver Almond preserved in the State papers: " For Oliver Alman (sic), the priest, I should find him about Ensome or Scotney, and he would bring me to some other Papists, who should relieve me and help me in anything." (Cf. *Foley's Records, S.J.*, Vol. 2, p. 243.) Clearly this was a case of exploiting the benevolence of devout Catholics and of abusing the kindness of a devoted priest.

Although of short duration, the Blessed John Almond's ministry in London appears to have included an arrest and an escape from prison. He was at first arrested and confined in the Gatehouse in the very cell in which the Jesuit martyr, Father Henry Garnet, had been imprisoned. This first arrest took place in 1608, and from the Gatehouse he was transferred to Newgate, from whence it is said he escaped along with seven other recusant prisoners. Among the priests who escaped with him were Father Thomas Cornforth, a Jesuit, and Father Henry Cooper, a secular priest, who had been instrumental in securing a safe passage overseas for a young English noblewoman to St. Monica's Convent, Louvain, where she was known as Sister Anne Tremaine. (*Foley's Records, S.J.*, Vol. 4, p. 588.)

The period of John Almond's liberty only lasted a few days, if not hours, for he was re-arrested again and the rest followed with dramatic quickness. In the Annual Letters of the English College, Rome, there is the following brief and dramatic notice: " While I am writing, news has just come from Flanders that the Rev. John Almond, a former student of this College, has been martyred. I reserve all particulars until we get a fuller and more authentic account." (*Foley's Records, S.J.,* Vol. 7, p. 1032.)

Another instance of the high esteem in which Father John Almond was held appears in a letter of Father Robert Jones, S.J., dated from London, 9th December, 1612, and addressed to the Cardinal, now St. Robert Bellarmine. In this letter the Jesuit missioner describes John Almond as " a learned and venerable priest . . . formerly a scholar of the English College, Rome." (*Foley's Records, S.J.,* Vol. 4, p. 378 and pp. 567, 568.)

On being recaptured, John Almond was again imprisoned in Newgate, and later thrust down into a subterranean dungeon called " Little Ease," sometimes called " Limbo." The martyr has described it in his own words: " We were all put down into the hole or dungeon or place of ' Little Ease,' whence was removed since we came thither, two or three cartloads of filth and dirt; we were kept twenty-four hours without bread, or meat or drink, loaded with irons, lodging on the damp ground, and so continued for ten days or thereabouts."

In addition to the excellent account given in the *Memoirs of Missionary Priests* (Challoner, pp. 329-338), there is the report most probably written by Father Richard Blount, S.J., who at that time was the " Socius " to the Jesuit Mission Superior at the time, Father Robert Jones. A rough paraphrase of this additional account is submitted as follows: " He was summoned for trial on 3rd December, 1612, and indicted for being a priest, but none could be found able to give evidence or to bring any accusation against him. Father

Almond refused to avail himself of a trial by jury, since there was no proof of any kind nor just reason why he should be condemned. He was unwilling, he said, that those twelve men should be guilty of his death, adding that they were as far from knowing whether he was a Frenchman, an Italian or a Spaniard, and not an Englishman, as his accusers were from being able to prove anything against him. Moreover, he added, to submit himself to their verdict would be to imbrue those twelve men in the shedding of his blood. The judge condemned him for being a priest and passed sentence against him according to custom, as a traitor against his King and country.

" Mr. Almond, standing at the bar, addressed the bishop of London, who was upon the Bench, taking the opportunity of alluding to a charge they had brought against him that, when examined before the same prelate, upon the oath of allegiance being tendered to him and upon his answering that it could not be lawfully taken, and the bishop having replied that he had himself taken it seven times, he (John Almond) had rejoined that he (the bishop) had seven times perjured himself . . . he now once more affirmed it before the judges, adding that he was ready to defend his assertion against the bishop by argument, if they would hear him. During all this time, although the bishop displayed great signs of anger and impatience, he nevertheless had not the courage to say a word, having in the past summer received rebukes of this kind at the hands of other martyrs to his own great confusion. Father Almond, however, still continued to urge the bishop, telling him that he was amazed at his sitting upon the Bench as a secular judge in a criminal cause and if he was a true bishop it was unbecoming in a cleric to occupy himself in secular affairs, especially in criminal matters; that if, said he, he were not a priest and consequently no bishop, he must hold him excused for not addressing him as My Lord bishop, the fact being that he really was not so, but simply a secular and private person, and that it were better for him to stay at home and attend his family, his wife and children, than to meddle in such matters. All this while, the bishop was swelling with rage but did not venture a word in reply.

The sentence of death having been pronounced, the martyr was remanded back to prison, where he was thrust down into the bottom of a tower with other priests for the whole of Friday, and he was executed on the following Saturday morning, 5th December, 1612.

" The martyr enjoyed great consolation in so happy a fate, and communicated no small share of it to his fellow-prisoners, spending all the time that remained to him in much prayer.

" On the next morning, he was engaged in his prayers, and declared that nothing could have afforded him such consolation as the arrival of the sheriff, and therefore he declined to take the little refreshment that was offered to him. The sheriff having arrived, the martyr took leave of his fellow-prisoners and received the blessings of those of them who were priests. It had been given out that he would be executed on the Monday, in order to deceive the public and thus prevent the assembling of a great concourse of spectators. However, although it was an early hour of the morning, a great multitude had gathered at the place of execution. The martyr was conducted there, ascended the cart, and, having obtained leave to speak, took the opportunity of telling the people that he had been thrust down into the hole at the bottom of the Tower, loaded with chains and deprived of food, except a mouthful, for the space of twenty-four hours; that he had been condemned without any evidence in proof of guilt and, for all they knew, he might have been a native of any other country . . . He spoke with great courage, inviting them to tear him alive piecemeal, lamenting that his torture had been so small on their first pinioning him. He added that there was nothing he so much regretted as that he had only one life to lose and had suffered so little. He begged them to bring a gridiron that he might suffer similarly and equally with St. Laurence, declaring himself ready for this.

" He scattered about much money on all sides, and in particular gave the hangman a gold piece, telling him, however, that this was not to gain any favour at his hands, but as wages for his labour. He did the same to the other officials. He gave the sheriff a ring wrapped up in a handkerchief, begging him, if he pleased, to hand it to Mr. Muscott, a priest in Newgate, who had given him the ring the preceding night, and begged the sheriff to accept the handkerchief as a token of his regard, which he did, adding that he would keep it out of affection for him for all the days of his life, and thereupon he was executed.

" After the Blessed John Almond had been hanged, the executioner took out his heart and threw it into the fire, when it suddenly of itself leaped out of the flames. Again he threw it in and a second time it sprang out, and by the providence of God came to the hands of one who concealed it and carried it away with him, and knowing to whom it would be most grateful, he gave it to the Father Socius of the Superior of the English Jesuits, who received it with all due reverence and devotion, and deposited it, as a most precious treasure, among the other relics of the blessed martyrs of the times."

Thus concludes Father Richard Blount's account, given in full in *Foley's Records, S.J.,* Vol. 7, pp. 1377-1381.

In a footnote, it is mentioned that Mr. Muscott (Father George Muscott), mentioned above, was also condemned to death for the priesthood, but was reprieved upon the very hurdle, at the intercession of the Queen of England (Anne of Denmark, who became a Catholic). Father Muscott had endured upwards of twenty years' imprisonment for the

Faith when he was released on bail. He was appointed by the Holy See to the Presidency of Douay College in 1642, and died there three years later, at the age of sixty-five.

A fuller account of the Blessed John Almond's trial is given in *The Memoirs of Missionary Priests*, Challoner, pp. 329-338. The execution took place at Tyburn, 5th December, 1612.

Mention is also made of a consoling sequel in connection with the prelate who was present at the trial of John Almond, Dr. King, bishop of London. He is said to have been a man of sorrows ever after the execution of his victim. It is asserted by Catholic writers of those times that he became a Catholic, and died in communion with the Church which he had so cruelly persecuted. In the preface of a book published in his name after his death and entitled *The Bishop of London's Legacy,* he is introduced as thus addressing the martyr:

" O happy Almond . . . in thy blood did I wash my hands; it was I that did further thy death. Be thou, O blessed saint, who now seest and hearest me (what does he not see, who sees Him that sees all things?), be thou, I say, out of thy seraphical charity as propitious to pray for the remitting of that crying sin as I am ready to acknowledge the sin; and let thy blood (guilty of no other treason than in not being a traitor to Christ and His Church) resemble not the blood of Abel, which cried for revenge against his brother, but rather the Blood of Christ, which prayed for the pardon of His crucifiers."

The martyr, John Thules, was born most likely in the pastoral district of Upholland, Lancashire. That locality, as the centre of an area of some four or five square miles, comprises the hallowed homesteads of many Lancashire martyrs like the Blessed John Finch, the Blessed John Rigby, and the Blessed Thomas Holland, S.J., probably a kinsman of the notable Holland family. The district of Upholland, if Down-holland is included, extends almost to Southport.

"About one and a half miles from St. Helens is Windle-shaw Catholic cemetery . . . It is an enclosed piece of ground about one statute acre with some ancient ruins at the upper end which have the appearance of having once belonged to a religious house, or more probably a mortuary chapel . . . Tradition marks them out as once a priory or abbey. This enclosure was for many years the burial ground for the Catholics of St. Helens, Portico, Ashton, Blackrock and Birchley. Sir John Gerard in the year 1835 gave a piece of land adjoining it to enlarge the burial ground . . . The spot is not far from Upholland or 'Holland,' the site of the monastery. Dugdale, however, makes no mention of the 'Priory' or 'Abbey' of Windleshaw, nor does the name 'Windleshaw' occur in the schedule there given of lands, etc., belonging to Upholland, or Holland Monastery. He says: 'The original foundation of Holland was a college or Chantry consisting of a Dean and twelve secular priests in the Church and Chapel of St. Thomas, the Martyr, here, which was changed A.D. 1319 by Walter, Bishop of Coventry and Lichfield, at the petition of Sir Robert de Holland, the then Patron, into a Priory of Benedictine monks . . . Four miles west of Wigan is the village of Holland or Upholland, whence the illustrious but ill-fated family of Holland derive their name. This family attained the highest offices of State, with the titles of Earls of Surrey and Kent, and Duke of Exeter, but was remarkable for their sufferings and miserable end. In this village was formerly a Priory of Benedictines, of which nothing now remains but the church and a few walls.' " (*Foley's Records, S.J.*, Vol. 5, pp. 406-407.)

Hardly a miserable end, since their "remarkable sufferings" evidently yielded glorious results in a descendant and martyr, the Blessed Thomas Holland.

Little is available concerning the early life of John Thules, who was born in the year 1568. Apparently he was still only a boy when he went overseas to Douay, and he remained in Flanders until his twenty-second year, when he proceeded to the English College, Rome, in 1590, to complete his ecclesiastical course. He was ordained priest in the early part of the year 1592, and one of the candidates ordained with him was a fellow-martyr, the Venerable Joseph Lambton. The two martyrs, along with a group of other missionary priests forming a party of eight, were sent to England on 22nd April, 1592. Both the future martyrs were arrested almost immediately after landing in England, and John Thules, heavily chained, was confined in Wisbech Castle, where he spent many years of suffering. He also was among those who about that time succeeded in escaping from Wisbech Castle. He made his way into Lancashire where he doubtlessly met Roger Wrenno, the Chorley weaver, and came to love and revere this steadfast and apostolic Catholic layman, who devoted himself to the dangerous task of harbouring priests and assisting them in their ministrations. The success of John Thules' short period of ministration in his homeland soon attracted the notice of the Earl of Derby, who issued an order for his immediate arrest. It is possible that John Thules was arrested at the same time as his friend and fellow-martyr, Roger Wrenno, and both were committed to Lancaster Castle.

It is said that, although of a fiery and combative disposition, he had so overcome that failing that whomsoever he met and wherever he went, he was loved by both friend and foe for his unfailing kindness and charity. As a prisoner at Lancaster Castle he not only won the esteem of his fellow-recusant prisoners but was definitely liked by the officials and gaolers. If the priest and his fellow-prisoner, Roger Wrenno, took advantage of this by making good their escape one evening from Lancaster Castle, they were both actuated by apostolic zeal and the knowledge that the needs of the Catholics in the county were urgent and many and that the number of available priests was far too small to meet these requirements.

John Thules and Roger Wrenno selected a suitable evening for escaping, having calculated that, by walking throughout the night at a good pace, they could cover the thirty odd miles separating them from the districts of their apostolate before sunrise. Most likely they had planned to cross the Ribble by one or other of the shallower fords east of Preston, possibly the one at Lower Brockholes, near Samlesbury. Their route would have had to be other than the main highway southwards, so that the initial trek eastwards from Lancaster would land them in the Trough of Bowland. They would then journey south, veering gradually westwards to strike the Ribble ford sought for. Those who know the region will easily realise the difficulties in the black of night by two pedestrians who dared not use a lantern or make inquiries. So it happened that the turn westwards was made too soon and resulted in the two fugitives completing a circle; for at dawn they found themselves almost under the walls of Lancaster Castle. They accepted this mishap as a sign that they were destined to become martyrs for the Faith, and their immediate re-arrest caused them no great sorrow.

Up to the last moment every effort was made to induce both to save their lives by conformity, even if only as an outward gesture. After the trial and after sentence of death had been passed, Father John Thules was approached more than once for this purpose, and even at the very gallows he was urged to save his life by taking the oath of supremacy. The priest replied, " Give me a form of civil allegiance, and I will take it." When urged again to take the oath on the plea that it was no more than an expression of civil allegiance, and that no other form of oath was available save that ordered by parliamentary statute, Father Thules refused it, stating that he could not take it in conscience, " for it contains," he said, " many things contrary to the Catholic Faith."

There was a general disposition at the time against taking the lives of these two prisoners, and a godson of John Thules, a Mr. Ashton of Lever, offered him an annuity for life if he would comply. However, such promises and offers had no influence upon either of the two martyrs. When he finally took leave of his fellow-prisoners who were priests, John Thules recommended them to foster mutual love and charity, the proper characteristics of the true disciples of Christ. These were the qualities which had drawn so many to Father Thules and no less than four of the malefactors who were to die that day had been reconciled to the Church by this good priest.

The Venerable John Thules was the first to be executed and his quarters were subsequently hung up at the four chief towns of the county, Lancaster, Preston, Wigan and Warrington. At Preston, the quarter assigned was affixed to the steeple of the parish church.

An edifying and noteworthy incident occurred at the execution of the Venerable Roger Wrenno who, after the hanging of the Venerable John Thules, was the next to be turned off the ladder. The rope broke with the weight of his body, and he fell down to the ground. For a few moments he was stunned and remained motionless. When he came to himself he rose and knelt up. He began to pray very devoutly with his eyes and hands raised up to heaven. Upon this, the ministers approached him and praised the providence and mercies of God in his regard, and likewise the King's clemency, who would give him his life, if he would condescend after all to take the oath. Roger Wrenno at once rose to his feet and cried out, " I am the same man I was, and in the same mind; use your pleasure with me." With these words he actually ran back to the ladder and climbed up as fast as he could. The spectacle was a touching one, and the sheriff cried out in his turn, " How now, what does this man mean, that he is in so great a haste to die?" Roger Wrenno answered at once in the remarkable words: " If you had seen that which I have just now seen, you would be as much in haste to die as I now am." A new and stronger rope had to be secured. The two friends were martyred at Lancaster on 18th March, 1616.

So terminated, for a matter of some ten years, a violent period of persecution. In 1613 the Blessed Edmund Arrowsmith came to England and began his missionary labours in Lancashire. For the first few years he was exposed to all the usual risks and dangers until the King, through changing dispositions among the people, was able to exercise his royal prerogative and suspend the executions of Papists.

CHAPTER 10

AN INTERLUDE

AFTER the execution for the priesthood of the Venerable William Southerne, a native of Durham, on 30th April, 1618, there were no public martyrdoms until the year 1628. In the meantime, however, the more well-to-do Catholics were being financially tortured by the favourites of James I, who were commissioned by the King to recoup themselves by collecting recusancy dues. Bad as this was, it was not enough for the parliamentary anti-Papists who demanded the enforcement of the death penalty on all Papist priests and their abettors. In order to induce the King and country to authorise that cruel policy, much publicity was given to what was called the " Blackfriars Disaster " of 1623, in which about ninety Catholics attending a Sunday evening service were killed in the collapse of the gallery and room where they were assembled. This was instanced by the enemies of the ancient Faith as proof positive of the growing numbers and boldness of the Papists.

In 1624, Robert Gee, a notorious apostate, was employed by the Puritan authorities to publish the famous " Gee's List," entitled " The Foot of the Snare," in order to arouse a popular demand for the revival of vigorous prosecution of the legal murder of Catholics. " The author is Robert Gee, an apostate and, as usual, replete with gall and bitterness against the Faith he had abandoned and against its adherents. His knowledge, as a one-time Catholic, of persons, etc., rendered him a very effective agent against them, and his list may be regarded as on the whole accurate." (Cf. *Foley's Records*, Vol. 1, p. 74; also Appendix, pp. 671-683.)

For the same purpose, much publicity was given in 1627 of a raid by the pursuivants on the Jesuit house in Clerkenwell, which was noised abroad at the time as " The Discovery of the Jesuit College in Clerkenwell." In point of fact the house was little more than a residence where the Jesuit missionaries occasionally assembled for the purpose of transacting necessary business in connection with their apostolate, and for spiritual retreats as well as for conferences which were attended by other missionary priests. Nevertheless, the slanderous propaganda resulting from these events brought about the imprisonment of many priests and recusants, including the untimely arrest in Lancashire of the Blessed John Southworth. Although it had no fatal results in London, the Blessed Edmund Arrowsmith and the Blessed Richard Hurst were indirectly its victims at Lancaster Castle.

One who lost his life in the " Blackfriars Disaster " was a Lancashire man, Father William Whittingham, S.J. An intrepid missioner, he was for many years confined for the Faith in the narrow cells of Newgate prison along with a Jesuit colleague, Father John Percy. " Father Whittingham entered the English College, Rome, as an alumnus on the 10th of October, 1607, aged seventeen years, and took the usual College oath on the 24th August, 1608, and in the same year received minor orders. He left the College for Lorraine on the 27th of September, 1611, and entered the Jesuit noviciate at Nancy. The Diary of the English College adds that he made there his philosophy and first year's theology and was always and universally beloved for his remarkable virtues and candour of soul. We subjoin a short autobiographical account extracted from the scholars' interrogatories, in the archives of the English College. ' 1607, William Whittingham. I was born on the Feast of the Purification of

the Blessed Virgin Mary, 1591, in a not very celebrated
village of Lancashire (Goosnargh), where I remained with
my Catholic parents, Richard and Anne, for only two years.
Afterwards I was taken to my grandmother to a town near
York, called Pocklington, and there until I was thirteen years
of age, I applied to my rudiments and alas unworthy of my
good education, I fell into the superstitions of the heretics,
and, without the least necessity, accompanied my school-
fellows to their churches. But afterwards, returning home in
half a year, by reading pious books I was restored to the
ancient Faith, and, before the lapse of another year, crossed
over to Douay with my father's consent.

" ' Both my parents are of respectable families, and well-
to-do, and, what is better than all, are Catholics. I have no
paternal, but four maternal uncles, of whom the eldest,
Robert Dowlman, and the youngest, William, are Catholics;
the other two, Marmaduke and Peter, are Protestants, but not
hostile ones. I made my elementary studies both at Pocklington and at Whalley in Lancashire.' " (*Foley's Records, S.J.*,
Vol. 1, pp. 87-88, footnote.)

It is mentioned that his brother, Paul Whittingham, also
became a Jesuit, having previously entered the English
College a year before his brother William. Paul gave a more
detailed account of his birthplace: " I am seventeen years
of age and was born in the county of Lancaster, near the
town of Preston, in the parish of Goosnargh, in the village
of Whittingham . . ." He died at the College a most holy
death on the 11th of July, 1611, after his admission as a
Jesuit. (Ibid.)

William Whittingham for his course of training as a Jesuit
also went to Central Europe, " Lotharinga." (*C.R.S.*, Vol. 37,
p. 149.) He is described as " a man from his infancy of a
most innocent life, of the mildest of manners, and a stranger

to all the more violent passions." As a devoted priest working in those perilous times among his flock in London, Father William Whittingham was known as " the Priest of the poor."

To the great loss of the English Mission he was killed in the disaster in Old Blackfriars. On Sunday, 26th October, 1623, an evening service was being conducted by Father Whittingham, assisted by another Jesuit, notable for his beautiful and instructive sermons, Father Robert Drury, in a large upper room with a large gallery, at Hunsden House, Old Blackfriars. Hunsden House then belonged to the French Embassy, and on that fateful Sunday afternoon about a hundred or more Catholics of both sexes were attending evening service. While Father Drury was delivering his sermon and Father Whittingham had momentarily gone to his room immediately underneath, the gallery packed with worshippers collapsed and the weight of its fall smashed the floor of the upper room. This in its turn collapsed, and the whole mass of doomed people, broken masonry and beams was precipitated through the floors of the lower storeys to the cellars beneath, carrying with it Father Whittingham's room, where he was at the time. It is said that over ninety people including the two priests were killed.

Father Henry More, in his *History of the Province* makes reference to this catastrophe and mentions that some " heretics, dead to all feeling, insulted and assailed those who had been dragged forth from the ruins (presumably survivors), not only with curses, but also with mud and stones, through the streets." Father John Floyd in his account mentions that among the survivors " some gentlewomen were forced to leave their coach to save themselves in the house of their friends." He adds, however, that English Protestants had no part in such behaviour, which was characteristic of any kind of mob out for horseplay. Some ministers, however, noisily ascribed the disaster to an act of divine retribution and refused to bury any of the victims in their churchyards.

These, however, cannot fairly be held as representative of the Puritan ministry, for a most touching account of the tragedy was written by a contemporary Puritan minister, the Rev. Samuel Clarke, to which he gave the title, " The Doleful Even-Song." In his account he states that the dreadful accident occurred at three o'clock on the fateful Sunday afternoon. His narrative was printed in 1623, and in the course of it he wrote: " Who can to the life express the face of death, presenting itself in so rueful and different shapes?" Of the two priests involved this kind-hearted man stated that they were doing the work appointed by God; they were " God's workmen," and to such he applied the words: " Happy that servant whom his Lord, when He cometh, shall find so doing." The narrative is given in *Foley's Records, S.J.,* Vol. 1, pp. 78-85.

Another minister, Richard Linton, Clerk, and late parson of Middleton, Norfolk, having heard of the disaster in London, made reference to it in his sermon on the Sunday before Christmas, when he preached on the text, " Thou knowest not what evil shall be upon the face of the earth." He took occasion to say of the accident, that he thought most of them were saints and martyrs, and as for himself he desired no worse death. (Ibid., p. 93.)

Not all, however, were so sympathetic and charitably minded. Lyson's *Environs of London,* Vol. IV, p. 410 (extracts from the *Eltham Register*), says: " Fatal accident. In 1623, the Vicar (of Eltham), in his zeal against Popery, has thus recorded a fatal accident which is mentioned by the historians of that time (Wilson in his *History of James I,* says, p. 141, that Father Drury, a Jesuit, the preacher, was amongst those who were killed): ' Let this be a pitiful remembrance to all posterity, that in the year of Our Lord, 1623, the 26th day of October, in the twenty-first year of King James his reign, there lay a French Ambassador in the Blackfriars in London, who being at Mass the same Sabbath day in the afternoon with a multitude of blind ignorant people, there fell . . . a gallery in the said chapel, and crushed to death four score and sixteen souls, besides a great multitude that had their arms and legs broken, so much was God offended with their detestable idolatry.' Thus the good parson of Eltham." (Ibid., p. 92.)

Very different was the sympathetic writer of " The Doleful Even-Song," who knew that Mass in those days was not celebrated at three o'clock in the afternoon, and in the Latin expression, *" quis talia fando temperet a lachrymis?"* (" who in the telling of such things can refrain from tears?")— expresses a sincere and heartfelt sorrow.

The bodies of the victims, since the bishop of London at the time forbade their burial in a churchyard, were buried under the site of the collapsed house. Many of these bodies, and some of them identified, were discovered in recent years during the reconstruction of St. Ethelreda's, Ely Place, and have been reverently re-interred in the crypt of that same London church. (Cf. *Foley's Records, S.J.,* Vol. 5, p. 1007.)

The Whittinghams of Goosnargh were apparently kinsfolk of the Catholic family of the Wadsworths of Haighton Hall, a part of which still exists as a large farm on a hillock at the eastern end of Durton Lane. In the cellar under the large living-room of the farm there is said to be a priests' hiding place, the entrance to which has been walled up with bricks.

In conclusion, it is reported in the Annual Letters of the Vice-Province of England for 1619-1623 that in the year of his death Father William Whittingham had made 150 converts to the Catholic Church. (Cf. *Foley's Records, S.J.,* Vol. 7, p. 1099.)

CHAPTER 11

TRAGEDY AND TRIUMPH AT LANCASTER CASTLE

B RIAN ARROWSMITH was born in the year 1585 at the farm of his parents at Haydock, near St. Helens. During his boyhood the widowed mother, Margery Arrowsmith, having struggled to maintain the farm and to support her growing children, had one great regret: she was unable to provide her son Brian with the education she judged necessary for him. The boy was compelled, therefore, to receive the rudiments of his education from local Protestant schoolmasters, who were kind to him and liked him, for all that he was in the beginning of a somewhat blunt and brusque disposition and uncouth in his manners. These were, however, only superficial defects and his kindly preceptors recognised them as such.

Apart from this he was a devout boy. On his way to school each morning he used to recite with his companions the Little Hours of Our Lady's Office, and the Vespers and Compline of the same when returning from school. At home in the evening, he withdrew into a little oratory in the house wherein he recited the Jesus Psalter and the Seven Penitential Psalms. At length, an old and virtuous priest in the district, in order to relieve the widow in her poverty, took the boy into his own service and gave him the necessary coaching in the humanities, which would serve him in good stead when eventually he went to Douay in the December of 1605. Soon after his arrival he received the Sacrament of Confirmation, taking the name Edmund after that of his uncle, Dr. Edmund

Arrowsmith, for whom he always had great love and admiration. It was doubtless the good services of his uncle that enabled him to go to Douay.

He had to return home for a while to recover health in his native air, for he had a weak constitution by contrast with his strength of character and soul. As soon as possible he returned, completed his course of philosophy and made a retreat of the Spiritual Exercises. During the course of it he felt that he had a vocation to become a Jesuit. He threw himself into his higher course of studies with such ardour and tireless industry that his superiors began to fear a second and more severe breakdown. So they recommended early ordination so that he could be sent to England where, while recruiting in his home county, he could usefully employ himself in ministering to the faithful.

He received minor orders in the church of St. Nicholas at Douay, 14th June, 1612, and before the end of the year was advanced to major orders at Arras, where he was ordained priest, 9th December. He was then sent to the English mission by Dr. Kellison, President of Douay, on 17th June, 1613.

At first his missionary labours in Lancashire covered an extensive area south of the Ribble. " There is little doubt that the last few years of Father Arrowsmith were spent in the neighbourhood of Brindle. He rode about on horseback a good deal, and a man often rode with him, and brought the horse back which Father Arrowsmith had ridden, after he had dismounted near the place where he was about to celebrate Mass. No doubt he had a large area. I have heard that he said Mass at Lower Hall, Church Bottoms; Fleetwood Hall, in Samlesbury; Jack Green, Brindle; Wickenhouse Farm, Withnell; Wheelton; Denham Hill, near Clayton Green; Woodcock Hall, Cuerdon; and Livessey Hall, near

Blackburn." Cited in *Forgotten Shrines,* Dom Bede Camm, O.S.B., p. 192.)

A house which he used may be seen at the present day at Gregson Lane, fortunately preserved as a memorial of the martyr. Here he said Mass for the last time before his final arrest. On the road to Walton-le-Dale, a few furlongs north of Gregson Lane, in a spot called " The Straits," is the site of another house which in later times became the " Blue Anchor Inn." It had been a comfortable and commodious cottage with a priests' hiding place. Here also Father Arrowsmith frequently said Mass and found safe shelter. Unhappily, this old house has been demolished.

An interesting description of Father Arrowsmith is given in the letter of a contemporary who knew him well: " Edmund Arrowsmith, although he was on the small side and of a homely and insignificant bearing, seasoned his zeal and fervour with a ready wit, especially in holding a controversy with any heretic whose arguments he would sew up in a kind of humorous relief. I often advised him in a friendly manner to carry salt in his pocket so as to season his witticisms lest too much zeal without discretion might bring him too soon into danger, considering the sudden vehement storms of persecution that often assailed us. Sometimes, I have been in his company when meeting with ministers sumptuously mounted, and I had much trouble in preventing him from approaching and disputing with ' the proud dogs,' as he called them." (Cf. *Foley's Records,* Vol. —, pp. 24 seq.)

About the year 1622 he was arrested and taken a prisoner to Lancaster to be examined by the State bishop of Chester, Dr. Bridgman. The bishop, a kindly man, was at supper with some of his clergy. It was during Lent, and he apologised to Father Arrowsmith for eating meat; being old and weak, he was dispensed. " But who has dispensed your lusty ministers here, for they have no such excuse?" asked Father Arrowsmith with Lancashire bluntness and a twinkle of humour.

Controversy developed. It became apparent that the priest was getting the better of the bishop, and several of the ministers began to argue all together. Whereupon Father Arrowsmith turned to the bishop and said laughingly: " Turn all your dogs loose at once against me, and let us have a loose bait." Dr. Bridgman appears to have taken Father Arrowsmith's controversial victories in good part and to have made the examination proceed amicably. The priest was set at liberty. It seems that not all the clergy present approved of the bishop's kindness and lenity, but for the moment they had to bear it with the best grace possible.

Being a small man, Arrowsmith had the better chances of disguising himself against pursuivancy, but he must have known that when set free his controversial successes would have direful repercussions. Retreat and retirement for a time might have been advisable. The martyrs, however, would not have accomplished their self-sacrificing task had their activities on all occasions been governed by the dictates of worldly prudence. Edmund Arrowsmith threw himself into his work as before and never yielded before the perils and fatigue of the mission.

In the year 1624 he was able to realise his vocation to become a Jesuit. He did not go abroad to make his noviceship, but retired only for two or three months into Essex, which time he employed in spiritual exercises. " In a list or catalogue of English Jesuits, which was seized with many other papers in the London house of the Jesuits at Clerkenwell during the attack on that establishment by the pursuivants in 1627-1628, Pater Edmondus Bradshaw (the alias used by Father Arrowsmith) appears as a novice. The date of this catalogue would be about 1624-1625." (*Foley's Records*, Vol. 2, p. 30, and footnote; also cf. p. 33.)

Father Arrowsmith returned to Lancashire and this time his arrest was due to a regrettable accident, as also his trial and condemnation at Lancaster Castle. It was through the personal vindictiveness of the judge, Sir Henry Yelverton, that the martyr was brought to the scaffold. At the time there was no violent spate of persecution, but Yelverton, in defiance of the royal wishes, was determined to have a Papist victim, and preferably a priest. " Charles I had professed his abhorrence of shedding blood on account of religion, and by his clemency he faithfully carried out that maxim from the time of his accession to the throne. It was felt to be very certain at the time, and history has since confirmed it, that His Majesty did in no way countenance or encourage the proceedings of (this) judge." (*Foley's Records, S.J.*, Vol. 2, p. 27.)

Father Arrowsmith was accustomed to visit the house of a Catholic family named Holden, the house which later became the " Blue Anchor Inn." When he was due to make a visit, the son, young Holden, his fiancée and his mother reported this to a Justice of the Peace, Captain Rawsthorn. The latter kindly enough sent word beforehand to Mr. Holden senior, that he had been summoned to search the house for the priest, and it was advisable for him to take Father Arrowsmith out of the way so that he would be safe while the search was in progress. Mr. Holden did so, but unfortunately they returned to his house too soon and met the magistrate, Mr. Rawsthorn, as he with his young son, a boy of tender years, and an attendant armed and mounted, were returning from the search which, as intended, had been in vain. Mr. Holden, the priest and a groom were mounted, and the three together could have avoided the arrest and made good their escape. Beyond tendering the unlawful oath, which Father Arrow-

smith rejected, the magistrate did nothing to notify the priest
that he was under arrest, so the actual capture of him was
effected by the servant and the boy. Neither Mr. Holden nor
his groom interfered and Mr. Rawsthorn himself took no
part in the capture. Later, Father Arrowsmith explained in
court this anomaly of his actual capture when he might so
easily have escaped.

It appears that Mr. Holden's son had married a non-
Catholic girl, who afterwards had expressed her desire to
become a Catholic. Father Arrowsmith had applied for a
dispensation to regularise the marriage in accordance with
the laws of the Church. Meantime, he enjoined the couple
to live apart until the marriage could be revalidated. The
injunction was a reasonable one and involved the couple
living as betrothed for fourteen days. Civil conventions could
scarcely have demanded less. The young couple, however,
took umbrage. They knew that Father Arrowsmith would
return shortly and, with the connivance of Mrs. Holden, the
young man's mother, they secretly sent word to the nearest
magistrate, Mr. Rawsthorn, who had perforce to call the
summons.

Sir Henry Yelverton, Father Arrowsmith's judge, was a
member of a notable Catholic Norfolk family, and unfortunately different members of it for financial reasons had
receded from the Church. Father Charles Yelverton, a Jesuit,
who had died of his hardships in England during the year
1609, mentions that his father died piously as a Catholic, but
of the father's five brothers, only one, Edward Yelverton,
remained steadfast in the Faith and he was entered in the
State papers of the time as a Popish recusant. The young
Charles Yelverton through the influence of his uncle, Edward,
was reconciled to the Faith and became a priest and a Jesuit.
Another of Charles' uncles, Sir Christopher Yelverton,
became a judge, and it was his son Henry who, following

the same profession, condemned Father Arrowsmith to death at Lancaster. (*Foley's Records,* Vol. 1, pp. 141-146 passim.)

Sir Henry hated Catholicism with all the venom of an apostate, and before the trial took despicable steps to inflame the jury against the martyr. In a letter written from England by a Douay priest, William Hart, to Thomas Blacklow, the clergy agent in Rome, and dated 27th December, 1628, the following is said in reference to Sir Henry Yelverton: " After the latter had asked Father Arrowsmith at the trial whether he was a priest or not, being dissatisfied with the information he had been able to extract from the prisoner, the judge said more publicly that, if he knew for certain that he was a priest, he should die for it, because some of his colleagues before proceeding to Lancaster from London had told him to his face that he durst not hang a priest. The fact of this savage monster having been thus chaffed in London helps to account in some measure for his great anxiety to induce the martyr to admit against himself the fact that he was a priest."

" Prudence," wrote Father Cornelius Morphy, S.J., in his life of the Blessed Edmund Arrowsmith, " has recommended those accused not to affirm that they are priests, in order not to betray Catholics who may have harboured them."

During the trial, Sir Henry Yelverton endeavoured by point blank questions to draw from the prisoner a definite admission that he was a priest. Arrowsmith's replies, such as, " Would I were worthy to be one," always thwarted his unjust efforts to extract admission from the prisoner of a fact which the court was assembled to prove or disprove.

One of the ministers, a Justice of the Peace, who had been present on the earlier occasion when Father Arrowsmith had outpointed the bishop of Chester in controversy, now whispered to the judge, and then began to revile the prisoner. The latter asked leave of the judge to hold a disputation with this parson, but permission was refused. The judge said that his doctrine could not be maintained but that probably he desired that those of his own religion should hear him talk. The priest answered that he would defend it by words, but would also be glad to seal it with his blood. In a savage voice, Sir Henry Yelverton cried out, " You shall seal it with your blood! " In spasms of rage, this tyrant kept repeating, " You shall die! " " And you, my lord, must die," replied Father Arrowsmith. Those words were verified in little more than a year's time, and Sir Henry remembered them.

Among the witnesses called against the martyr were the Justice of Peace who had committed him, the young son, and the servant. This magistrate stated that at the time of the arrest, he had tendered the oath of supremacy to the prisoner, Father Arrowsmith, who had refused to take it and was thereupon committed to the common gaol. By the judge's direction two indictments were prepared: one accusing Arrowsmith of being a priest and a Jesuit, upon the strength of a letter written by the young Holden and by his mother to the Justice of the Peace, when Father Arrowsmith was first examined; the other of being a perverter in religion. The servant who had apprehended the martyr was summoned to the witness-box and swore that Father Arrowsmith had tried to persuade him to become a Catholic. The boy of twelve affirmed, though not on oath, that the prisoner had endeavoured to withdraw him from Protestantism. Realising that the circumstances of his arrest could easily be misunderstood, and to enable himself more easily to avoid any admission which would give a handle to his cruel judge, Father Arrowsmith begged leave to explain the manner of his arrest. When this was granted, the martyr took care in his narrative to avoid any detail which might show the Justice of Peace's disinclination to arrest him. Father Arrowsmith's horse had stubbornly refused to gallop away when its rider had urged it on. This made it necessary for the priest to dismount, since the horse was useless. Father Arrowsmith's account is given in his own words:

"My lord, as I was upon the road, that very man, as I take it, rushed out upon me with a drawn sword. He was meanly dressed and on horseback. I made what haste I could from him, but being weak and sickly was forced by him at last to the moss, where I alighted and fled with all speed I was able; which yet could not be very great, seeing that I was loaded with heavy clothes, books, and other things. At length he came up to me at a moss-ditch, and struck at me, though I had nothing to defend myself with but a little walking stick and a sword which I did not draw; with a blow he cut the stick close to my hand, and did me some little hurt. I then asked him whether his design was to take my purse and my life. He answered that perhaps it was; and then I fled from him, but was soon overtaken (he being mounted). Then came up this youth, who has offered to give evidence against me, with others to assist him. They used me with great indignity and took me to an alehouse, and searched me to the skin, offering insults which modesty forbids me to relate, and which I resisted as far as I was able. That done, they fell to drinking and spent nine shillings of my money in an hour; they told me that the Justice of the Peace, by whose warrant I had been apprehended, was there in person, but that, I would not believe. Upon this occasion, my lords, I began to find fault with the man's wicked and rude behaviour, who seemed to be the ringleader; and I besought him for the *love of Our Saviour* to make an end of his disordered life of drinking, dissolute talk and whatever might offend Almighty God. Upon my word and my life, this or to this effect is all I said to him. Let him look on me and gainsay it if he can. As for that youth, I do not deny having told him that I hoped when he came to riper years, he would look more closely into himself and become a true Catholic, for that, and that alone, would be the means of saving his soul; to which he made no answer at all. And I hope, my lords, that neither they nor any other can prove ill against me."

The Justice of Peace in question, presumably Mr. Rawsthorn, rose up and sought safety for himself in invective, denouncing Father Arrowsmith as a dangerous seducer, to whom no favour should be shown. This Justice's real or pretended fear made the prisoner smile, for which he was strongly rebuked in court.

The rebuke did not remove Father Arrowsmith's smile, for that was his customary expression. Neither was there any irony intended, for the martyr had explained to the best of his power the anomaly of his actual seizure by one man and a boy, when apparently the way was open for him to escape. He told the simple truth without implying any animadversion either on the elder Mr. Holden and the serving-man with him, who had made no attempt to render him assistance when his stubborn horse landed him into a mossy bog, or on the Justice of the Peace, who had in the first instance been palpably reluctant to arrest him.

Having been forced to dismount in that bog, had he been a stronger man and not small, emaciated and in a weak state of health, he would hardly have been able to defend himself with any hope of success against the attendant of the Justice of Peace, who, besides being a strong and healthy man, was well mounted and well armed. On foot and loaded with his luggage, all he could do was to ward off the savage blows aimed at him. Like all the martyrs, Edmund Arrowsmith was a giant in God's service and his case cannot be measured solely by human standards.

At this point of the trial, Sir Henry Yelverton, although the judge of the case, so far forgot himself that he made himself counsel for the prosecution by thus addressing the jury: "Look you, gentlemen of the jury, how he wishes God to confound us all and root out heresy, by which he means our religion." Not that Sir Henry Yelverton had any serious interest in religion of any kind.

Father Arrowsmith, who was suffering violently from toothache, was relieved and glad of a respite when the jury retired to consider their verdict. They were not long in doing so, having been inflamed by the judge, and when they returned they gave a verdict of guilty. Sir Henry Yelverton then rose up, and with a pompous display of magnanimity asked the prisoner what he had to say for himself, why he should not die according to the law. Edmund Arrowsmith made no reply, but merely lifted up his hands and raised his eyes to heaven. The judge then pronounced the sentence: "You shall go from hence to the place from whence you came; from thence you shall go down to the place of execution upon a hurdle. You shall there be hanged by the neck, till you be half dead; your members shall be cut off before your eyes and thrown into the fire, where likewise your bowels shall be burnt. Your head shall be cut off and set upon a pole, and your quarters shall be set upon the four corners of the Castle. And may God have mercy on your soul."

The calm and prayerful demeanour of the martyr provoked the judge to add a little more to the accustomed formula: "Know shortly that thou shalt die aloft between heaven and earth, as unworthy of either: and may thy soul go to hell, with thy followers." This diabolical imprecation did not perturb the martyr, who was absorbed in prayer, and so that this disgraceful man continued in fury: "I would that all priests in England might undergo the same sentence."

When he had quite finished, Father Arrowsmith fell down on his knees and said, "Deo gratias." The gaolers came to take him away to the filthiest cell in the prison and were ordered to load him with chains. He was then thrust down into a narrow hole, where he could not lie down but was forced to sit supported by a bolster which the humanity of the keeper allowed him to have. Only Mr. Leigh, the parson Justice of the Peace, was allowed to visit the prisoner, and his vaunt that he had secured a controversial victory in the prison cell was detected by the Protestants for what it was worth as a poor sort of evasion, and they asked him why then had he refused to accept Father Arrowsmith's challenge to a dispute in court. Many townsfolk of Lancaster were dissatisfied with the trial but intimidated by the brutality of the judge.

There was considerable difficulty in finding an executioner. A butcher, himself ashamed to become the executioner, engaged for five pounds that his servant should dispatch the martyr. This servant, however, when informed of his master's shameful contract, fled from his service and was never seen by him again. Felons and malefactors were offered their own lives, but refused to undertake the murder. At length a deserter under sentence of death was prevailed upon to undertake the gruesome task on promise of freedom, a sum of money and the victim's clothes. The sheriff himself awaited the warrant for execution, for an assistant judge refused to sign. So the signature of Sir Henry Yelverton was the only one on the warrant and the sheriff made difficulties until by a ruse the warrant was doctored and disguised by a legal officer under the direction of Yelverton.

A Catholic gentleman succeeded in making his way to Father Arrowsmith in his prison cell, and was arrested and brought to trial for that act. He was, however, able to give a sufficient reason for his presence in the prison and the case against him was dismissed. It may be surmised that this gentleman was Mr. Southworth, the father of the Blessed

John Southworth, a prisoner at the time in Lancaster Castle under sentence of death but reprieved. It seems likely enough that in this way an arrangement was made that the Blessed Edmund Arrowsmith should stop on his way to execution opposite the cell of Father Southworth who, from a barred window, would administer the last sacramental Absolution.

This in fact was actually given. 28th August was the day fixed for the execution and on the way, probably as he was walking to the hurdle, Edmund Arrowsmith paused by the window of Father Southworth's cell and received from him the Absolution and Last Blessing. Several final attempts were made to persuade the martyr to take the oath of supremacy and receive the King's pardon, a thing which Judge Yelverton by no means desired. He was intent only upon making good his vaunt that in spite of the King's displeasure he would hang a priest. At Tyburn for over ten years there had been no execution of a martyr for the Faith. Indeed, two Queens had knelt down at that scaffold and prayed in honour of those martyred there; Anne of Denmark, who had become a Catholic, and Henrietta Maria, the saintly wife of Charles I.

Mr. Leigh himself, the parson Justice of the Peace, who a few years ago had been worsted in controversy with Father Arrowsmith, sincerely wished to save his adversary from death. " Take the oath of allegiance and your life shall be spared," he said. " Good sir, accept your life. I desire you to live. Here is one come from the judge to offer you mercy. You may live if you conform to the Protestant religion." Meanwhile the judge had selected a suitable place from which he could view the execution, providing himself with a thick pair of magnifying spectacles to obtain a better view of the gruesome scene so soon to follow. In reply to Mr. Leigh's urgent appeal, Father Arrowsmith pulled the cap over his face. He said many prayers aloud and among them one of the most beautiful passages was, " I freely and willingly offer to Thee, Sweetest Jesus, this my death in satisfaction for my sins; and I wish that this little blood of mine may be a sacrifice for them." Again: " Give me, good Jesus, constancy to the last moment, and let me not live one instant without Thee, for since Thou art true life, I cannot live unless Thou livest in me."

The awful sentence was carried out in the usual brutal way, and the Blessed Edmund Arrowsmith was crowned a martyr on 28th August, 1628. His quarters were parboiled and by the order of Sir Henry Yelverton were collected and brought to him so that he could gloat over the fulfilment of his boast. There was something of the primitive baseness of the cannibal in this horrible man, for as a special meal was being prepared for him and some colleagues and the haunches of venison for the feast were brought in, he sent for the parboiled quarters of his victim and compared them with these haunches. He had successfully hounded to death that rare quarry, a Catholic priest, in the teeth of the royal displeasure. The judge in question had taken an oath not to sit down to a meal until Edmund Arrowsmith was dead. He now whetted his appetite in that disgusting way.

Little more than a year after this, on 29th-30th January, Sir Henry Yelverton, while sitting at supper, felt a sudden blow on his head, as if someone had struck him heavily with his fist. In a passion he turned and rounded on the waiter who stood behind him. The waiter protested, saying that he had neither struck him nor seen anyone else striking him. While vituperating the waiter, the judge received a second blow and was carried out of the supper room and put to bed. Next morning, he was found struggling with death and crying out, " That dog Arrowsmith has killed me." Two blows killed this judge; one for the Blessed Edmund Arrowsmith and one for another of his victims, the Blessed Richard Hurst or Hayhurst.

How different was Father Arrowsmith's death; Mr. Southworth, the father of the Blessed John Southworth, who witnessed the execution, declared to those who spoke to him afterwards that at the moment of the martyr's death he saw a very brilliant light extending in a luminous stream from the prison to the gallows like resplendent glass; he had never in the course of his life witnessed anything like it.

In spite of every precaution, relics of the Blessed Edmund Arrowsmith were secured. Local Protestants who were present put themselves out to help Catholics to collect them. Thus those concerned in the actual execution, when ordered to clear away the blood of the martyr with sand, dipped pieces of straw into the blood and passed them to the Catholics present. One of the prison-keepers at Lancaster Castle helped to secure some more relics, and wrote a testimonial signed by himself and a colleague affirming that the relics he had collected were those of Father Arrowsmith. This testimonial was enclosed in a letter from a Mr. Henry Holme and addressed to Mr. Thomas Metcalfe, thought to be a priest, and dated 5th November, 1629. The reference in *Foley's Records,* Vol. 2, page 59, gives the superscription of this letter as follows: "A letter from Henry Holme, endorsed by Thomas Thornburgh and John Rigmaden, addressed to Mr. Thomas Metcalfe, 5th November, 1629, attesting the relics of Father Arrowsmith. Rigmaden was the keeper of Lancaster Castle."

A paraphrased letter runs: " Worthy Sir,—My duty remembered; for the certification of these things which I did deliver to you, when you were at Lancaster, I assert that they are true relics, for the hair and the pieces of the ribs I collected myself, when the plumbers went up to see the leads in order to repair them, and the handkerchief was dipped in his blood when his quarters were being brought back from the scaffold to the Castle. You know the handkerchief was your own, which you gave me at your departure: and as regards the piece of the quarter, both I and some others had taken part of it for our friends, which facts Mr. Southworth can witness; and that part which I gave you, John Rigmaden, our keeper, gave me leave to take and to bring the rest which I delivered to you again as I had promised; and since you desired them all, I explained everything to him, and secured the parcel with my own hands. This same package I delivered to my daughter, who placed it in your hands when you came to the Castle, and she received your acknowledgment. All these were the relics of Mr. Arrowsmith, who was executed here at Lancaster the 28th of August, 1628, upon the statute of persuasions. I testify that I collected all the things I delivered to you, and more at different times, and received none from any man's hands but my own. Thus, with my love and due respect, I remain at your service to the best of my power,—Henry Holme."

The testimonial originally written in Latin and signed by the two witnesses previously referred to is, roughly translated, as follows:

" We, the undersigned, solemnly affirm and attest that the above letter was written by a man worthy of belief; wherefore there cannot be the shadow of a legitimate doubt of any kind but that the said articles that were handed to Mr. Thomas Metcalfe were the true relics belonging to Edmund Arrowsmith of happy memory, and what gives a fuller and weightier testimony in this matter is the attestation in regard to the same of the keeper of this Lancaster Castle, in whose custody the said relics were placed.

" Date, Nov. 5, A.D. 1629.—Thomas Thornburgh.
John Rigmaden."

(*Foley's Records, S.J.*, Vol. 2, pp. 59-60.)

One of these relics, the hand of the Blessed Edmund Arrowsmith, is preserved at St. Oswald's, Ashton-in-Makerfield, to which some well-authenticated miraculous cures are attributed.

The account of this great Lancashire martyr is concluded in *Foley's Records, S.J.*, with a citation from the MSS. belonging to the archives of the Southwark diocese, a passage from which is transliterated here as follows: " As the martyr was being drawn to the place of execution on the hurdle, a Catholic girl approached him. Her father and mother, who were Catholics, dwelt in a part of the Castle and were acquainted with Father Arrowsmith, both being Catholics. ' Well, Margery,' asked Father Arrowsmith, ' is there anything you wish me to do for you?' Margery replied that she did not desire anything but wished to bear him company. Father Arrowsmith then exhorted her to continue in her Faith and be faithful to her religious duties, and not to have any doubt that the time would come when she would be a happy soul in Heaven. When they arrived at the place of execution, the sheriff sent the girl away (no doubt out of consideration for her feelings).

" The girl went home; and that night, when she went to bed in a room which she shared with one of the keepers' wives, she had a dream during her sleep. Apparently the sleeping girl gave a great sigh and began to speak: ' Lord, Father Arrowsmith, in what a stately place you now live, which is so bright, composed of silver and gold; would to God I might be with you and stay with you, for I think the place is most sweet, like flowers or perfumes.' When Margery awoke next morning, the woman who shared the room with her asked what she had dreamed of, but the girl replied that she could not remember having dreamed of anything. This woman, who was a Protestant, was greatly astonished at the girl's reply, having obviously heard what the latter had said in her sleep. This incident in point of fact caused the woman in question to reflect very seriously about her own faith and religion. And this is all the narrator can say for his part." (*Foley's Records, S.J.*, Vol. 2, pp. 72-74.)

CHAPTER 12

THE LANCASHIRE FARMER

JUDGE Henry Yelverton had still one more victim, who had been arrested and was a prisoner in Lancaster Castle along with the Blessed Edmund Arrowsmith. This was the Lancashire farmer, now honoured as the Blessed Richard Hurst or Hayhurst. He had a farm in Broughton some four miles north of Preston. This country district is adjacent to Goosnargh and Whittingham, where Richard Hurst is thought to have been born. He was known to be a firm recusant and devout Catholic, and pursuivants with warrants went out to arrest him and to bring him before the bishop of Chester for examination. The warrants were placed in the hands of one Christopher Norcross, who was in the service of the State bishop. The pursuivant selected one Wilkinson and a man named Dewhurst to assist him in the projected arrest. The latter was a man of mean and despicable character and had been leading such an infamous life that the officer of the parish had at that very time a warrant in his hands to arrest Dewhurst and place him for his lewdness in a house of correction.

When the pursuivant and his two assistants armed with staves arrived in the field, Mr. Hurst was guiding the plough while a youth drove the horses. There was also a farm-maid, who was leading a harrow. The three men advanced towards Hurst with the warrant. For some unaccountable reason, one of Norcross's men, named Wilkinson, struck at the farmer with his staff, and the maid who witnessed the action ran to the farm-house to summon help, crying out that the three men were killing her master in the field.

A man-servant and another man called Bullen were in the house at the time and hastened into the field to help farmer Hurst. Wilkinson and Dewhurst turned and met them and Wilkinson struck down both. In the scuffle, the farm-maid struck Dewhurst on the head with some implement she was holding. The blow did not fell Dewhurst, who was able to run unsteadily in the direction, it seems, of Wilkinson. Running over the rough, ploughed land, Dewhurst fell down and broke his leg.

After thirteen days, the poison from the broken leg, striking upwards into the body, brought about his death, since he was some distance from needful attention. However, before then the wound on the head from the blow given by the maid had healed up and could not have been the cause of his death. Dewhurst himself before he died declared that he was grieved to have been employed in such a business, and that he had been brought to death's door by no other wound than the injury resulting from his fall. This was verified afterwards by two witnesses. It was, moreover, certain that when the farm-maid struck Dewhurst on the head, the farmer Hurst was more than thirty yards away from both, and also that Hurst had given no direction or encouragement for any such means taken in his defence.

" Thus stood the case," continued Bishop Challoner in the *Memoirs*, " and how should this be made a case of wilful murder against Hurst, 'tis hard to conceive, yet it was arranged that such a charge should be made," and the same judge, Sir Henry Yelverton, accepted that charge and delivered sentence of death, and Richard Hurst was executed at Lancaster Castle on 29th August, the day after the martyr-dom of the Blessed Edmund Arrowsmith. In the meantime he was consigned to the prison-cells, and his life was promised if he would but take the oath of supremacy; but Richard Hurst refused to save his life on any such conditions as were inconsistent with his conscience.

" A gentleman of our country solicited the judge for Mr. Hurst's life, which was granted upon condition that he would take the oath of supremacy. Hereupon the gentleman in question went to the prison with these tidings and told the prisoner what he had done on his behalf. Richard Hurst thanked him most heartily, stating that his visitor had been a friend to him in many things, but in this especially that whereas before he was to die on suspicion of a foul murder, but now through the gentleman's good services he was to die for his conscience and for the Catholic religion. Many wished him to take the oath and to save his life; but Mrs. Hurst, his wife, a courageous woman, told them that she loved her husband as well as other women did theirs, yet she had rather see him die many deaths than once wrong his conscience." (From Father Harte's letter to Father Blackloe in Rome, dated 8th September, 1628. Cf. *Foley's Records, S.J.,* Vol. 2, pp. 34-36.)

To continue Bishop Challoner's narrative: " The day before he was to suffer, he was called upon to attend a service in a State church and hear a sermon there along with other prisoners; but Mr. Hurst assured them that if he had a thousand lives, he would rather lose them all than go willingly there. But the High Sheriff ordered him to be dragged there by force, whilst he on his part made all the resistance that he could, and not without receiving serious injuries. He was trailed upon the ground, hauled by his legs over a rugged and stony way for about a hundred or more yards from the prison to the church. Arriving there, the martyr cast himself upon the ground, and thrust his fingers into his ears so that he might not hear their doctrine. When he was returned to the prison afterwards, he said pleasantly to some Catholics: 'They have tortured my body, but I thank God they have done no hurt to my soul.'

"Two of his friends found means of seeing the martyr on the evening before his execution and remained with him till midnight, engaged in prayer and spiritual devotions. The next morning, the same two friends paid a visit and found Mr. Hurst fearless and full of the desire to be dissolved and to be with Christ. Often during the course of that morning he said: 'What a long time they are taking; when do you think they will come?'

"It was about one o'clock in the afternoon when the Sheriff came to the prison to take those condemned to death to the scaffold. He read out to the prisoners the names of those who had been condemned to death, including the name of Father Arrowsmith. On hearing that name, Mr. Richard Hurst exclaimed: 'You have already sent him to heaven; and I hope I shall not be long after him, for I have the greatest trust in his prayers.' While saying these words, the Blessed Richard Hurst gazed upwards to the top of the castle, where the head of the Blessed Edmund Arrowsmith was fixed. On being asked by one of the officials what he was looking at, the martyr replied: 'I look at the head of that blessed martyr whom you have sent on before to prepare the way for us,' meaning himself and one other who had been reconciled to the Faith in prison. On the way to execution, he gave away alms according to his means, as he had done before to poor prisoners in the castle.

"Being met in the street by Mr. King, the vicar of the town, who questioned him about his faith, he answered: 'I believe according to the faith of the Holy Catholic Church.' The vicar demanded further of him, how he meant to be saved. He answered with his usual cheerfulness, 'Not by your religion, Mr. King.' Mr. King then asked whether he meant to be saved by the merits of Jesus Christ. To this, Mr. Hurst answered shortly, ' Does it do credit to your profession as a divine to ask me a question like that?'

" On the way to execution he carried in his hand a picture of Christ crucified, on which his eyes were fixed; and frequently repeated to himself short ejaculatory prayers. When he came in sight of the gallows, he said: ' Gallows! of you I have no fear.' He approached them and kissed one of the posts. Some few ministers were present to importune him again on questions of religion, but he regarded them not. When the Sheriff told him that he was to be the first to be executed, the Blessed Richard Hurst most devoutly recommended himself to the mercy of God; begging the prayers and intercession of Our Blessed Lady, his Angel Guardian and all the saints, especially St. John the Baptist, the day being the Feast of his Beheading.

" He then looked up, as a farmer would, at the executioner, who was busy fastening the rope, but did not seem to know how to do it properly. Merrily he addressed him by his name, saying, ' Tom, I think I must come and help you.' Such was his courage and serenity of mind upon the very brink of death. Then ascending the ladder, after repeating some devotional prayers and the names of Jesus and Mary three or four times, he was turned off, and so passed from this mortal life to a glorious and happy eternity on 29th August, 1629."

The Blessed Richard Hurst left behind him six young children and a loving wife, who was at that time expecting her seventh. This wife and mother, who had so explicitly and with such faith shared in the temporal sacrifices of her martyred husband, was a widow with a difference. She would know how to train her children to pray to, rather than pray for, their glorious father.

While in prison, the Blessed Richard Hurst had taken care to commit to writing a further testimony of his own innocence regarding the death of Dewhurst. The declaration runs: " Whereas I have been a humble petitioner to His Excellent Majesty for a pardon for the death of one Henry Dewhurst, and his gracious pleasure was that I should have a legal trial before my appeal could be forwarded; and I trusting in the innocency of my cause submitted myself to arrest and imprisonment and placed myself in the hands of Judge Yelverton for fair trial. He, however, informed the jury that I was a recusant and had resisted the bishop of Chester's authority, and that the jury must see to it that I would be made an example of, by bringing in a verdict of murder against me. Whereas the jury, after learning of the affair, was unwilling to find for murder, and three of them in company with the foreman went to the judge in his room after dinner; the judge took the foreman by the hand and told him that the jury must bring in a verdict of murder, so that I could be made an example of. This did one of the jury testify to me when I left the court, and repeated the same to my friends that he had been one of the three that had been to the judge.

" And now the judge has certified, my lord keeper, that it is the foulest murder he has ever heard of, and upon which certificate my appeal was stayed, and because of that fact I am to lose my life. Wherefore for the satisfaction of everyone and in order to clear my friends who have sued for pardon on my behalf, and especially for the sake of the Queen's Excellent Majesty, who has begged most earnestly for my life, I testify that the man had no serious injury except in the leg, which was found to be the cause of his death, and he confessed on his deathbed that he had broken it himself. All this was given in evidence before the coroner, as is manifest from the coroner's verdict and from the examination of witnesses, whose evidence was taken before Sir Ralph Ashton and the coroner. That verdict and the evidence resulting from the examination will easily be seen to contradict the judge's certificate; the verdict given at the inquest was that the man had no mortal wound except in his leg, and that I had never touched him, much less given him a blow, for I was some thirty yards or more away from him when he received his injury. All this will be found to be true from the examination and depositions taken before Sir Ralph Ashton and the coroner, which was all the actual evidence that came against me at the assizes. I have made this declaration for the satisfaction of the public and not now to save my life, but to manifest the true facts of the case, as I hope to be saved."

The Blessed Richard Hurst also wrote three letters to his spiritual director a little before his death, and three citations from them will exhibit something of the great soul of this farmer-martyr.

The first reads: " Dear and Reverend Sir,—I received your letter with the news of death, at which I was not much dismayed, I thank my Lord and Saviour. The more malicious my enemies are, the greater is my comfort; for I do constantly believe that my religion is the cause of their malice, and my greatest desire is to offer my blood in so good a cause. And although from the human point of view I feel afraid and even terrified, I still find great comfort in spirit, when I cast myself upon my sweet Saviour with most fervent love, when I consider what he has done and suffered for me, and my greatest desire is to suffer with Him. And I would rather choose to die a thousand deaths than to possess a kingdom and live in mortal sin; for there is nothing so hateful to me as sin, and that only for the love of my Saviour. I do most constantly believe that He has afflicted me to save me; and

I trust I shall die truly humbled, and for this I desire your good prayers, that I may persevere to the end; for myself I can do nothing without His grace."

In the second letter, he writes: " Now I am preparing for my soul, and I ask you to pray for me: and I likewise wish you to commend my case to the prayers of some good priests and Catholics. And I do freely offer myself into the hands of my sweet Saviour, neither desiring life nor death, but according to His blessed will, hoping that He will dispose all things for the good of my soul."

In the third letter, written the very day of his execution: " Dear and Reverend Sir,—Now I take my last leave. I am now dying and I am as willing to die as ever I was to live, I thank my Lord and Saviour, who I trust, will never fail me. I have comfort in Christ Jesus and His blessed Mother, my good Angel, and all the blessed Saints; and I am much comforted in the valiant and triumphant martyr who has gone before me, and I do much trust his good prayers. How I have been treated you will hear, and likewise what I had offered to me, if I would have taken the oath. I hope my friends will truly understand that my greatest desire is to suffer, and I would I had as many lives to offer as I have committed sins. Now, dear Sir, prepare yourself also to suffer, and animate your spiritual children in suffering. Once again I desire you to say and to procure some Masses for my sinful soul, and if it please God to receive me into His Kingdom, I shall not be unmindful of you and all my good friends. I beg of you to remember my poor children, and encourage my friends about my debts; and let it appear and be known that my greatest worldly care is to satisfy them as far as my means will extend. Once again, adieu: I desire to be dissolved and to be with Christ Jesus. I trust we shall meet some time in heaven to our eternal comfort. Now I take my last leave this execution day, about eight of the clock, and commit you to Christ Jesus." (*Foley's Records, S.J.,* Vol. 2, p. 55.)

It is not unlikely that the Blessed Richard Hurst was also acquainted with another close friend of the Blessed Edmund Arrowsmith, Father Edward Barlow, O.S.B., who some eleven years later was to be the next martyr to be executed at Lancaster Castle. The Blessed Ambrose (Edward) Barlow's home where he was born, Barlow Hall, may still be seen in the outer districts of Manchester. It is situated in Barlow-more Road, Withington, formerly in the parish of Didsbury. Although the area is now built-up and coal-pits and large chimneys have disfigured the site, Barlow Hall, in its own grounds, has been preserved in something of its original pastoral seclusion. The grounds are not entirely surrounded by buildings, since one part of them descends to the banks of the Mersey.

CHAPTER 13

THE PURITAN PERSECUTION

THIS phase of the persecution of Papists commenced in the sixteen-twenties, and claimed its two victims at Lancaster Castle as described in the preceding chapter. Such executions were suspended by royal intervention until 1640 when the Long Parliament became powerful enough to over-rule the King. Very much against his will, Charles I signed the death warrants of some of the martyrs, until he raised the royal standard at Oxford. Catholics understood and appreciated the King's attitude, and as an instance of this " a contemporary Jesuit priest, William Malone, born at Manchester in the year 1592, and later, the Rector of the Irish College, Rome, dedicated one of his learned written works to Charles I." (*Foley's Records, S.J.*, Vol. 7, p. 481.)

The first Lancashire martyr to suffer during this violent outburst was the Blessed Ambrose Barlow, O.S.B., born at Barlow Hall, Manchester, in the year 1585. His baptismal name was Edward, and he was the grandson of that steadfast Catholic, Sir Alexander Barlow, who had rebuilt Barlow Hall. He had died in custody, a prisoner for his Faith, after having converted his custodian. His eldest son, also Sir Alexander Barlow, was a life-long recusant and locally well known for his holy and exemplary character. He married Mary, the daughter of Sir Uryan Brereton of the county of Cheshire. There was a numerous family and the fourth son was Edward Barlow, the martyr, who later, as a Benedictine, took the name Ambrose.

Both his parents suffered terribly from recusancy fines, and more so from the enforced removal of their young children from a Catholic home to be farmed out in Protestant households and brought up in the reformed religion.

In lists of Lancashire recusants drawn up by the ecclesiastical State commissioners and endorsed 15th February, 1583, the recusancy of the Manchester Barlows is mentioned more than once, and the head of the family, after having been previously and perhaps prematurely reported as " conformed," was again bound over for continued recusancy. (*C.R.S.*, Vol. 5, pp. 70-71.) A sufficient number of instances has already been mentioned of the practice of the enemies of the Faith to spread false rumours of the conformity of influential Catholics, so that their dependants might become more tractable.

The following incident in the case of Sir Alexander Barlow, the martyr's father, is no doubt an instance in point. He had all his children baptised privately by a Catholic priest beforehand. But they had to be registered as christened in the nearest State parish church of the Didsbury district. Edward Barlow was christened in this way, but the function was little more than a kind of civil registration of birth, and the attendance of the parents there on such occasions could easily be notified and rumoured as conformity. The falseness of such rumours is proved by the fact that Sir Alexander Barlow continued paying his recusancy fines to the end of his life. As previously mentioned, James I, to save his own purse, empowered his favourites to collect for their own pockets from wealthier Catholics all recusancy fines due to the Crown. In this way a herd of blackmailing vampires was let loose on Catholics, and the torture of systematic impoverishment became a kind of martyrdom hardly less cruel than the thumb-screw or the rack. It brought the devoted household of Barlow Hall to financial ruin. Sir Alexander Barlow lived to have two of his sons priests and Benedictines; William Barlow, the elder son, became Dom Rudesind Barlow and the Administrator-General of the Benedictine Congregation at Douay, while his younger brother was destined to be raised to the Altars of the Church as the Blessed Ambrose Barlow. After a long life of fidelity and holiness, Sir Alexander Barlow died on 20th April, 1620. There appears to be some ground for believing that he had superficially conformed for a time through financial pressure, but was reconciled through the apostolic zeal of a Catholic lady, Margaret Davenport, the widow of Sir William Davenport of Bramhall, Cheshire. Since he had never been a conformist by conviction and continued to pay heavy fines all his life for non-attendance at the State church services, his reconciliation can hardly be called a conversion.

In his earlier years, Edward Barlow, like the friend of his later years, Edmund Arrowsmith, went to a Protestant high school, and at the age of twelve years had perforce to go as a page into the household of a noble Protestant kinsman, Sir Uryan Legh of High Legh Hall, Cheshire. Here the boy was being brought up a Protestant, until the Catholic widow, Margaret Davenport, intervened and most likely at the instance of his parents, took the child under her wing. Years later, when the young Edward had become Dom Ambrose Barlow, he confided to a friend, "I had more cause to remember . . . that a certain lady who was the widow of Sir William Davenport and mother of the now Lord Chief Baron of the Exchequer, was the cause of my conversion and my father's about the same time, her residence being near to her sister Talbot's, which I think is not many miles from the place where he suffered for his conscience." (Cf. *Forgotten Shrines*, Dom Bede Camm, O.S.B., p. 221.)

The latter words of the citation refer to the martyr, the Venerable John Talbot, who was hanged at Durham on 9th

August, 1600, along with the priest, the Venerable Thomas
Palasor, whom he had been sheltering. The martyr, John
Talbot, was a kinsman of the Talbots of Salesbury, near
Ribchester, Lancashire, a family into which Margaret Davenport's sister had married. Margaret Davenport herself was
the daughter of Richard Assheton of Middleton, near Manchester. She not only reconciled Edward Barlow to the
ancient Faith, but also fostered within his soul an ardent
desire to become a priest.

In due course Edward Barlow went to Douay, providen-
tially at a time when Dr. Thomas Worthington was the
President, well known to the youth's own family, and from
whom he acquired a strong purpose to devote his life to the
service of the Catholic farming folk of Lancashire. While
at Douay he attended with others the humanities courses at
the College of Anchin, directed by the Jesuits, and then went
to Valladolid for the course in philosophy. In the year 1610,
for reasons of health he returned to Douay, where he followed
the example of his brother, William Rudesind Barlow, and
became a Benedictine. The year of his ordination to priesthood is variously given as 1615 and 1617, but there was no
delay after being raised to the priesthood in the fulfilment
of his apostolic purpose, for he at once went to England as
an itinerant missionary in Lancashire, never apparently
journeying south of the Mersey.

Although many applications were made for his ministrations from noble Catholic families, where the services of a
man of his culture would have been invaluable, he preferred
to minister to the needs of the poorer Catholics. For a time
he apparently was associated with his friend, Edmund
Arrowsmith, working as an itinerant missioner in a district
for the most part a little south of the area served by the
Jesuit. Some of the places where Ambrose Barlow had his
Mass-centres were Winwick, Warrington, Aughton, near

Liverpool, Ormskirk, and his more lengthy missionary journeys took him northwards across the Ribble as far as Lancaster. (Cf. Recently discovered list of Clergy in 1638 among the Towneley Papers by Godfrey Anstruther, O.P. *Recusant History*, Vol. 4, pp. 38-46. Arundel Press, Bognor Regis.)

In all his journeys, Ambrose Barlow refused a horse and did not carry the accustomed sword, but travelled on foot from village to village and from cottage to cottage, disguised as a humble countryman and living for the most part with Catholic farmers.

Being a close friend of Edmund Arrowsmith, he would also be a close friend of the Blessed John Southworth, and for a time the three friends and martyrs were working together in Lancashire.

The following curious incident in connection with the execution of the Blessed Edmund Arrowsmith on 28th August, 1628, at Lancaster Castle, is related by Father Cornelius Morphy, S.J., in his life of Arrowsmith. On the same evening of the day of that execution, the apparition of Father Arrowsmith appeared at the bedside of the Blessed Ambrose Barlow, who at the time was several miles away from Lancaster. In the words of Father Morphy: " How different was the death of Father Arrowsmith, who on the very day of his memorable combat appeared to the Reverend Father Ambrose Barlow, an English Benedictine monk, then at a great distance and ignorant of what had taken place at Lancaster; and related to him his happy conflict and triumph, foretelling at the same time that Father Ambrose would share in a like glorious end. But let us hear the martyr himself describe this apparition of Father Arrowsmith. Father Barlow was the next who was executed at Lancaster, on 10th September, 1641 (i.e., the next priest), at the age of forty-four (sic); and from his prison-cell he tells of his future death, and narrates the prediction of Father Arrowsmith, when writing to his brother, the Rev. Father Rudesind Barlow, then at Douay, on 17th May, 1641. This letter is quoted in his brother's MS. narrative of the martyrdom, addressed to the Abbot and monks of Cellanova, dated 1st January, 1642, and contains these words: ' I believe I shall suffer; for Mr. Bradshaw (Arrowsmith), the last (priest) that suffered martyrdom (at Lancaster), the night after he suffered, whereas I knew nothing of his death, spoke thus to me, standing at my bedside: " I have suffered, and now you will be to suffer; say little, for they will endeavour to take hold of your words." ' " (*Foley's Records, S.J.,* Vol. 2, pp. 54-55.)

In the meantime, Father Ambrose Barlow continued his missionary labours in Lancashire in spite of the growing dangers and the warnings of friends to move further afield from the surrounding menaces, for the " iniquitous joint-stock company " of paid spies had their agents in Lancashire. The good priest could easily have gone to live for a time with a kinsman, who had a house in Cheshire. The labours and exposures to which his apostolate subjected him brought on a serious illness, which he dealt with and endured as best he could on his rounds.

He could not be persuaded to leave his flock to seek his own safety. Rather did he pursue his tasks with his usual ardour. " On the eves of the principal Feasts of the year, the Catholics resorted to him from distant places, and spent the night after the manner of the early Church, in watching, prayer and spiritual colloquies; whilst for his part, he was employed for almost all the night in hearing Confessions. On the next day he treated them all with dinner, where he and some of the better classes amongst his flock served them that were poor, and waited upon them, and then dined on what they had left. When he sent them home, he gave each of them some money by way of alms; and when all had dined, he distributed what remained to the poor of the parish. His zeal, therefore, made him as well known in that neighbourhood as the very parson of the parish." (Cf. *Memoirs of Missionary Priests,* p. 396.)

This last statement of Bishop Challoner has a special significance, since the last actual minister referred to was a Puritan of a kind obnoxious to the Protestant Royalist ministry.

At the time of his arrest, Father Ambrose Barlow was only beginning to recover from his illness, and the details of that arrest he later from his prison-cell communicated to Dom Rudesind Barlow. In this letter to his brother, Ambrose Barlow refrained from mentioning any names of persons or places owing to the danger of such correspondence falling into the hands of spies and pursuivants.

Although he had visited his home, Barlow Hall, and had been harboured at the home of his Catholic kinsfolk, the Downes of Wardley Hall, Manchester, where at the present time the Blessed martyr's skull is enshrined, Father Ambrose Barlow for the most part selected as his apostolic headquarters Morleys Hall, Leigh. Here he was more accessible and freer to serve his beloved Catholic poor.

" The principal place of his residence was the old hall of Morleys in Astley, in the parish of Leigh, about seven miles from Manchester and about as far from Barlow Hall. The owner of Morleys was Mr. (afterwards Sir Thomas) Tyldesley, the famous knight, *sans peur et sans reproche,* who was Major-General in the Royal army and Governor of Lichfield. He was slain at the Battle of Wigan in 1651. Sir Thomas was a devout Catholic, as all his forbears had been. His grandfather, Thomas Tyldesley, of Morleys Hall and Myerscough Lodge, Preston (near Claughton-on-Brock), was himself a grandson of Thurstan Tyldesley of Wardley Hall, where Father Barlow's kinsfolk, the Downes, now resided.

" This older Thomas Tyldesley was specially obnoxious to the Elizabethan government, and Lord Burghley has placed a cross against Morleys Hall on his famous map of Lancashire, to signify that its owner was a specially stiff Papist and would require extra coercion. In a report presented to the Privy Council in 1591, it is said that ' his children and family are very greatly corrupted, and few or none of them come to church.' His widow, Elizabeth, daughter of Christopher Anderton of Lostock Hall, was reported to Lord Burghley in 1598 as ' one of the most obstinate recusants,' and so she continued till the day of her death. She survived until Father Ambrose Barlow came on the mission, for we are told that he assisted her at her death, and she left a pension of £8 a year to a priest that would take charge of the poor Catholics in the neighbourhood of her residence.

" This charge was undertaken by our martyr himself, and he therefore with the consent of Sir Thomas took up his abode at Morleys. Of the £8 a year, he gave £6 to the poor man with whom he lodged for his diet, though he was absent for almost a fourth part of the year. ' For his custom was to be three weeks at home, the fourth in circuit, excepting only the week in Advent. At two places on his circuit, I have been with him; the one was a widow's house (who is a tenant of my Lord Stranges) some twenty miles from Morleys where there was a great number of people. That widow's house is very near a park of my Lord Molineux (Cf. Footnote, Sir Richard Molyneux of Croxteth Hall, and Sefton Hall . . .) whose good father (though then a Protestant) gave his horses leave to feed in that park of his.' . . . Unhappily, Morleys Hall has been pulled down, and nothing now remains to remind us of the martyr." (*Forgotten Shrines*, Dom Bede Camm, O.S.B., pp. 225-226.)

The final arrest of this much-hunted priest took place at Morleys Hall. On the Easter Sunday of 1641, a neighbouring minister, James Gatley, the vicar, emboldened by the effective resistance of the Long Parliament to the King, instead of conducting an Easter-day service for his congregation of some 400 people, proposed that they should all then and there set out in a body under his leadership to arrest the noted Popish priest, who was at the time sure to be holding a service for his flock at Morleys Hall. A minister of that type even in those days was something of an oddity, for he even went so far as to state that if they waited until church-time was over, they would miss the opportunity. Therefore he marshalled his congregation, armed with clubs and sticks, and, vested in his surplice, led them to the house where Father Barlow was finishing the celebration of the Easter Mass.

When this mob reached the house, the good priest, having completed the Mass, was delivering an exhortation to his congregation of about a hundred people. Realising that the house was being besieged, the Catholics urged Father Barlow to take refuge at once in one of the many hiding-places which were available. Father Barlow " would by no means consent to secure himself and leave his flock to the mercy of these wolves. Wherefore, exhorting them all to constancy, and reminding them that these light and momentary tribulations would work in them an eternal weight of glory; and telling them withal how ready he was for his part to suffer all things for Christ, he ordered them to open the doors." (*Memoirs of Missionary Priests*, p. 397.)

The mob of some four hundred rushed into the house, crying out: " Where is Barlow? Where is Barlow? He is the man we want." In the meantime they searched the entire house, and finding Father Barlow's box, they broke it open in the hopes of finding money therein. There was in fact a bag inside the case which contained a sizeable sum of money given him by a charitable gentleman for distribution among his poor. Although the marauders rummaged about and turned over all the priest's clothes, they failed to find this bag, which remained safe, and its contents were at length by Father Barlow's orders distributed to the poor according to the intention of the donor.

As he was being led to the nearest Justice of the Peace for commitment, since the parson and his followers had no warrant, many of the Catholics would have attempted to rescue their priest and might easily have succeeded had not Father Barlow dissuaded them earnestly from doing so. He was therefore duly arrested and committed to Lancaster gaol in the Castle. He was, however, in such a weak state of health that he could not sit on horseback without someone behind him to give him support.

After some four months' imprisonment, he was brought to trial before the judge, Sir Robert Heath, who appears to have had instructions from Parliament that if any priest were convicted at Lancaster, the full penalty of the law was to be executed upon him as an example to all Catholics, who were still numerous in the county. Father Barlow made an open admission of his Faith and priesthood, but warned the judge solemnly of the danger of his own damnation in passing a sentence that amounted in its injustice to murder. On receiving the death-sentence, the martyr said aloud: " Thanks be to God." He then prayed heartily to the Divine Majesty for forgiveness on behalf of all those who had been in any way accessory to his death. It was a final prayer in court which touched the heart of the judge, who applauded the charity of the prisoner and granted the boon he had petitioned for—namely, a room to himself in the Castle during the brief remainder of his earthly life.

The day of his execution was Friday, 10th September, 1641. Lying down on the hurdle, he carried all the way in his hand a wooden cross, which he himself had made while in prison. When he arrived at the scaffold, he walked three times round it, holding the cross before him and reciting the " Miserere." He refused to discuss anything with the ministers present, having, as he said, much more important matters to attend to at the moment. The Blessed Ambrose Barlow, O.S.B., was hanged, drawn and quartered at Lancaster in the fifty-fifth year of his age, after devoting twenty-four years to missionary labour in his native county.

A precious relic, the head of the Blessed Ambrose Barlow, was rescued by Francis Downes of Wardley Hall, and is still preserved there. The Hall is about five miles from Morleys Hall, and by good fortune Wardley Hall is in Catholic hands, being the residence and headquarters of the Bishop of Salford. The hand of the martyr is also preserved, in a handsome reliquary at Stanbrook Abbey.

Moreover, it should be mentioned that Father Ambrose Barlow paid probably more than one visit to the Catholic prisoners in Lancaster Castle and, twelve years before his own execution there, he had administered the Last Sacraments to the Blessed Edmund Arrowsmith, when he lay in prison awaiting his execution. " Though the biographers of Father Arrowsmith do not mention this incident, Challoner's authorities are so good that we may accept it as a fact. Perhaps this is the reason why this holy Jesuit appeared, after his martyrdom, to our Benedictine, as already related." (*Forgotten Shrines,* Dom Bede Camm, O.S.B., p. 236.)

There are also some precious details of the Blessed Ambrose Barlow's personal appearance culled from some early records cited in *Forgotten Shrines,* pages 232-233. " Remembering how Sir Thomas More jested at his beard, it put me in mind that our martyr was ever careless of his; for he did not trouble himself or anyone else with the trimming or shaving of it, but let it alone as nature had framed it. It was forked and not long, much hair about his cheeks.

The hair of his head curled naturally, which sure was sometimes cut, for it was never long. Hair of a chestnut colour was still adhering to the skull when found at Wardley Hall. His clothes were still of grey-frise, the fashion thereof for the oldness might be the same that was in use when he first did leave or return into England; a long-waisted jerkin and doublet, his breeches tied above the knees. The best hat that ever I saw him wear, I would not have given him two groats for; the band about his neck of the country folks' fashion, as poor a one as is ordinarily worn by any, tied with a round threaden point, as I remember: no cuffs at all. Instead of pantofles, a pair of scurvy old slip-shoes, which he continually wore within doors. I adventuring once to find fault with those slip-shoes said to him: ' Alas, Sir, why do you not get a pair of warm slippers? Besides, you walk with difficulty in those trashes.' His answer was, ' We must have something to look at.' Although it is a usual thing among many good men that would be loath to fight to wear swords, yet our martyr would wear none; and thus merrily he answered me when I took notice of it, saying, ' Indeed, I dare not wear a sword, because I am of a choleric disposition.' And then he told me in these words that on one occasion he had felt a strong urge to have crossed swords with an individual who was on the point of arresting him, but in the end his own heels proved to have been his best weapon.

"He loved to observe how time passed, but he had no pocket watch; and once I asked him why he had not a watch to take abroad with, as this was usual: and he answered me that it was pride, pride. He had a clock at home for that purpose, which nobody kept but himself." (Ibid., p. 233.)

The Blessed Ambrose Barlow also possessed a ready wit and for the most part he directed it against himself and left the rest to the Great Master whom he had served so well. Of him his ancient biographer wrote: " He has now concluded his days with the master-piece of charity, and so sealed his doctrine with his own innocent blood."

Another missionary priest in Lancashire about the same period was a Jesuit, Richard Bradley, who was born in Lancashire in 1605. He became a Jesuit in 1623 at the age of eighteen, and beyond these meagre details little is known of his early years. Before coming to labour as a missionary in Lancashire during the last years of his life, he appears to have spent most of his priestly life as a military chaplain to English and Irish troops in the Continental wars of the period. An early biographer and fellow-Jesuit, Father Tanner, writes of him as " a man of great soul, and prodigal alike of blood and life, as often as occasion and necessity occurred. He entered the Society of Jesus at the age of eighteen, under the discipline of which he was formed by virtue and learning, a most apt instrument of divine glory. In due course he was solemnly professed." (*Foley's Records, S.J.*, Vol. 2, pp. 178-180.)

Two of his contemporary Jesuit associates, the Blessed Henry Morse and the Blessed Ralph Corby, had been drawn to the work of a military chaplain, but neither of them had visualised it seemingly as a life-long profession. Richard Bradley, a learned and proficient man, appeared ready to take up his appointment as a life's work, and perhaps few priests had a greater and longer experience of the horrors of the battle-line than he.

The same biographer writes: " In an engagement more sanguinary than the rest, he ran through the dense shower of bullets flying about his head, regardless of his own safety, to hear the confessions of the wounded, when a certain soldier, seeing his imminent danger, and apprehensive for the priest's safety, took off his own helmet and placed it on the head of Father Bradley, so that one might have suspected him to have been his good angel guardian, for no sooner had the trooper performed this act of charity, when a musket ball struck the priest on the head, and must have shattered it, had it not been turned off by the helmet." (Ibid.)

By the year 1639, Father Richard Bradley had apparently been appointed to the English mission to labour in his native county. According to the recently discovered list of clergy ministering in Lancashire and dated 1639, a Father Bradley, S.J., is included as working in Wigan. It appears certain that this is Richard Bradley, who was at length arrested by the Parliamentary pursuivants. In the words of the biographer, " It is easy to foresee the sufferings he would have to undergo in those difficult times, on being appointed to the English mission, from those of others, since there was no opportunity of going abroad in open daylight to visit, console and encourage the faithful, but this could alone be accomplished under cover of the darkness of the night. And although Father Richard did this with the utmost caution, he was nevertheless seized and thrust into the gaol of Manchester."

There is an ominous reference in the above quotation to a particularly insidious and diabolic form of pursuivancy that had been fairly recently engineered in which, unfortunately, some wretched apostate priests and renegade Catholics, only too well provided with the needful evidence, played their despicable parts. Father Richard Bradley was arraigned for trial at Manchester, convicted of his priesthood and minis-trations and condemned to be hanged, drawn and quartered in the usual brutal manner. He was then returned to his filthy prison cell to suffer a worse pain than death from the appalling stench, darkened dampness and verminous state of his dungeon. He was left to rot there until the authorities could make up their minds whether to have a public execution in Manchester of a convicted priest. But before they could come to a decision, the inevitable gaol fever laid hold of the condemned priest and finally relieved the executioners of their gruesome task. The devoted priest died of gaol fever on 30th January, 1645, at the age of forty-one.

The special menace of the time for all devoted missionary priests and steadfast recusants, which hindered their apostolic labours, is described in *Foley's Records, S.J.*, Vol. 1, page 514: " Frequent mention occurs in these *Records* of this middle period of the seventeenth century of a gang of notorious pursuivants, comprising a so-called Captain Wadsworth (James Wadsworth, an apostate), Francis Newton, Thomas Cross, John Gray and others employed by the Privy Council, to hunt down their victims, the Catholic clergy, like wild beasts, and to hound them to death and exile. These men appear to have formed themselves into a kind of joint-stock company for unholy purposes, and no doubt made large pecuniary profits."

Dr. Lingard refers to the same in the *History of England*, Vol. 8, page 645, Appendix (Note " G " for p. 396). An original document is given here containing the names and fate of such Catholic priests as were prosecuted in London alone between the end of 1640 and the summer of 1651 by four individuals who banded themselves together for that purpose, and who solicited from the Privy Council some reward for their services. It should, however, be remembered, Dr. Lingard adds, that many others were engaged in the same pursuit, and consequently there were many other victims besides those enumerated. These two references will explain something of the difficulties which beset the Blessed Thomas Holland, S.J., during his all too brief missionary apostolate in London. A short survey of his life will be largely the subject of the following chapter, and besides showing forth the glory of his martyrdom, will also present the sad spectacle of the degradation and disgrace of an apostate priest who, having turned pursuivant, had become a member of what has been described as an infamous joint-stock company. The full account given in the *Records* from documents written by members of the "gang," shows how widespread over England its diabolic activities had become. As a sample of the claims upon the Privy purse for successful pursuivancy on the part of members of the notorious joint-stock company, the following quotation of a few of the victims from a much larger list reads as follows:

"Thomas Sanderson, alias Hammond (The Blessed Thomas Holland), executed at Tyburn.

Ralph Corby (The Blessed Ralph Corby, S.J.), executed at Tyburn.

Henry Morse (The Blessed Henry Morse, S.J.), executed at Tyburn.

Thomas Worsley, alias Harvey, indicted and proved, and reprieved by the Spanish Ambassador and others.

Andrew White, indicted and proved, reprieved before judgment and banished.

Peter Beale, alias Wright (The Blessed Peter Wright, S.J.), executed at Tyburn.

George Gage, indicted by us, and found guilty, and since is dead.

The list is signed:

"James Wadsworth.
Francis Newton.
Thomas Mayo.
Robert de Luke."

Father Andrew White, a Jesuit, lived to be the founder of the mission in Maryland. Father George Gage, died of cancer, a prisoner for his priesthood. He was a secular priest and the apostasy of his younger brother, a priest and a religious, and a member of the iniquitous company, broke his heart.

Chapter 14

A MARTYR FROM ST. HELENS

THOMAS HOLLAND was born at Sutton, near St. Helens, in the year 1600, his parents being devout Catholics. His father, Richard Holland, was a descendant of the noble Holland family. The young Thomas was educated St. Omer's and, on a bursary supplied from the Jesuit College, went to the English College, Valladolid, for his higher studies and thence proceeded to Belgium to become a Jesuit. He had an uncle, Father Henry Holland, who laboured for many years in Lancashire and was instrumental in reconciling to the Faith Mr. James Anderton of Lostock Hall, near Preston. For a time, Father Henry Holland was associated with Father Henry Garnet, S.J., and was present at his martyrdom in 1606 in St. Paul's churchyard. Henry Holland survived his nephew, the Blessed Thomas Holland, who won the crown of martyrdom in 1642. The uncle, who had become a Jesuit in 1609, exercised a salutary and exemplary influence on his nephew and both were arrested almost at the same time.

The older priest was tried and condemned to death in 1648, but was reprieved and sent into perpetual exile where he lived to be an octogenarian. It was this good priest who arranged for Thomas's admission into the English College at St. Omer's. Both at Valladolid and at the Jesuit novitiate at Watten in Belgium, Thomas Holland became acquainted with the Blessed Ralph Corby, S.J., and with his brother, Father Ambrose Corby, S.J. Catholics are indebted to the latter for an admirable book, *The Triple Combat*, which describes the heroic conflicts of the three Jesuit martyrs who were executed during the Puritan Persecution: the Blessed Ralph Corby, the Blessed Henry Morse and the Blessed Thomas Holland, S.J.

A Catholic prisoner for the Faith, who was for a time incarcerated with each of these priests in Newgate, contrived with almost miraculous skill to paint a strikingly life-like portrait of all three. These miniatures were and still are preserved at the Carmelite Convent of St. Columba, Lanherne. " They were brought to our Venerable Rev. Mother by a novice, Miss Mary Gifford of Staffordshire, who made her Profession in our convent of Antwerp on the 8th of April, 1681, aged forty-two years, and was named in religion Mary of the Martyrs, in honour of the English Martyrs. Her father, Mr. Gifford, being their fellow-prisoner, was filled with a veneration for them, and conceived an ardent desire to take their portraits, and though he knew nothing of the art of painting, he felt a strong impulse to try, which having done, he succeeded so well that it was considered miraculous, he having taken the likeness of each of the three martyrs only on the night before the day of their execution at Tyburn, or day on which they expected to receive the crown. Mr. Gifford desired his daughter to give these portraits as relics to the ' English Nuns at Antwerp.' Very much later, actual photographs of the three miniatures in the same size were taken by the Woodbury Process Company, Great Portland Street, London, and these have been reproduced and in certain cases enlarged. Unquestionably the portraits are strikingly lifelike." (Cf. *Foley's Records, S.J.*, Vol. 1, pp. 542-543. Footnote.)

" Thomas Holland was very young when he went to study the humanities in the College of St. Omer's, and there he was esteemed for his great abilities and for his quiet and pious character. He was elected Prefect of the Sodality of

Our Blessed Lady, and in this post he not only gave his fellow-students the benefit of a good example, but by a singular grace and tact was of much influence in familiarly exhorting his companions to acts of piety. He was no less prominent in Exercises spoken from the rostrum, or in plays, which were performed in the College theatre. On the termination of his course of rhetoric, he was sent by his superiors in August, 1621, to the English College of *the Jesuits* in Valladolid to study philosophy. When Charles, the Prince of Wales, afterwards Charles I, visited Madrid . . . it seemed fitting that the youth of England, who by the munificence of His Catholic Majesty (King of Spain) were pursuing their studies in his kingdom, should give some proof of their loyalty on the arrival amongst them of their future Sovereign, and of their reviving hopes of more favourable times for their religion. This was entrusted to Thomas Holland, who was sent for the purpose from Valladolid to Madrid. In the name of the rest, he assured His Royal Highness of their loyalty and good wishes, and addressed him in a Latin oration of which the Prince was pleased to express his admiration and approval." (*Foley's Records, S.J.* Ibid., p. 544.)

After some three years at Valladolid in the study of philosophy, Thomas Holland's health broke down and he had to return to Flanders to complete his full course. In 1624 he entered the Jesuit novitiate at Watten. In due course, he passed on to the College at Liege for theology and was eventually ordained priest. For a short time he was minister at the house of the third year of probation at Ghent. He then returned to the English Jesuit College at St. Omer's to become spiritual director and confessor of the pupils. As long as Father Thomas Holland's health lasted—for his was a delicate constitution—no pains were spared by him in the fulfilment of those necessary labours in the training of youths for an arduous apostolate. He was eminently successful with the youths under his direction, and had that most rare character of being able to guide and direct boys without any kind of punishment or of even the shadow of any threat of it.

A paraphrase of the written testimony of a contemporary, Father Thomas Carey, S.J., who was with him at the College in Liege, will bear out the above remarks: " I heard it most constantly reported at the English Seminary of St. Omer's that our glorious Father Thomas Holland, being prefect there in the year 1623, perceiving one of the scholars, William Norice (sic), now Alferus (Alfredus) Westby, to be very melancholy and disconsolate, told him to go and rest on his bed, whilst he himself went into his own room which was near by and took a discipline for him (i.e., Father Holland went to his own room and gave himself some strokes with a scourge, so that by punishing himself, this friend in need might secure blessings and graces for his unhappy and home-sick pupil). He was extremely charitable to the sick, and of this I had long experience, for, while he was prefect, I was in ill-health and sickly, though not in the infirmary. Nevertheless, he made my bed for me several times.

" Being in charge of the scholars' dormitory in summer time, he was much troubled with flies (fleas), and on being told that he had many on his face and cap, he would not beat them off. I think I was present when to some that showed him the inside of his cap, all swarming with them, he only smiled and put in on his head without removing one of them.

" On another occasion, some scholars, meeting him in the dark and either unwittingly or jokingly taking him to be one of their companions that had donned the prefect's cornered hat, made a rush at him and knocked his hat down to his ears. All this he took patiently, and took it all to have been an innocent mistake. He showed not the slightest sign of displeasure and readily forgave them. But when speaking of

Almighty God, he appeared to become all inflamed and his eyes would sparkle; and in chiding those whose misdemeanours savoured of sin he would with much emphasis and spirit repeat the words: 'Dominus Deus videt vos' ('the Lord God sees you'). While speaking thus, he manifested a very vivid consciousness he had of His Divine Majesty, and, although while chiding in this way with voice and gesture like a man on fire, we could clearly see that he was not angry, but was speaking only out of zeal, for as soon as ever he had ended his speech he became his tranquil and quiet self instantaneously, as if he had in no way been moved . . .

"He was an exceedingly able spiritual director and was so beloved that four or five years after he had left the Seminary his name remained famous for his extraordinary gifts as a director of souls and a confessor. His many penitents and clients proclaimed that he never could be replaced. He would very often encourage us in confession by saying: 'My soul for yours,' and in such a tone of voice and expression that one could not fail to perceive that it proceeded from a true and noble heart.

"Liege, 4th February, 1643.   THOMAS CARY (sic)."

(Foley's Records, S.J., Vol. 1, pp. 545-546.)

While he was the minister at Ghent he took his final vows, on 28th May, 1634. His health having again broken down, it was thought that the native air of his own country would help to restore his constitution. Hence he proceeded to England in the year 1635, and became a chaplain in a Catholic household, the name of which in those dangerous times was not divulged. His weak state of health including loss of appetite, and insomnia prevented him from embarking upon those strenuous missionary labours which were his heart's desire.

For the most part he was constrained to confine himself to the house and garden during the daytime, but at dusk and early dawn, he visited isolated Catholics who depended upon such help for the Sacraments and the fulfilment of their other religious duties. At these times also he ministered to the sick. Although the times were more tranquil, Father Thomas Holland was assiduous and skilful in disguising himself on all these occasions. He could speak fluently French, Flemish and Spanish, and found little difficulty in speaking broken English to any dangerous person who showed a tendency to cross-examine him.

Unfortunately his movements did not escape the watchful eyes of some apostate members of the disgraceful " joint-stock company." One of these, who had been a contemporary at St. Omer's, recognised Father Thomas Holland one evening when he was making a sick-call. This wretched man, thought to have been Thomas Gage, caused one of his assistants in the same diabolical group to approach Father Holland, whom he identified as a priest and gave into custody. This was on 4th October, 1642, the Feast of St. Francis of Assisi. The martyr was taken before a magistrate and committed to what was then called the " New Prison " in the suburbs of London.

Thomas Gage had lately deserted and abandoned his Faith, his priesthood and his religious vows for degraded motives. This unhappy man was the brother of the devout priest, Father George Gage, and of the gallant Colonel, Sir Henry Gage, who lost his life in the Royal cause at the fight of Culham, near Abingdon, Berks., 11th January, 1644.

At the trial of the Blessed Thomas Holland, Father Ambrose Corby, S.J., in the *Certamen Triplex*, mentions the four witnesses brought against him, " whose names," he wrote, " I forbear to mention. May God forgive them, and bring them all into His Church. One especially who was born of a noble family, and once a priest and a religious, by this act no less disgraced the dignity of his family, and the honour of his blood, than he had by foul and wicked apostasy disgraced his Faith and religious vows." (*Foley's Records, S.J.*, Vol. 1, p. 549, footnote.)

To protect those who had harboured him, received him into their houses and received his priestly ministrations, Father Holland neither affirmed nor denied his priesthood, having pointed out at the commencement of the trial that his accusers had to prove their statements. The judge on this occasion was the Recorder, who asked him if he were prepared now to swear that he was not a priest. " It is not the custom of the English law," replied Father Holland, " for the accused to clear himself by oath; but that either the crimes laid in the indictment be clearly proved, or else that the accused be acquitted and set at liberty."

The four witnesses against him were members of the mercenary band of apostates and their names were John Cooke, James Wadsworth, Francis Newton and Thomas Gage. In court, Francis Newton stated that without any success he had endeavoured to arrest Father Holland, whom he had known to have been much in the company of a Jesuit priest, Father Ffloyd, for many years past, but that eventually his servant, John Cooke, had effected the arrest, assisted most likely by the guidance of Thomas Gage. The evidence of both Newton and Cooke at the trial was a tissue of asseverations neither could substantiate, and the martyr's long association with Father Ffloyd, S.J., did not prove that Holland was a priest.

Captain Wadsworth's statements were confined for the most part to Thomas Holland's address to the then Prince of Wales, while he was at Madrid. Wadsworth stated that Sir Tobie Matthew, " that archest of all Jesuits," as this witness described him, had brought Thomas Holland to Madrid to pronounce an oration " in the name of all the Jesuits " before His Majesty, then Prince of Wales, and that the latter had refused to proffer his hand to be kissed, deeming it a disgrace to let any Jesuit touch his hand. Father Thomas Holland denied that he knew any such arch-Jesuit, and stated that far from refusing, the Prince of Wales had allowed him to kiss his hand. Although Father Sir Tobie Matthew was always devoted to the Jesuits, having been received into the Church by Father Robert Parsons, S.J., and later ordained priest by a Jesuit Saint, Cardinal Robert Bellarmine, there appears to be no proof that he ever became a Jesuit. It is true that he finally retired to Ghent and lived and died in the Jesuit house there. He proved himself a benefactor there by helping students from England to reach the various seminaries on the Continent and by assisting many English postulants to reach the English communities of nuns in Flanders. It appears likely that Father Thomas Holland was well acquainted with Father Matthew, but not as an " arch-Jesuit."

After the evidence had been given in the manner described, the jury retired and soon returned, bringing in a verdict of guilty. Many were astonished. " Indeed, the Lord Mayor himself and another member on the bench declared that had they been members of the jury they would not have given in the same verdict on evidence that was so weak." (Ibid., p. 550.)

The death sentence, to be hanged, cut down alive, drawn and quartered, was passed upon Father Holland by the judge, to which the martyr replied in a very audible voice with humble acknowledgment: " Deo gratias." He was then taken back to Newgate to await his execution. When he arrived at the prison, he induced his fellow-Catholic prisoners to sing with him the " Te Deum." In his prison, Father Thomas

Holland, through the services of several members of the Catholic embassies and his fellow-prisoners for the Faith, was able to celebrate the Holy Mass.

Also, he received a most touching letter of apology from the Rev. George Gage, the saintly brother of the apostate, Thomas Gage:

" Reverend Sir,

" No sooner did I hear of your happiness in being destined to become a martyr than I was also shaken to the very depths of my heart with grief, when I learned that my miscreant of a brother had been secured as a witness against you. Since in the latter's regard, I rightly fear that he who accused you will not have the grace to ask your pardon, I thought it my duty to do so on his behalf, and that however much his person cannot be cleansed from the guilt of so foul a sin, except by his own personal repentance, at all events to save our name and family honour, I in the name of the whole family and all his brothers and sisters will not be wanting in making at once this disavowal and deprecation of the crimes committed and basely done by one bearing our family name, and moreover of crimes of such sort that the entire family blush to behold. In this, all the family are joined, and as for myself, I am so confounded and out of countenance, that I am ashamed to show my face.

" In brief, Reverend Sir, if I could do so without grave and severe censure, being at the moment seriously ill, I would come to you in person and beg at once for your blessing and pardon, the first for myself, the second for my graceless brother, who has now so basely apostatised from the honoured Catholic pedigree and fair name of his family, as he had done before from his Faith and religious vows.

" Dear Sir, I beg to call to mind the more than ordinary correspondence which was maintained in a most friendly manner between yourself and myself, and the intimate friendship we had at St. Omer's. I remember so well that even in those youthful years your spiritual counsels and exhortations on a virtuous life made a salutary and lasting impression upon me. Remember, I pray, those familiar days we then had, and because of them I hope you will afford me such a share of your sufferings as your kind nature can bestow on your friends, and this favour I beg of you, bowed down as I am as low as the earth. For my part, I shall pray that God will aid you in like manner through the passage of martyrdom; I am heart-broken about my brother, his apostasy and his betrayal of you; it is a grief I cannot find words to describe: I hope still that you will pardon him, and that after your martyrdom you may help many sinners to repentance and to Heaven, whom you leave behind you on earth, amongst whom none shall more need your aids than myself.

"Your most affectionate brother in Christ and ready servant,—GEORGE GAGE.   December 10/20, 1642.

"P.S.—I beseech you, Reverend Sir, to give my best respects to my cousin Powel, your happy associate in this your glorious combat, where God and Angels as well as the lower world are your spectators."

A paraphrase of a letter cited (*Foley's Records, S.J.*, Ibid., p. 563.)

The "Powel" mentioned in the post-script refers to the saintly Benedictine priest and monk, then in prison, the Blessed Philip Powel, O.S.B., who was later martyred for the priesthood at Tyburn on 30th June, 1646.

Although Father Thomas Holland declined to have his portrait drawn by his fellow-Catholic prisoner and artist, Mr. Gifford, the former's objections were fortunately over-ruled and on the very night preceding his execution the perseverance of his friends contrived that, whilst he was placidly asleep, the lineaments of his face were taken by Mr. Gifford.

The good priest constantly declined also the title of "martyr," repeating over and over again that he was no martyr before his execution. When so many were even then helping themselves to relics of his hair and vestments and were kissing his feet, he would say, as though commiserating his own fate: " I am forced to suffer these things against my will."

On 12th December, 1642, the day of his execution, Father Thomas Holland rose early and celebrated Mass, and he had hardly finished his thanksgiving when news was brought to him, that the hurdle was ready at the prison-door to draw him to Tyburn. Neither of the sheriffs of London and Middlesex were in attendance, being unwilling, it is thought, to be present at what they considered to be a judicial murder. Hence the cortege appears to have been in the charge of a serjeant-at-law, who answered to all inquiries that the priest was going to die contrary to law, right and justice.

At Tyburn, the martyr for the most part said his own prayers and then explained the injustice of his trial and condemnation. Since there was no longer any reason to maintain silence, he proclaimed his Faith, and gave public thanks to God for his priesthood and for his vocation as a Jesuit.

After praying for the King, Queen and the Royal family, and, be it added, for the Parliament and the whole nation, he said aloud: " If I had as many lives as there are hairs on my head, drops in the ocean, stars in the firmament, perfections in the Lord of Heaven, I would most willingly lay them all down for this purpose," which last sentence the people received with much applause. Then, turning to the executioner, he said: " Well, Gregory, I also willingly pardon you for carrying out my sentence, and with the permission of my superiors, whom under God I obey, do you take what money I have," at the same time giving him two gold crowns.

Father Thomas Holland then gave a signal to a fellow-

Jesuit priest, who was disguised. This friend approached and spoke to him words of encouragement and then gave him the last Absolution. He was then hanged and, moved by some impulse, a Catholic present removed the head-gear covering his face. " The spectacle was indeed admirable, for his hands were joined before his breast and pointed upwards, and his eyes, which one of the soldiers two or three times endeavoured in vain to close, were directed towards heaven. His face, at first suffused, some moments afterwards returned to its original complexion. Nor were his features hideously distorted, as often happens in the case of persons who are hanged, nor were his arms or feet or any of his limbs agitated by any painful quivering; but, hanging with unmoved body, he ceased, says Father Ambrose Corby, to lengthen out the earthly pilgrimage of that soul of his, which angels, as one might well believe, were vying with each other to conduct in triumph to heaven.

" One of the ministers, perceiving that he was still alive, admonished the hangman, that it was his duty to cut him down and disembowel him whilst half dead. But this man, more humane than the other, occupied himself with something else until it was clear that life was extinct, and then at length he cut the rope. This Blessed Lancashire martyr suffered in his forty-second year, after he had passed eight years on the English mission, chiefly in London. In stature he was below the middle size; he had a handsome face, florid complexion, auburn beard, dark hair, large and prominent eyes, the expression of which was subdued by his sweet and pleasing manners."

A non-Catholic witness of this execution at Tyburn on 12th December, 1642, was heard to say in reference to the Blessed Thomas Holland: " When in all our life shall we see any other—when shall we see anyone of our religion die so nobly?"

One of the prison-keepers at Newgate, as he looked upon the limbs of the quartered body of this martyr, holding in his hand and lifting up the neck and throat of the severed head, exclaimed: "See, this is the throat through which went so many excellent sermons and so much wise counsel."

It is fitting to mention here that a few years later, in 1651, the blessed martyr, Father Peter Wright, S.J., met with an unexpected happiness when the hurdle on which he was borne reached Tyburn. He found himself assisted in rising from the hurdle by the outstretched hand of Father Edward Latham, a fellow-Jesuit and a member of the recusant family of the Lathams of Mosborough Hall, Lancashire. The latter was disguised perfectly as a country yokel. The Blessed Peter Wright recognised him at once, and during those hurried moments of earnest talk, Father Latham in the guise of one asking a favour gave his friend the last blessing and Absolution. The officers, annoyed at the delay, struck Father Latham several blows, crying, "Be off, you troublesome clodhopper; what do you mean by annoying a dying man?" (*Foley's Records, S.J.*, Vol. 2, p. 544.)

CHAPTER 15

MORE LANCASHIRE VICTIMS

IN 1643 Charles I broke with the Long Parliament and established his headquarters at Oxford. The Civil War commenced but in no way distracted the Puritan politicians from violent persecution of Catholics. Sometimes priests who had escaped the gallows were beaten up and murdered. The Presbyterian Scottish allies had instilled their hatred of Papists into the rough Roundhead soldiers and, after their victory at Marston Moor in the early spring of 1644, marauding bands added priest-hunting to the loot and robbery of Royalist homesteads.

Thus two Benedictines died for the Faith at York in 1644. Dom Boniface Kemp was a Londoner. He joined the Order in 1603 and was one of the original Benedictine community at St. Malo in 1611, and its Superior in the following year. Returning to England, he was imprisoned in 1613 or 1614. He is briefly described as " a Londoner, learned and observant: he is in prison." He was examined at Newgate in 1615 and banished at the end of the year with thirteen other priests. Back in England again, he was stationed in York in 1644.

Dom Ildephonse Hesketh was a native of Lancashire, born at Barrowford. As a priest he was at Seville in 1614. After his profession he was sent to England and later recalled to Douay to teach in the Benedictine house of studies, and later transferred to Paris for the same duties. He was again in England as a missionary priest in the danger zone of Yorkshire. About ten or twelve days after the Battle of Marston Moor, Dom Boniface and Dom Ildephonse were seized by a gang of Roundhead soldiers and tortured to death at York, martyrs for the priesthood. (Cf. *C.R.S.*, Vol. 33, pp. 212-213.)

Brian Cansfield, a Jesuit martyr, was born in 1581 or 1582 at Robert Hall, comprising an estate that apparently included Tatham, Hornby and some districts a few miles north of Lancaster. The Cansfield family was well-to-do, Catholic and strongly recusant, and so Brian's early life was in a devout Catholic atmosphere. He was sent to various schools, notably at Lancaster, Tunstall, Blackburn, Orswick, Warton, near Lytham, and Thornton, near Fleetwood. At Lytham Hall, the Catholic family of the Cliftons supported a number of junior students who were destined eventually to complete their studies at one or other of the English seminaries on the Continent.

Brian Cansfield at the age of sixteen went to the College of the English Jesuits at St. Omer, where he spent three years. Although his two brothers and three sisters were apparently devout and steadfast Catholics, Brian Cansfield surprisingly states that he himself had been, for a space it may be presumed, brought up a Protestant until the age of sixteen, when through the good influence and example of one of his brothers, he made up his mind, was reconciled by Father Stanney, S.J., and received into the Church by Father Fleck. (Cf. *Foley's Records, S.J.*, Vol. 3, pp. 140-142.)

Perhaps not all the schools he had attended during his earlier impressionable years were Catholic, and he may have fallen away for a time in spite of the care and solicitude of his Catholic relatives. On 15th October, 1601, he went to the English College, Rome, for his higher studies, and in that year he mentioned that both his pious parents were dead. On 14th November, 1604, he became a Jesuit.

His lapse as a youth appears all the more strange when it is remembered that his eldest sister, Elizabeth Cansfield, was one of the first to enter the new foundation of English religious at Brussels. She arrived there on 4th November, 1598, taking in religion the name of Anne. The following English ladies made their sacred vows on 21st November, 1600: Mary Percy, Dorothy Arundel, Gertrude Arundel, Elizabeth Cansfield, Frances Gawen, Elizabeth Southcote, Winifred Thomson and Renata Smith, and thus the new Brussels Convent was founded. It was at the instance of Mary Percy that the new foundation was to be affiliated to the Benedictine Order. Elizabeth Cansfield died in religion, aged thirty-four. She was of a sweet disposition and, being devoted to the sick, served in her convent as infirmarian. (*Foley's Records, S.J.*, Vol. 4, p. 680.)

Brian was talented and studious, and convinced that he had much cause for repentance, led in the Order a very mortified life; it was enough to know anything to be gratifying for him to reject it. While generous to others, he was unduly hard on himself. It is said of him that " the thirty-nine years of his religious life were for him a perfect school of martyrdom." (*Foley's Records, S.J.*, Vol. 6, p. 220.)

After his ordination to the priesthood, he made his profession on 7th February, 1619, remaining for a few more years on the Continent, although he yearned always to give his life as a martyr on the English mission. This prayer was eventually granted. For some years he devoted his ministerial labours to the service of Catholics in Lincolnshire and became the local Jesuit Superior. After that, he went to Lancashire, and for some time lived at Scarisbrick Hall. The Cansfield estate at Robert Hall later passed into the posses-

sion of the Gerards of Brynn and Garswood when the heiress,
Mary Cansfield, married Sir William Gerard of Brynn, the
fifth baronet. (*Foley's Records, S.J.*, Vol. 3, p. 140, footnote.)

His apostolate was blessed with many reconciliations to the
ancient Faith. He was conspicuously successful and so was
assiduously hunted by the pursuivants. Although his final
missionary adventures took him into Yorkshire during the
dangerous period of the Civil War, his residence remained
at Scarisbrick Hall, and there, whenever he allowed himself
the indulgence, he devoted himself to theological study.
Father Cansfield left a fine library there.

He was over sixty years of age when he was arrested by
a troop of Roundhead soldiers while he was labouring in
Yorkshire, where his activities had made him a marked man.
A certain judge, living in Yorkshire, whose name and address
are not available, had married a Catholic lady whom he had
induced to apostatise, he himself being violently anti-Catholic.
His wife, however, had recently been reconciled to the Faith
by a Jesuit priest, and when the fact became known to the
judge, he declared that he would not rest until he had
discovered that priest and had him hanged, drawn and
quartered.

This declaration was no idle remark, for he had the pursuivants and soldiery searching and ransacking every place
in the region, where there was the least suspicion of Mass
being said. By an unlucky chance for the Catholics assembled,
these searchers discovered Father Cansfield actually vested
and at the altar. They dragged him at once to the angry
judge's house, who apparently knew of this Jesuit's widespread activities, and assumed at once that he was the priest
who had reconciled his wife to her old Faith. The wretched
man's fury boiled over at once and Father Cansfield, before
he was allowed to say a word, was brutally beaten up in a
most cruel and foul manner, and then sent to one or other

of the York prisons, battered and bruised all over. The gaolers here were encouraged to flog and beat this elderly man in the same way.

The judge eventually made another discovery, and this was that he had grievously maltreated the wrong man, for it was not Father Brian Cansfield who had reclaimed his wife to the Faith.

Meanwhile this good priest had been all but kicked, beaten and starved to death when the hurried order for his release came to the prison. The order was too late, for the martyr died of his punishments at York, 3rd August, 1645. Brian Cansfield is stated to have been arrested by pursuivants. But the rough treatment he received strongly points to the presence among them of Roundhead soldiers, as in the case of the two murdered Benedictine priests and martyrs. The case of these three murders raises a possible question whether the three victims had not been suspected in turn of being the unnamed priest for whom a determined search was being made at the time.

The Roundhead troopers who arrested the Blessed Henry Morse on the eastern borders of Cumberland were in reality searching for another priest. (*Foley's Records, S.J.,* Vol. 1, p. 591.) It is probable that they knew that Henry Morse was not the priest and Jesuit for whom they were searching, and consequently was not treated with undue roughness. Although the search for the unknown priest was most likely in progress at the time, the Blessed Ralph Corby and the Blessed John Duckett, arrested by Presbyterian soldiers, were apparently under no suspicion of being the priest in question.

There were similar murders of Papists committed by Roundhead troops in those places where the Parliamentary forces were in occupation. In fine, so much depended upon the varying dispositions of different gangs of troopers. On 30th June, 1646, the Blessed Philip Powel, O.S.B., was hanged, drawn and quartered for his priesthood at Tyburn, and his execution was followed in the August of the same year by the martyrdom at Lancaster Castle of three Lancashire men, all priests, Edward Bamber, John Woodcock, a Franciscan, and Thomas Whitaker.

Edward Bamber was the son of Mr. Richard Bamber, a rich landowner, whose mansion was situated near Poulton-le-Fylde and was known as "The Moor." "The Moor in Carleton, the seat of the staunch Catholic family of Bamber, of which the martyred priest, Edward Bamber, was a member, continued as a missionary station till the end of the seventeenth century." (*C.R.S.*, Vol. 16, p. 581.) No doubt Edward Bamber attended in his early years the Catholic junior colleges maintained at his own home and at Lytham Hall. Of Edward Bamber, Bishop Challoner writes in *The Memoirs*: "Having made good progress in his humanities at home, he was sent abroad into Spain to the English College of Valladolid." He arrived there in 1625 and was ordained priest some three years later in 1628. Shortly after his ordination he was laid low with a severe fever, and when able, returned to Belgium and Douay in Flanders to recuperate. It is mentioned in the Valladolid registers that he paid his own travelling expenses and most probably left the journey cash, granted by the royal bounty of the King of Spain, for others who had more need of it. (Cf. *C.R.S.*, Vol. 30, p. 145.)

Father Bamber cannot have been more than a year, if as much, at Douay before he embarked for the English mission and landed at Dover. His first action on landing was to kneel down and thank God for a safe voyage overseas. The Governor of Dover Castle happened to observe this, and at once suspected that the kneeling man was a priest. The latter was arrested and confessed that he was a priest, but pleaded that he had not yet been on English soil for the space of time mentioned in the statute. This plea was accepted and

Edward Bamber was sent into banishment. But a priest of his apostolic character was not disposed of so easily, for he was again in England and at work in Lancashire by the year 1631, and was noted to have been labouring in his home county in the following year. He was arrested for the second time at Standish, near Wigan, and committed to Lancaster Castle.

Father Bamber's journey there under escort took him through Preston, and the cortege reached Broughton village by nightfall, where his guards made a night of it in the inn after locking their prisoner in a garret and removing his clothes. Nearby was " Broughton Tower, abutting on Sharoe Green in Broughton, which for centuries was the seat of the knightly and powerful family of Singleton, formerly seated at Singleton." (Cf. *C.R.S.*, Vol. 15, p. 312.) In spite of seques-trations and numerous mortgages and the insidious methods introduced by James I of collecting recusancy dues, the Catholic Singletons held on to Broughton Tower until the rack of financial persecution forced them to vacate the estate.

At the period under review a devout Catholic, Mr. Edward Singleton, was the gentleman in residence at Broughton Tower, and he was the means of assisting Edward Bamber. Round about midnight, while his guards were in a drunken sleep, Father Bamber made good his escape through a window, having no other clothes to his back but his shirt. He made for the nearest field to seek some safe shelter. In the meantime, Mr. Singleton was actually dreaming that a hunted priest was at large in a certain field hard by. The householder rose at once, fully dressed himself and proceeded to the field of which he had dreamed. There he found the fugitive, whom he at once conducted to his house and provided him with all the care he needed.

It is also a significant fact that a Protestant kinsman of John Woodcock, the Franciscan martyr and prison

companion at Lancaster of Edward Bamber, Mr. Richard
Woodcock of Walton-le-Dale, had at the time a stake in
Broughton Tower. (Ibid.)

Edward Bamber was able to resume his active ministry
until the times became grave and terrible for Catholics and
Royalist Protestants alike. He was eventually arrested for a
third time and securely lodged in Lancaster Castle, from
which he succeeded in making his escape, hoping by travelling
all night to find safety among friends further afield. He lost
his way, however, and unwittingly completed a circle, finding
himself once more at the walls of Lancaster Castle. He was
at once seized and incarcerated for the last time, where he
rejoined his companions who were destined to be crowned
martyrs with him, John Woodcock, O.F.M., and Thomas
Whitaker.

At the subsequent trial, two apostate Catholics gave
evidence against Edward Bamber, that they had witnessed
ministrations proving him to be a priest. The names of the
two apostates were Malden and Osbaldeston, and on their
evidence Edward Bamber was condemned to death for his
priesthood. At the gallows he was not allowed to give the
usual address, and so instead Father Bamber gave a most
edifying and instructive object lesson of the Faith. He had
while in prison taken under his wing a prisoner named Croft,
who had been condemned to death for felony and was to die
with the three priests that same day, 7th August, 1646.
Edward Bamber had already instructed Croft in the Faith,
and at that supreme moment, in the sight of all the spectators
at the very foot of the scaffold, he received Croft into the
Church in full ritual. Croft with great fervour and in a very
audible voice, made his profession of Faith and abjuration of
heresy. Then Father Bamber in an equally audible voice gave
him the necessary Absolutions. This brave priest still kept
the executioners waiting, for he immediately moved away a

pace to say a few words of encouragement to Thomas Whitaker, who was showing signs of fear. The authorities, however, were exasperated with Father Bamber's behaviour, and ordered him at once to mount the ladder. The priest obeyed cheerfully and, after taking leave of some friends, he said smilingly as he mounted the ladder, that they were not to grieve for him since he was hoping soon to be praying for them in heaven. He paused for a moment while he put his hand in his pocket and drew out all the money he had. Still smiling, he threw it all among the people, saying, " God loves a cheerful giver." He then spent a few moments in private prayer, after which he managed to catch the eye of Thomas Whitaker, quaking somewhat at the sight of the preparations for the coming slaughter, and surrounded by would-be friends exhorting him to save his life by conforming. At that supreme moment, Father Bamber gently warned him to be on his guard and to beware of the enemy in that critical hour on which the welfare of his soul was to depend for all eternity.

The sheriff put a stop to this address and ordered Edward Bamber's immediate execution. The good priest was only allowed to hang for a short time before he was cut down and butchered in a most cruel and savage manner, on 7th August, 1646.

Meanwhile John Woodcock continued the duty of encouraging the young priest, Thomas Whitaker, to follow the counsel and example of Edward Bamber. The noble Franciscan remained with him while preparations for his own slaughter were being made.

The entry in the Diary of the English College, Rome, reads: " Farrington, John, vere Woodcock, Lancashire, aged twenty-six . . . after living in the College for half a year, left for Paris, and there entered among the Capuchins, 16th May, 1630. A youth who afforded a remarkable example of

the mildest disposition . . . John Woodcock states that he was
the son of Thomas and Dorothy Woodcock, and was born
at Leyland, and brought up at Clayton in Lancashire until
he was nineteen years of age. His parents were of the middle
class. He had an elder brother but no sisters. His father
had lapsed from the Faith; his mother was a pious Catholic.
He studied for one year at St. Omer's, after having been a
Protestant until nearly twenty years of age, when he was
converted to the Catholic Faith, and suffered much for a long
time from a cruel father on that account. He went to live
with his grandfather, a Catholic gentleman, Mr. Anderton
of Clayton. At length, under the care of Edward Squire, a
Jesuit Father, he crossed over with others to Belgium (St.
Omer's College)."

He proceeded from there to the English College, Rome,
and thence to the Capuchins, but was transferred from that
Order to the Friars Minor. He received the Franciscan habit
from Father Paul Heath, O.F.M., and a year afterwards made
his profession in the hands of Father Francis Bell. Both of
these Franciscan Fathers became martyrs at Tyburn in the
year 1643—the Venerable Henry Paul Heath, hanged, drawn
and quartered on 17th April, and the Venerable Arthur Bell,
similarly slaughtered for the priesthood on 11th December.
(Cf. *Foley's Records, S.J.*, Vol. 6, p. 322.)

Father John Woodcock, after suffering two years of painful
imprisonment at Lancaster Castle, was tried and condemned
to death upon his own confession of his priestly character,
together with two priests, his companions, the Revv. Edward
Bamber, alias "Reading," and Thomas Whitaker, and he
was executed the following day, 7th August, 1646.

The circumstances attending his execution were singularly
brutal and cruel. Being flung off the ladder, the rope broke,
and he fell to the ground perfectly conscious; he was ordered

to be drawn up again, and a second time was cut down and butchered alive.

Within a year or two after his religious profession, John Woodcock was ordained priest. Being of a weak constitution, he went to live for some time at Arras with a Catholic gentleman, a Mr. Sheldon, in the quality of chaplain and confessor until his superiors called him away in order to send him on to the English mission. In England, he laboured zealously and industriously for some time in spite of his frequent illnesses and infirmities. Desiring to end his days among his religious brethren, he at length obtained leave to return to the community life at Douay, where he lived a most exemplary life. He had therefore the privilege of being present at the conventual house of the English Franciscans at Douay on the occasion of the solemn service of thanksgiving held there in due honour of the two venerable Franciscan martyrs, Venerable Henry Paul Heath and Venerable Arthur Francis Bell.

The immediate call to return to the English mission came through the words of a French Capuchin, who preached a most moving sermon on the occasion of the thanksgiving service. The subject of the sermon was " The happiness of suffering in so great a cause." John Woodcock was so stirred with that sermon that he begged again and again to be sent once more on to the English mission. His superiors acceded to his request, and for a second time he embarked for his native land. He landed at Newcastle-upon-Tyne and thence made his way to Lancashire. He was arrested on the very first night after his arrival at the home where he was born, and was committed at once by a neighbouring magistrate to Lancaster Castle. The story of this final adventure is given as follows:

John Woodcock was born at Woodcock Hall. Up to the present time, the house still exists as a farm and is divided

into two tenements. Its site is on the road from Bamber
Bridge to Leyland, and because it is in a bad condition, the
news to hand during October, 1956, is that the old building
is to be pulled down. A smaller house has already been built
beside it.

John Woodcock landed at Newcastle-upon-Tyne in 1644,
and at once proceeded to Lancashire and reached Woodcock
Hall on the Eve of the Assumption. He made arrangements
at once to celebrate Mass on the morrow at Woodend, the
house of the Catholic family of the Burgesses almost next
door to Woodcock Hall. On the morning of 15th August,
while vesting for Mass, the alarm was suddenly given of the
approach of the pursuivants, and Father Woodcock immediately unvested, closed the cupboard-like altar, and withdrew
into the hiding place. With equal alacrity, Mrs. Burgess
became a sick woman with a turn for the worse, attended by
the congregation acting the rôle of sympathetic neighbours
who had hurried into the house to give kindly help. Thus
the erstwhile chapel had become a sick-room and the pursuivants departed, leaving Father Woodcock free to enter,
re-vest and celebrate Holy Mass and administer Holy Communion. The altar in question had formerly been in the
possession of Mr. Burgess, a bailiff of the Towneleys of
Burnley, at whose house services for Catholics were held in
earlier penal days. This cupboard-altar was in the possession
of Mr. Thomas Clarkson of Bolton-le-Sands, and is reverently
preserved there.

In the meantime, the traitor who had notified the pursuivants of John Woodcock's presence at Woodend also told
them as they were departing that he knew the whereabouts
at Woodend of the hiding place. Therefore they returned to
Woodend but by then John Woodcock had finished the
service and had returned to the home of his parents at
Woodcock Hall.

Here the good priest spent the night, but early next morning his father ordered him to leave the house after giving him his breakfast. Father Woodcock complied and fled towards Preston, but was overtaken by the pursuivants at Bamber Bridge and placed under arrest. It is said that the actual arrest took place nearer Preston at Walton-le-Dale. (*Haydock Papers*, pp. 87-88.)

In the first instance, there had been much opposition to John Woodcock's entry into the Order of the Capuchins on the part of those of his relatives who were averse to the religious State in any capacity. Added to that fact was the unsatisfactory state of his health, and in consequence of these disabilities, he had to leave the Capuchins.

Nevertheless, his desire for the religious life had been so strong, that he wrote to a relative, Father William Anderton, a letter, an extract from which is given herewith: " The more conscious I am that it is better to be poor in the House of the Lord than to abide in the tabernacles of sinners, so much the more the conviction of my soul, still unaccomplished, grows stronger in the day and night, and the former direction of my conscience, disturbed in spite of myself from its original seat and form, incessantly solicits and urges me on; so much, that the desire for its reformation, no less than that sudden fall, which threw both it and my whole being into confusion, inflames my soul. Wherefore, my dear Father William, I beseech you by our old friendship, which in this misfortune intercedes for me with you, to take pity on my miserable state, and apply yourself to obtain my pardon and the favour of my restoration. This is my desire, this I ask, this I wait for, for this I sigh and groan, and I desire it for no other motive than the pure love of God and His glory. That which you saw me previously desire lightly, strive now for Christ's sake to obtain for me more efficaciously. This

will be my greatest happiness, and nothing whatever can add
thereto." (*Mementoes of the English Martyrs and Confessors,*
H. S. Bowden. Orat., p. 284.)

His devout uncle, Father William Anderton, secured for
Father Woodcock his admission into the Order of Friars
Minor. In the words of Bishop Challoner, Father John
Woodcock " suffered at Lancaster in the forty-fourth year of
his age, the fifteenth of his religious profession, and the thir-
teenth of his priesthood. His head is preserved in the cloister
of the English Franciscans at Douay." (*Memoirs,* p. 485.)

The English martyrs suffered and with God's help braced
themselves to endure, and it was this intensified suffering
which added merit to the heoism of the third victim at
Lancaster Castle on 7th August, 1646.

The Venerable Thomas Whitaker was born at Burnley and
was the son of Thomas and Helen Whitaker. The former
was the headmaster of a noted free school in Burnley, where
the youthful Thomas made his preliminary studies under the
care and supervision of his father. These were sufficiently
successful to qualify the boy for a higher course of studies
in the English seminaries abroad, and having a vocation for
the priesthood he was sent on the Continent. All his expenses
were paid by the neighbouring Catholic family of the
Towneleys of Towneley. Thomas Whitaker made his final
studies at the English College in Valladolid and was there
ordained priest and sent on to the English mission in the
year 1638.

He laboured for five years with notable success in his
native county. He was arrested by the pursuivants in 1643,
but managed to escape, very much in the same way that his
fellow-martyr, the Venerable Edward Bamber, effected his
first escape. It was while he was being taken to Lancaster
that Thomas Whitaker eluded his captors. He was not at that
time familiar with the countryside north of Preston, but since

the guards employed in conducting prisoners northwards to Lancaster were, seemingly, accustomed to refresh themselves en route at the various inns and hostels, and for the most part at the expense of their prisoner, Thomas Whitaker, taking advantage of the drunken state of his guard, slipped away during the night. He had had no time to dress himself or to provide himself with any clothes. Thus he wandered for some miles with the intention of putting distance between himself and the guard. " He ventured at length to sit down and take breath awhile, being at a loss what to do for clothes and for the security of his person." Apparently Catholics were on the watch for hunted priests in those parts, and one of them happened to be near by, and on being informed by Father Whitaker, a complete stranger in those parts, this friend in need took him to his own house, where he was kept in concealment for a short time until it was safe for him to return to his field of labour.

For a time, he ministered to the Catholics of Claughton-on-Brock, where he was sheltered by the Midgeall family. A relic of the Venerable Thomas Whitaker is the plain oaken desk in which he stored his vestments and other requisites for the Sacred Mysteries. Another relic is a box about seven inches square, in which he used to keep the Blessed Sacrament. This is elaborately carved on its panels. These relics of the martyr were preserved by the Midgeall family and afterwards by the family of the Fitzherbert Brockholes.

Thomas Whitaker's second period of freedom lasted only a few months, for in the same year 1643, he was arrested again at the house of Mr. Midgeall (Mitchell?), Place Hall, Goosnargh. The mob of priest-hunters that caught Father Whitaker were armed with clubs and swords. The good priest was severely beaten up, until the confession that he was a priest had been extracted from him.

In prison at Lancaster Castle, he was at first treated with " an uncommon severity," having been cast into a filthy dungeon in complete black-out and solitary confinement, where he remained for six weeks before he was " allowed the liberty of the common gaol, and the company of his fellow confessors." For three years, he remained a prisoner until his trial and condemnation to death. Bishop Challoner in *The Memoirs*, cites the testimony of an old priest, who was at the time a prisoner at Lancaster Castle along with Father Thomas Whitaker, of whom he wrote a short account: " He always speaks of Father Whitaker as a person of a most saintly life; and declares, from his own observation and knowledge (having been an eye-witness of his conduct for a long time), that he was still the first and last at prayer; or rather that his whole employment was a continual communication with God, either in mental or vocal prayer; and that the little time which he spared from his holy exercise was constantly employed in charitable offices about such of his fellow prisoners as by sicknesses or age stood in need of help. He was particularly assiduous with regard to his brethren, the other three priests, because, being the youngest by far, he looked upon it as a duty to serve them and assist them upon all occasions; and this he performed with pleasure, and at the same time with so much humility, deference and respect, as if he had verily believed them not only his seniors in years, but his superiors in authority, and was glad to be serviceable to them even in the lowest menial offices." (*Memoirs*, pp. 487-488.)

It has been stated that the Venerable Thomas Whitaker was of a timorous disposition, and showed evident marks of dread and anguish, which troubled him and made the prayers and encouragements of his two fellow-martyrs a most needful support, without which he would have fallen.

There were other glorious martyrs who had endured a

similar terror, anguish and dread, and nevertheless won the great crown. Furthermore, it should be remembered that Father Thomas Whitaker at his arrest had been severely and cruelly beaten up and he had had to endure that almost unbearable and gruelling torture of witnessing in detail the terrible slaughter of his two companions. When at length his own turn came, the last efforts of many to induce him to save his life by conformity entirely failed.

" Use your pleasure with me," he said, " a reprieve or even a pardon upon such conditions I utterly refuse."

After some moments spent in earnest prayer, he was suddenly flung from the ladder, cut down and butchered in the same brutal manner as his companions, at Lancaster Castle on 7th August, 1646.

Chapter 16

TROUBLE DURING THE COMMONWEALTH

A LTHOUGH there were fewer public executions for the Faith during the years of the Protectorate, the pursuit and hunting of Catholics was personally and vigorously undertaken by parties of Cromwellian soldiers, who were infected with a fierce and fanatical hatred of Papists. " From the year 1646 till the year 1651," wrote Bishop Challoner, " I find not any priests put to death for their priesthood; though otherwise the persecution against Catholics did not cease and the sequestrators were everywhere busy . . . in plundering their estates and property, as well real as personal." (*Memoirs*, p. 491.)

In pursuance of an act made by the " regicides " in the Rump Parliament, 16th July, 1651, and a later act, 18th November, 1652, these sequestrations were carried out with vigour against Royalist landowners and Catholics in particular. There is no space to record the number of Lancashire Catholics who suffered the forfeiture of their property for their Faith and loyalty—for example, Mr. Thomas Tyldesley, a steadfast Catholic, who lost his life in the royal cause, also lost his estates, attached to Myerscough Lodge, which were sold. For some time longer, the family managed to retain Fox Hall, near Blackpool. Similar sufferers for the Faith were William and Robert Latham, Charles Towneley, Thomas Langtree, Hugh Anderton of Euxton, William Anderton of Anderton, near Chorley, James Anderton of

Clayton, Richard Chorley of Chorley, Marmaduke Langdale and his son, both killed, and William Shireburn of Shireburn, Stonyhurst.

The Venerable Thomas Whitaker was not the last priest to be executed at Lancaster Castle. There was a later instance in the case of a devoted Jesuit priest, Father John Smith, alias Harrison, who was hanged, drawn and quartered at the Castle in the year 1651.

The story of this good priest of Lancashire is given in the following extract: " Rixton was the seat of the old Catholic family of Massey, whose members rank amongst the benefactors of the Jesuits in that district. The Jesuits of the district continued to serve there, until it was given up to the Benedictine Fathers in 1825-6. The earliest Jesuit Father who can be traced there (in consequence of the loss of records) is Father John Smith, alias Harrison, 1650, and the only information we possess regarding him is derived from Dodd's *Church History,* Vol. 3, p. 312, from which we quote: ' John Smith, whose true name was Harrison, was born near Liverpool, and being sent to study amongst the Jesuits abroad, became one of that Society. At his return from the (English) mission, he resided with Mr. Massey of Wrexen (Rixton), near Warrington, in the county of Lancaster. He had not been long in those parts, before he was apprehended, tried and condemned to death.

" ' His case was a singular one. Several gentlemen, who had served in King Charles I's army, entered into a combination to plunder the parsonage of Winwick, whereof one Mr. Erle was Rector. This Mr. Erle, as Anthony à Wood observes, had always been regarded as a Puritan; sided with the Presbyterian party; took the covenant; was elected one of the assembly of divines in 1643, &c. Now whether an aversion against the man, or a wild notion that he had no right to what he was possessed of, induced them to this desperate undertaking, the following persons raided the parsonage—viz., Mr. Catterall, Mr. Massey, a younger brother of Rixton (i.e., the householder), a French gentleman and some others. The robbery being discovered, search was immediately made to find out the offenders. The Frenchman was the only person apprehended, but unable to speak English, they could draw nothing from him; but happening to name Wrexen (Rixton), the searchers were immediately ordered thither.

" ' They found Father Smith in his chamber and, looking about, discovered a red cap which was known to belong to Mr. Erle, and as we may suppose, was left there by one of those concerned in the robbery. This was judged sufficient ground to suspect Father Smith, and not being able to give any satisfactory account by reason of his character (see footnote), he was committed prisoner to Lancaster Castle, and at the next assizes was tried, condemned and executed as an accomplice in the aforesaid fact.

" ' Many severe reflections were made on the Catholics upon account of this unfortunate occurrence, which were increased by a certain pamphlet which charged Father Heton, the Superior of the Jesuits in Lancashire, and Father Orton, the Superior of the secular clergy in the said county, with being accessories to robbery. But this . . . was contradicted by the actual author of the pamphlet, who subscribes himself R. M. N. In his recantation, which I have read, he begs pardon of Almighty God, and of those two gentlemen, for defaming them on the occasion mentioned.

" ' Most people lamented Father Smith's hard fate; but such were the circumstances of his person, his religion and the disposition of those times, that no favourable construction would be admitted. The particulars of this story I have not only read in a well-attested manuscript, but also received them by word of mouth from a gentleman, who was well acquainted with Father John Smith, and had a great opinion of him for his many excellent qualities.'" (End of Dodd's account.)

In *Foley's Records, S.J.*, from which the above narrative is taken, there is a footnote referred to above and quoted as follows: "His character or position as a Catholic priest, bound under the sacred seal of confession; for we can readily imagine that the young gentlemen in question were actuated in their dangerous and unjustifiable assault upon the house of the 'churlish' (as we believe A. Wood calls him) Puritan parson of Winwick, rather out of youthful bravado than for the mere purpose of plunder; and that one or more of the party, repenting his fault, had been to Father Smith to make his sacramental confession, and had by accident left the worthy rector's red night-cap behind him. The high character that Father Smith bore forbids us to suppose that he was himself one of the party. His priestly character was no doubt the leading motive for the severe sentence." (*Foley's Records*, Vol. 1, pp. 664-665.)

During his march in 1648 to capture Preston, which was occupied by a Scottish Royalist army under the Duke of Hamilton, Oliver Cromwell is said to have spent a night in the Stonyhurst mansion of the Shireburns. The long table on which he slept is preserved in the boys' refectory at Stonyhurst. His army was advancing for the most part along the Fell road and from Chaigley to Longridge, which was held by a fairly strong Cavalier force under Sir Marmaduke Langdale and his son. It is thought that had the Scottish army advanced and joined forces at Longridge, as Sir Marmaduke Langdale had urged, the Royalists would have defeated Cromwell's army and, incidentally, the life of Charles I might have been saved, if not his throne.

At the time, sections of Cromwell's troops were billeted in the farms and cottages in the neighbourhood, and it is believed that a party of Roundheads, who had spent the night in one or other of the cottages at Kemple End, the easterly spur of the Longridge Fell overlooking Stonyhurst, rose early and began priest-hunting. Thus it happened that an atrocious priest-murder was perpetrated before Oliver Cromwell at the Stonyhurst mansion had completely awakened to the new day.

The priest in question is traditionally thought to have been Father Holden, who was being harboured at the time in Chaigley Hall, the home of his parents. The good priest was actually celebrating Mass, most likely in the chapel-house of St. Chad, about a mile away from Chaigley Hall and belonging to the Holden family. The raiders entered the chapel and, before the small congregation could interfere, rushed the altar.

They not merely dragged the priest, clothed in his white vestments, away from the altar, but brutally beheaded him on the altar steps in the sight of the little congregation, including, it is said, his own relatives. The severed head rolled down the altar-steps and was caught by one of the soldiers and placed on a pike. The tradition relates that it was Father Holden's mother who intervened and begged for the head of her martyred son. The soldier took it from the pike and threw it to her. Mrs. Holden caught the head and wrapped it in her apron, and since that time, the head of the martyred priest, the bloodstained white vestment in which he was murdered, the apron or cloth in which it was wrapped and the rest of the altar requisites were reverently preserved by the pious descendants of the Holden family.

All these relics were placed in an oaken chest, which was carefully guarded by the Holden family long after the members of it had been compelled through hardships to leave Chaigley Hall and the chapel-house. The oaken chest contains a large linen altar-cloth, or Communion-cloth, two chasubles, one of green silk embroidered with lilies, with a centre-piece of red silk in the form of a Cross.

The other chasuble is the white one in which the priest was murdered, and has a stain of blood across it. The altar-cloth itself bears blood-stains. In addition, there is a Missal, a pewter chalice and an altar-stone, and the severed head of the martyr. The story is contained in *Forgotten Shrines*, by Dom Bede Camm, pages 247-252.

The oaken chest and its contents are now preserved at St. Robert's, Catforth, near Preston; a church dedicated to the English martyrs, whose acts are pictured in stained glass windows. The terrible and sacrilegious murder of the priest at Chaigley and his relics, including the severed head, are established facts, and the tradition that the priest in question was Father Holden is a very strong one; there is an opinion that the skull may be that of an earlier martyred priest.

The Cromwellian troops at the period under review left a trail of woe in this part of Lancashire, which had hitherto been comparatively peaceful and unmolested. Several loyal Catholic families of the district were ruined and had to leave their homesteads and mansions, and such was the fate of the Crombleholmes, the Hothersalls and the Osbaldestons.

Nor were Royalist Protestant ministers spared from the brutality of the Roundhead troops; in 1647, the State church minister, Christopher Hindley, who had been vicar of Ribchester parish church since 1618, a much beloved and respected man, was brutally evicted because of his loyal adherence to his lawful King. In spite of this, the old man dutifully returned to his pulpit, and when in 1649 Charles I was beheaded at Whitehall, Christopher Hindley, shortly after, mounted the pulpit of Ribchester parish church, and denounced the regicides. Although at the time there were many of Cromwell's soldiers present, the old vicar did not mince his words, and stated that the execution of Charles I was a scandalous sin of bloody murder of a most sacred person, of more value than ten thousand of his best subjects: " an act so horrible and prodigious, that no language can describe it." Some of the soldiers left the church, and having formed a troop, re-entered the church to rush the pulpit. There was an unseemly struggle, and the brave old man was dragged out of the pulpit in a rough and violent manner to be flung out on to the road. It appears he was roughly escorted on to the Preston road and then cruelly beaten up. ("Local Records," cf. *Lancashire's Fair Face,* by Jessica Lofthouse.)

The ferocity of the Presbyterian element that the Scottish covenanters brought into the country knew no bounds. It had infected nearly the whole of Cromwell's armies, and uniformity of worship and doctrine were enforced with unmerciful violence: " The clergy of the established church were ejected from their livings and the professors of the Catholic Faith were condemned to forfeit two-thirds of their property, or to abjure their religion." (*History of England,* Lingard, Vol. 8, p. 395.)

" When the Independents succeeded to the exercise of the supreme power, both persecuted parties indulged a hope of more lenient treatment, and both were disappointed. The Independents, indeed, proclaimed themselves the champions of religious liberty; they repealed the statutes, imposing penalties for absence from church; and they declared that men were free to serve God according to the dictates of conscience. Yet their notions of toleration were very confined: they refused to extend it either to prelacy or Popery, to the service of the church of England or the church of Rome. The ejected clergymen were still excluded from the pulpit, and the Catholics were still the victims of persecuting statutes. In 1650 an act was passed offering to the discoverers of priests and Jesuits, or their receivers or abettors, the same reward as had been granted to the apprehenders of highway-men. Immediately officers and informers were employed in every direction; the houses of Catholics were broken open and searched at all hours of the day and night; many clergy-men were apprehended, and several were tried and received judgment of death. Of these, only one, Peter Wright, chaplain to the Marquess of Winchester, suffered. (This was the Jesuit martyr, the Blessed Peter Wright, priest, who was hanged, drawn and quartered for his priesthood at Tyburn, 19th May, 1651.) The leaders shrank from the odium of such sanguinary exhibitions, and transported the rest of the prisoners to the Continent.

"But if the zeal of the Independents was more sparing of blood than that of the Presbyterians, it was not inferior in point of rapacity. The ordinances for sequestration and for-feiture were executed with unrelenting severity. It is difficult to say which suffered from them most cruelly—families with small fortunes who were thus reduced to a state of penury; or husbandmen, servants and mechanics, who, on their refusal to take the oath of abjuration, were deprived of two-thirds of their scanty earnings, even of their household goods and wearing apparel . . . (Footnote: 'In proof, may I be allowed to mention one instance of a Catholic servant maid, an orphan, who, during a servitude of seventeen years, at seven nobles a year, had saved twenty pounds. The seques-trators, having discovered with whom she had deposited her money, took two-thirds, thirteen pounds, six shillings and eightpence, for the use of the Commonwealth, and left her the remainder, six pounds, thirteen shillings and fourpence. In March, 1652, she appealed to the commissioners at Haber-dashers' Hall, who replied they could afford her no relief unless she took the oath of abjuration.')" (*History of England,* Lingard, Vol. VIII, pp. 395-397.)

A further and more terrible instance of cruelty to Catholics is the case of the girl martyr of Lostock Hall, Dorothy Anderton, the daughter of Mr. Christopher Anderton and his wife, Alethea Anderton. An account of the incident is given in a letter of the Abbess of the Benedictine nuns at Dunkirk, Dame Mary Caryll, to her brother, the first Lord Caryll. An extract is given here in a paraphrase. The main characters of the story are the two young daughters, Alethea and Dorothy Anderton, and a young brother:

" Alethea, so called in baptism, was the daughter of Mr. Christopher Anderton of Lostock, a man of fair estate, who fell awhile from the Church about a suit of law; but it pleased our Lord to deal with him mercifully and he returned soon to the Faith. By his first marriage he had one daughter. After his return to the Church, he went for a while to the Low Countries, and after that, returning home, he married Mistress Alethea Smythe, sister of Frances Smythe, who was an Augustinian nun at Louvain . . .

" Mr. and Mrs. Anderton both suffered very much for their conscience in the time of the Parliamentary revolt against Charles I, having their goods plundered and their land in such hands, that the good gentlewoman had scarcely enough left to maintain herself and her children, of whom she had fourteen, with the result that one of them being sick, she had to contrive to roast a piece of meat for her with the aid of two sticks. In addition to this, she had a far greater cross to bear, for they took away from her one son and two daughters, to make them heretics, and forcibly boarded them out in a place where they were most cruelly used, although the parents had to pay more for the board and lodging of those three unhappy children than was left to maintain all the rest.

" In this worse than prison, the three Anderton children were kept barelegged in sackcloth, and their food was flour and water sodden together; if sometimes these inhuman householders thought fit to vary the diet, they threw the three young victims a bone from their table, which scarce had any meat on it. Besides this, they flogged them with whips that had crooked pins in them, and on one such occasion hit one of the girls with the same kind of whip in the face and over the eyes, with the result that for some time she was almost blind and was laid up and helpless for a long time until cured. This was the elder of the two girls, Alethea, who later was professed as a nun at Louvain. The younger sister, Dorothy, they put daily to fetch water in a sort of pail for their use, the weight of which being far too heavy for one of her tender years, so that with such hard treatment, and being compelled to eat such filthy scraps that she could manage to get hold of, it is thought that she contracted the disease of which she died in 1653, being then only eleven years old.

" The good mother, on learning how cruelly her children were being treated, made all the efforts of which she was capable to get them out of their tormentors' hands, after they had been with them, suffering this hard life, for more than two years. At length, she succeeded in having them boarded with some of their tenants, where from the bodily point of view, they were very much more comfortable.

" The condition, however, was strictly to be adhered to, that the new householders should be Protestant, and that the children should be brought up in the then Cromwellian Protestant way. This process of perversion was resorted to without undue force or cruelty, so that as it were by stealth these guardians endeavoured to instil their own hatred of Catholicism into the youthful hearts of their young charges. The elder daughter, Alethea, became infected and began to concentrate on the Bible rather than the Catechism, until after three years Mrs. Anderton succeeded in getting her

children home again. At first, Alethea gave her devoted
mother a great deal of trouble in the matter of prayers and
the Catechism, but in the end her mother's influence prevailed, and Alethea became a good Catholic . . ."

Dame Mary Caryll's letter concludes with the notice of the
death of the little girl martyr, Dorothy Anderton of Lostock
Hall, from the effects of the cruelties inflicted upon her, and
also of her sister Alethea's vocation to the religious life in
the convent of Louvain, where she took the habit in 1656,
and made her profession at about the age of eighteen. (Cf.
Foley's Record's S.J., Vol. 3, pp. 779-781.)

The second of the two public executions during the Cromwellian period of Martyrs for the Faith was that of the
Blessed John Southworth at Tyburn on 28th June, 1654.

There is little available concerning the early years of this
great martyr beyond the fact that he was born in Lancashire
and was a member of a younger branch of the Southworths
of Samlesbury. He went to Douay in 1613, and as a theola-
gian in his first year was obliged to return to his native
county to recuperate his health on 3rd May, 1616. He went
back to Douay on 25th March, 1617, and was ordained priest
on 14th April, 1618, being sent to the English mission on
13th December, 1619. He was apparently at Douay again in
the year 1624, and for a time was confessor at the Benedictine convent at Brussels. He had a desire to join the
Benedictine Order, but there was before him a laborious and
heroic apostolate of many years as a missionary priest in
the London area. On his second journey to England, he was
arrested in Lancashire and remained a prisoner in Lancaster
Castle under sentence of death, until a royal reprieve released
him for what was to prove his life-work among the plague-
stricken in London. The year of his release from Lancaster
Castle appears to have been between 1629-1630.

From then onwards until his death in 1654, he was in and out of prison, an object of especial hatred by Mr. Prynne and a gang of despicable apostate informers and pursuivants. For a time John Southworth was able to devote himself to his plague-stricken flocks in the district of Clerkenwell, as long as the King and Archbishop Laud were able to afford him some protection. Being so often a virtual prisoner for the priesthood, he made no attempt to disguise the fact, but openly professed the same, and the members of the iniquitous " joint-stock company " kept their political Puritan paymasters constantly informed of the devoted priest's ceaseless spiritual and corporal works of mercy. Towards the end, the martyr was apprehended upon the information of one Jefferies, whom Mr. Prynne had in fee, and Father Southworth was taken out of bed at night and thrust into prison. (*Memoirs*, pp. 506-507.)

He had been removed from one of his prisons, along with other prisoners for the Faith, to the Gatehouse, whence he was allowed out on parole, and was able to continue his work among the sick, mostly in Clerkenwell. He reconciled many to the ancient Faith, and one of his last labours was the instruction of two stricken men, whom he converted. These were named William Baldwin and William Styles, and their reconciliation proved to be one of the chief circumstances which led to the martyr's final arrest, trial, condemnation, and glorious death on the scaffold. William Styles died after having piously received the Last Sacraments from John Southworth. This incident and the conversion of William Baldwin of Kemp Yard, Westminster, as instances of the good priest's activities were reported by the sub-curate of the locality, and the matter was brought to the notice of Mr. Prynne, the arch-dissenter.

In spite of all Mr. Prynne's efforts to the contrary, coupled with those of the sub-curate of St. Margaret's, Westminster, the martyr was not at once made a " close " prisoner, but was still permitted out on parole, a prisoner at large, to continue his works of mercy. At length, the authorities in 1654 decided that the time was ripe for one more public execution of a priest at Tyburn, to provide another example of the fate in store for incorrigible Papists.

The final trial of the Blessed John Southworth at the Old Bailey had by no means the approval of all the dissenters and followers of Cromwell. On the subject of this trial, a dissenter, a gentleman of some political influence, wrote a pamphlet entitled: " A letter from a Gentleman in the City to a Gentleman in the Country, about the Odiousness of Persecution." This letter was printed in the year 1687, though written and circulated long before the " Titus Oates' Plot," and concerns the trial and martyrdom at Tyburn of the Blessed John Southworth.

The account of this letter is taken from Bishop Challoner's *Memoirs of Missionary Priests,* and is cited as follows:

" The last Popish priest that was put to death in England for being a priest of the Romish Church was put to death in the time of Cromwell. I suppose we are not to doubt of the passionate heat which inflamed those who were then in authority against the Papist and Popery. They looked upon the Papists as mortal enemies to their government, and as fast friends and devoted servants to the Crown and Royal family. Notwithstanding which, when the said priest (Father John Southworth) came upon his trial at the sessions house in the Old Bailey, and upon his arraignment pleaded that he was not guilty of treason, but acknowledging himself a priest of the Roman Church, it clearly appeared that those who were his judges did their utmost to preserve his life, and to prevent the execution against him of those laws upon which he stood indicted; for they did for many hours suspend the recording of his confession, making it their endeavour to prevail with him to plead not guilty to the indictment. They pressed him to this in the public court, assuring him that if he would so plead his life should be safe, and that they had no evidence which could prove him to be a priest. And when the old man (probably close on eighty) would not be drawn to deny himself to be a priest, taking it to be a denying of his religion, and that the court was compelled to give judgment against him, the magistrate who gave the sentence (Serjeant Steel, Recorder of London) was so drowned in tears upon that sad occasion that it was long before he could pronounce the sentence, which the law compelled him, as he professed, to give." (*Memoirs of Missionary Priests,* Challoner, p. 507.)

A witness at Tyburn states that thousands were assembled at the execution, and that the crowds apparently could by no means be described as hostile to the martyr. An extract from the final speech of the Blessed John Southworth at Tyburn is given as follows: " Good people, I was born in Lancashire. This is the third time I have been apprehended, and now I am about to die, and so would gladly witness and openly profess my Faith for which I suffer. And though my time be short, yet in what I shall be deficient in my words, I hope I shall make good with my blood, which I most willingly spend to the last drop for my Faith. Neither my intent in coming into England, nor my practice was to do anything against the secular government. Hither I was sent by my lawful superiors to teach Christ's doctrine, not to meddle with temporal affairs. Christ sent His Apostles, their successors; and their successors, me. I did what I was commanded by those who had power to command me, being ever taught that I ought to obey them in matters ecclesiastical, and my temporal governors in business, only temporal. I have never acted nor thought any hurt against the present Protector. I had only a care to do my own duty, and discharge that duty in saving my own and the souls of others.

"This, and only this, according to my poor abilities, I laboured to perform. I had a commission to do it from him, to whom our Saviour, in His predecessor, St. Peter, gave power to other to progagate His faith. This is the reason for which I die. O holy cause! But not for any treason against the laws. My Faith and obedience to my superiors is all the treason charged against me; nay; I die for Christ's law, which no human law, by whomsoever made, ought to withstand or contradict . . ."

At the time of the execution it began pouring with rain, but the lightning and thunder had no terrors for the Blessed John Southworth, who was hanged, drawn and quartered for the priesthood at Tyburn on 28th June, 1654. In view of the well-known fact that the martyr had previously been arraigned at Lancaster Castle, condemned to death for his priesthood but reprieved, the authorities knew he was a priest. Besides this, his ministrations performed openly as a priest, when free and in prison, made the fact of his priesthood widely and publicly known. Hence the Blessed John Southworth could not have availed himself of kindly-meant legal counsel to plead not guilty until the fact of his priesthood had been proved, without giving scandal to multitudes of humble people whom he had served. For the most part he had been a prisoner on parole, and by his open profession of the priesthood he endangered no one. So when dragged out of bed in the dead of the night by the pursuivant, Colonel Worsley, he at once professed his priesthood.

A Protestant minister present at the execution wrote a Latin epigram which expressed his profound admiration of the Blessed John Southworth's constancy:

"Martyr erat, vindex quia religionis avitae,
    Unica quae nobis ducta per aeva fuit."
("Martyr, vindicating the ancient Faith handed down
        to us through the ages.")

Fortunately the Blessed John Southworth's body was secured in its entirety and sent overseas to the English College at Douay, and there remained until it was brought back to England again, to rest in the shrine prepared for it in Westminster Cathedral.

CHAPTER 17

LANCASHIRE MARTYRS IN THE OATES' PLOT PERSECUTION

FROM the year 1660 and onwards for some nineteen years, Charles II suspended the execution of the penal statutes against Catholics and sought by the Declaration of Indulgence to have them abolished. However, the preceding Commonwealth régime, though suppressed, had disseminated throughout the country among large sections of the people a virulent hatred of Papistry, subdued but like a smouldering fire.

The mantle of Mr. Prynne with his personal and political hatred of Catholicism appeared to have descended on Lord Shaftesbury, the Chancellor of the Exchequer. This influential member of the Privy Council and his partisans in their hatred of Catholics and anxiety to exclude the Duke of York, who had become a Catholic, from succession to the throne as James II, were largely responsible for kindling the smouldering fire into a terrible conflagration of persecution. To this end, they made use of a bogus convert and criminal, expelled for bad conduct from the seminaries abroad, by name, Titus Oates.

This wretched man and his associates fabricated the slander involving the Duke of York, and even the virtuous and devout Queen herself, Catharine of Braganza, but especially the Jesuits and their Papist associates, in a plot to kill the King and place his brother James on the throne. Under the leadership of Shaftesbury, this notorious liar and his perfidious intimates were afforded every opportunity to publicize their atrocious calumnies.

The murder at Primrose Hill of Sir Edmundbury Godfrey was attributed to Jesuit machinations, and numbers of innocent persons were arrested and imprisoned as suspects and promised freedom if they would supply fabricated evidence implicating the Jesuits in the murder. William Bedloe, criminal, gaol-bird and one of Titus Oates' associates, actually got himself arrested at Bristol as a suspect of the murder so that he could launch the slander implicating the Jesuits and Papists as the principal agents. (Cf. Lingard: *History of England*, Vol. IX, p. 374.) Shaftesbury had also the services of " the Chief Justice, Scroggs, a lawyer of profligate habits and inferior acquirements, who acted the part of prosecutor rather than of judge." (Ibid., p. 383.)

Thus an epidemic of terror began to spread over London and the whole country, disseminated by a group of atrocious blackmailers who were invested with authority and let loose on the public. By no means all the victims so arrested as suspects could be punished into bearing false witness on a promise of pardon and monetary reward. The following incident gives proof of this and shows at the same time what kind of man Lord Shaftesbury was: ". . . The most remarkable instance was that of Francis Corral, a hackney coachman, who was arrested upon a charge of having taken the body of Sir E. Godfrey to Primrose Hill. In answer to Shaftesbury, he denied all knowledge of it. He (Shaftesbury) laid £500 down upon the table and promised it to the poor man if he would confess the truth, and the fullest protection if he feared to speak. The man again repeated his utter ignorance. The Earl replied that if he would not confess, he should be put into a barrel of nails and rolled down a hill.

" The man answered: ' What would you have me say, my lord? I know nothing of the matter. Would you have me to accuse other people, to bring them into my condition?' The Earl then threatened him with death, and he was committed to Newgate. Here he was laid 'in vast heavy irons' in a dungeon, and after some hours was taken out again so faint with the foulness of the place that he swooned away, and had to be restored by cordials. The same day he was again examined by Shaftesbury and in reply to his bullying, said hastily: 'What will you have me confess? I know no more than your lordship does, and it may be not so much.' The Earl then told the gaoler to take him and starve him to death, 'at which the poor man wept,' and with imprecations declared that he knew no more than the child unborn. He was accordingly kept in Newgate heavily ironed, in the condemned hole, from Thursday evening until Sunday noon, without food or drink, which drove the poor man into such despair that he was tempted to commit suicide, but was prevented by the knife dropping out of his hand. On the next Monday, he was taken to the lord's secret committee. Shaftesbury, assuming a pleasant countenance, again offered him the former great rewards to confess. Upon which the poor man, falling on his knees, said: 'I know nothing of it; and before I wrong any man, I will die immediately.'

The Earl, changing his tone, threatened him that he should rot in Newgate for a while, and then be tried and hung; and again urged him to confess rather than hear the dreadful sentence. 'Yes, my lord,' cried the man, 'it will be a dreadful hearing; but, my lord, it will be a more dreadful hearing for me at the Lord's Bar, if I should wrongfully accuse any man. It will be a more dreadful hearing, when it shall be said: "Take him away, devil, for he hath falsely accused those he knew no hurt by."'

"The brutal Shaftesbury ordered him back to Newgate. The man pleaded he had a wife and children. The Earl said: 'Let them starve.' The man was kept heavily chained in the same hole for nearly seven weeks, and afterwards without fetters for seven more, when at length another person swore that Godfrey was carried there on horseback, and thereupon the poor coachman was released on bail, but so injured by the irons that he could not drive a coach for eight weeks after. Such, adds Echard (loco citato. *History of England*), were the arbitrary proceedings of the great pretenders against arbitrary power . . ." (Cf. *Foley's Records, S.J.*, Vol. 5, p. 29. In Footnote.)

The first Lancashire man to win the martyr's crown at Tyburn, during the ensuing violent persecution, was the Blessed William Barrow, a Jesuit priest who had made use of the various aliases of " Harcourt," " Wareing," and others. He was born in the Fylde at Weeton-cum-Presall in the year 1609, and while yet a boy was sent to the English Jesuit College of St. Omer's, and after his ordination, entered the Jesuit Order at Watten in 1632. He was professed on 24th November, 1646, having completed his third year of proba-tion at Ghent in 1642. For a time he was Procurator of the English Jesuit Province in London, and at the time of the " Plot " was the Rector of the Jesuits of the London district, under the English Provincial, his fellow-martyr, the Blessed Thomas Whitbread. From the commencement of the " Plot," Father Barrow was marked out by Titus Oates for one of his victims, and was diligently sought after. An attempt was made by Oates and his satellites to arrest him on Michaelmas night, 1678, at the same time as his Provincial, Father Thomas Whitbread, but Father Barrow received timely notice, and for the moment escaped. He was thus enabled to warn his brethren to provide for their own safety, and to be especially on their guard against the snare of any forged letters they might receive, such as had been sent to Father Mumford, vere Bedingfield, at Windsor, who died of his sufferings in prison.

The charity of Father Barrow induced him to risk his life for his brethren. He was already proclaimed a traitor by the

Privy Council, and a large reward was offered for his appre-
hension. His remaining in London exposed him to the
certainty of arrest, the vigilance of the pursuivants being
quickened by the money which the Government offered for
his capture, and he himself being well known there. But he
resolved to remain, that he might render spiritual and temporal aid to his brethren in distress, especially to those
already in prison, whose number was daily increased by fresh
captures. Almost every day he changed his dress, his
lodgings, and even his name and general appearance. Although he had received permission from his Superior to
repair to safety in Holland along with two other Jesuits, he
did not avail himself of it and remained in the danger zone.
He made every exertion to remove all his brethren to places
of greater security than London afforded, nor would he consent to delegate to others less known than himself the duty
of attending his brethren in prisons. He continued this course
unmolested for several months, even to his own surprise.
However, he who had been so long protected by disguise was
at length betrayed by his own modesty; for a female servant
of the house in which he lodged, observing the gravity of his
manner and his temperate manner of living, suspected him
of being a Jesuit, and basely betrayed him to the pursuivants,
who readily recognised and seized him. (Cf. Account in
Foley's Records, S.J., Vol. 5, pp. 240 seq.)

Being brought before the Privy Council, his white hairs
and venerable appearance excited the commiseration of many
of its members. Nevertheless, at his trial, he was condemned
with his four Jesuit companions for complicity in the fabricated plot, and on 20th June, 1679, was placed on the same
hurdle with his Provincial, the Blessed Thomas Whitbread,
to be drawn to Tyburn. His final address at the gallows is
given as follows: " The words of dying persons have always
been esteemed as of greatest authority, because uttered then

when, shortly after, they are to be cited before the high tribunal of Almighty God. This gives me hopes that mine may be looked upon as such. Therefore I do here declare, in the presence of Almighty God and the whole court of Heaven, and this numerous assembly, that, as I hope by the merits and Passion of my Lord and sweet Saviour Jesus Christ for eternal bliss, I am as innocent as the child unborn of anything laid to my charge, and for which I am to die."

The Sheriff: "How? Or Sir Edmundbury Godfrey's death?"

Father Harcourt (Barrow): " Or Sir Edmundbury Godfrey's death?"

The Sheriff: "How? Did you not write that letter concerning the despatch of Sir Edmundbury Godfrey?"

Father Waring (Barrow): " No, sir. These are the words of a dying man: I would not do it for a thousand worlds."

The Sheriff: "How have you lived?"

Father Waring (Barrow): "I have lived like a man of repute all my life, and never was before the face of a judge till my trial. No man can accuse me. I have from my youth been bred up in the execution of my duty to God and man. And I do utterly abhor and detest that abominably false doctrine laid to our charge, that we can have licences to commit perjury or any sin to advance our cause, being expressly against the doctrine of St. Paul, saying, ' Non sunt facienda mala ut eveniant bona ' (' Evil is not to be done that good may come thereof.') And, therefore, we hold it in all cases unlawful to kill or murder any person whatsoever, much more our lawful King now reigning, whose person and temporal dominions we are ready to defend with our lives and fortunes against any opponent whatsoever, none excepted. I forgive all that have contrived my death, and humbly beg pardon of Almighty God for them. And I ask pardon of all the world. I pray God bless His Majesty and grant him a prosperous reign. The like I wish to his royal consort, the best of Queen. I humbly beg the prayers of all those who are in the communion of the Roman Church, if any such be present." (Ibid., p. 243.)

At the crucial moment, just as the execution was about to take place, a horseman rode up with a reprieve from the King. As read out to the five martyrs, a condition was added that they should admit there and then their complicity in the plot to kill the King, a condition, which the martyrs irrevocably refused to accept, since to have done so, would have been to save their lives by admitting a gross and foul lie. It is worth mentioning, that as Father William Barrow was being led to the hurdle, the Protestant chaplain of Newgate approached him and said: " Sir, you did not think fit to admit me to your chamber to any discourse, but now that you are on the very borders of death, and must be judged to an eternal state of happiness or misery, consider how heinous the crime is for which you are to suffer death. Beg of God to give you true repentance unto life eternal, and do not stand out in the denying or extenuation of your crime." Father Barrow recognised an unusual simpleton in his profession and charitably answered that he need not trouble himself concerning him or the others condemned with him, for he and they knew their duty.

The minister in question had made a similar advance to each one of the five martyrs, who felt with pity, that the poor man had been cruelly fooled by the fabricators of the " Plot."

On 20th June, 1679, the Blessed Thomas Whitbread, the Blessed William Harcourt, vere Barrow, the Blessed John Fenwick, the Blessed John Gavan, and the Blessed Anthony Turner, five Jesuit priests, were hanged, drawn and quartered at Tyburn.

Another Lancashire Catholic to be martyred during this violent period was John or William Plesington, a surname that could be spelt " Pleasington," denoting at the present time the rural district a little west of Blackburn on the road to Bamber Bridge and Preston. The name is that of the distinguished Catholic family whose estate was situated in the locality and of which family John Plesington was a member. To-day this spot is beautifully and appropriately indicated by the handsome and large gothic church dedicated to St. Mary and St. John the Baptist, which was built in 1819 and is served by the clergy of the Salford Diocese.

The following notice is taken from the Registers of the English College, Valladolid, under the date 1663: " (The Blessed) John Plessington (sic) alias Scarisbrick; born about 1637; youngest son of Robert Plessington, Dimples Hall, near Garstang, Co. Lancaster, and his wife, Alice, daughter of Laurence Rawstorne, of Newhall in Tollington, whose wife was the daughter of Robert Hesketh of Rufford; (as a young boy John Plesington) was sent to a school privately kept by the Jesuits at Scarisbrick Hall, and he adopted the alias ' Scarisbrick ' when he came to Valladolid . . . He was ordained priest at Segovia (in the Cathedral), 25th March, 1662. He went to England on account of his health, April, 1663; lived chiefly with Mr. William Massey of Puddington, Cheshire; he was arrested during the Titus Oates Plot Persecution, imprisoned in Chester Castle gaol, and executed, 19th July, 1679, on Gallows Hill, now known as Barrel Well Hill, Boughton, west of Chester. (His quartered body lies buried in the graveyard of the Parish church at Burton-in-Wirral, Cheshire.)"

Incidentally, it is mentioned in the same Registers that Titus Oates was expelled from the College at Valladolid, 30th October, 1677. (*C.R.S.*, Vol. 30, p. 169.)

It is not mentioned in the Registers that first of all John Plesington went to St. Omer's College, Flanders, for his preliminary course, and it is possible that he met there Richard

Shireburn, the son of the Mr. Shireburn of Stonyhurst, who had to billet for the night an unwelcome guest in the person of Oliver Cromwell. John Plesington's two sisters, Mary and Grace, became Poor Clare nuns at Gravelines in Flanders, and when he went to Valladolid he met at the College another Lancashire man, Thomas Wilkinson, who later as a priest and a Jesuit laboured in Durham and Northumberland, and after a long period in prison, a victim of the Titus Oates Plot, was murdered by being poisoned in Morpeth gaol by a surgeon who hated the patient he was summoned to assist because he was a priest and a Jesuit. Father Thomas Wilkinson was killed for his Faith and priesthood on 12th January, 1681. (Cf. An Article, *Stonyhurst Magazine*, " St. Omer's Roll of Honour, 10: Blessed John Plesington." April, 1955, pp. 108-111.)

In the *Memoirs of Missionary Priests,* pages 541 seq., it is mentioned by Bishop Challoner that John or William Plesington was descended from the Pleasingtons of Pleasington, near Blackburn, and was the younger son of Mr. Robert Plesington, who in the time of the Civil War was Governor for the King, Charles I, of Greenough or Greenhalgh Castle, Garstang, and who suffered imprisonment and the loss of his estates for his loyalty.

Father Plesington's first appointment, when he came to England, was at Holywell in Flintshire, and his zeal as a missioner there and elsewhere " joined to a certain candour and agreeableness in conversation," made him esteemed and loved by the well-disposed, but these good qualities raised against him enemies who were not so well disposed. These latter betrayed him and caused him to be arrested and prosecuted on the score of his priesthood. The charge made against him during his trial at Chester was that of high treason for having taken orders in the Church of Rome and of remaining in England contrary to the Statute 27 of Elizabeth Tudor. The

Blessed John Plesington did not suffer by reason of any false accusation of being involved in the Plot, but solely for his Faith and priesthood; " The Plot " was an opportunity and served as an occasion for the violent enforcement of the penal laws against priests and recusants.

It was unfortunate for themselves that the three witnesses that appeared against him were bad Catholics: they were, Margaret Plat, George Massey and Robert Wood. These swore that they had witnessed John Plesington's priestly functions, and upon their testimony the verdict against him was brought in as guilty, and he received sentence of death. In regard to the three perverted witnesses the following is an extract from a paper endorsed " Martyrs of England " in the Stonyhurst Collection: " The accusers of Mr. Plessington (sic) who was put to death at Chester, a city by the sea, were three in number, and all three died in strange ways a little after his condemnation but before his death. The first whilst helping to lift a vessel was crushed under it, and was the only one that died then, though there were twelve others who were in a more dangerous place and remained uninjured; and the ministers of justice who made the examination related under oath that, considering the circumstances of the place and the position in which the corpse was found, it seemed impossible that the vessel or any other thing should have touched him, and yet he was found so crushed that it was impossible to recognise him. The second was a woman who went altogether mad and so died. The third was found drowned in a ditch, where there was not above a foot of water." (*Foley's Records, S.J.,* Vol. 5, p. 410.)

An extract of John Plesington's last address at the scaffold is given as follows: " Thieves and robbers that rob on the highways would have served God in greater perfection than I have done, had they received so many favours and graces from Him as I have. But as there was never sinner who truly repented and heartily called to Jesus for mercy to whom He did not show mercy, so I hope by the merits of His passion He will have mercy on me, who am heartily sorry that I ever offended Him.

" Bear witness, good hearers, that I profess that I undoubtedly and firmly believe all the articles of the Roman Catholic Faith, and for the truth of any of them, by the help of God, I am willing to die; and I had rather die than doubt of any point of Faith taught by our Holy Mother, the Roman Catholic Church.

" In what condition Margaret Plat, one of the chiefest witnesses against me, was, before and after she was with me, let her nearest relatives declare. George Massey, another witness, swore falsely when he swore I gave him the sacrament and said Mass at the time and place he mentioned; and I verily think that he never spoke to me, or I to him, or saw each other except during the assizes week. The third witness, Robert Wood, was suddenly killed. But of the dead why should I speak? . . . That which remains is that I recommend myself to the mercy of my Jesus. O Jesus, be to me a Jesus." The Blessed John Plesington was hanged, drawn and quartered at Chester on 19th July, 1679.

Sixteen days later, another native of Lancashire was martyred at Worcester for his priesthood, the Blessed John Wall, O.F.M. He was born in 1620 at Chingle or Singleton Hall, Goosnargh and Whittingham, near Preston. He was the fourth son of Anthony Wall, the first of the name to hold the Chingle estates. His younger brother, William, also became a priest, and having survived the persecution finally retired as a Benedictine monk to Lambspring. Father William Wall, O.S.B., along with Father James Corker, O.S.B., both victims of Titus Oates, were arrested and acquitted of implication in the Plot, but tried again for their priesthood, and were condemned to death but reprieved and imprisoned in Newgate until their release at the accession of James II.

John Wall, the martyr, entered the English College, Rome, at the age of twenty-one on 5th November, 1641, and had resolved to enter as a paying-student, but his father, being unable, with his numerous family to support, to supply the money, John Wall took the College oath and was admitted among the Pope's alumni. He was finally ordained priest on 3rd December, 1645. He then returned to Douay and received the habit of St. Francis in the Convent of St. Bonaventure on New Year's Day, 1651, and took the name of Joachim of St. Anne, the parents of our Blessed Lady. After some years as Vicar of the Franciscan house at Douay, he became Master of Novices. In 1656, with a company of Franciscan missionaries, he went on to the English mission. Here he assumed the names of "Johnson" and "Webb," but during his sojourn in the Midlands and the scenes of his devoted missionary labours, he spent some time in London, where he met and conferred with that great apostle of the Devotion to the Sacred Heart, the Blessed Claude de la Colombière, who was then residing in the household of the Duke of York at St. James' Palace. The story of this holy meeting is reproduced here from *Brother Foley's Records, S.J.*, Vol. 5, pages 867-868:

"Just two years before, the apostle of the Sacred Heart of Jesus had been sent over by his superiors to visit the Court of the Duchess of York, in order to impart spiritual instruction to the numerous foreigners who had gathered round her in London. He came fresh from Paray-le-Monial, and was full of ardent zeal to propagate the beautiful devotion so lately revealed by our Blessed Lord Himself to the holy nun of the Visitation. During two years he had preached those lessons of Divine love in the Chapel of St. James's, and had kindled the sacred flame in many a breast amid the obloquy and persecution which overshadowed the Faith in England. Some few of our countrymen had contrived to slip in and hearken to his consolatory discourses. They may have imbibed such fervour from the revelations which he disclosed as to have enabled them to bear the terrible trials in store for them.

" The love of the Sacred Heart was no new doctrine. It had been revealed to the beloved disciple as he lay upon his Master's breast in the Coenaculum, and was well known to St. Augustine, St. Bernard and St. Gertrude; but it had recently been manifested to the Blessed (now Saint) Margaret Mary in the Chapel and the garden at Paray. The flame then kindled, smouldered imperceptibly, and was often seemingly extinct, until two centuries later it burst forth again among our Catholic countrymen when a pilgrimage departed from our shores to suspend the banners of England over the shrine where the mystery was revealed.

" Father Wall had heard of the famous young Jesuit, and was prepared to meet with one deeply versed in the science of Divine love; but when he found himself in the presence of the holy priest, it seemed to him as if the Apostle St. John had reappeared on earth to rekindle those flames from the Heart of Jesus with which his writings abound. His calm and beautiful countenance was precisely such as one may picture that of the beloved disciple, who stood beside the Cross when the lance pierced his Master's side, and revealed the material tabernacle of His ardent charity.

" ' Father,' he said, ' I am a poor minorite of St. Francis, come to seek strength and counsel of the Sacred Heart of Jesus, of which you are known far and wide among us as the Apostle. Among the friends I longed to see in London is one of your own Society, Father Turner (The Blessed Anthony Turner), now a prisoner in Newgate, looking forward to the blessed crown of martyrdom. Had I not been called away by my superiors I should ere this have been in prison, with the certain prospect of a similar reward, if God but grants me the grace to merit it by my constancy.'

" ' My friend,' said the holy man, ' you have indeed come to the fount of graces for the strength you need, and yet none can probe the mysteries of His Heart without tasting the cup of bitterness which He drained in the Garden of Gethsemini. Whoever takes up His Cross and follows in His wake, though he gain an hundredfold even in this life in the way of consolations, must yet feel the sharp edge of persecution. Oh, that I were granted this great grace which your English priests are reaping in this land of crosses; but God may yet have something in store for me.'

" ' Our Lord will not let you go hence, may be, without much suffering,' said Father Joachim of St. Anne (John Wall); ' but I foresee that your life will be spared to propagate this sweet Devotion, and re-kindle the flagging zeal in many hearts.'

" Thus communing, they spent together that day, which was the vigil of All Saints, in sweet converse on the love of Jesus; and it was not until after Father Wall had said Mass at the little Altar of the Sacred Heart, which Father de la Colombière had erected in his oratory, that they finally parted at dawn on the Feast. The former proceeded in the direction of Charing Cross, with a view of returning to his friend's house near to Clerkenwell, where he had left his horse."

Father John Wall's visit to the Blessed Claude de la Colombière was made during his arduous and dangerous apostolate in the Midlands, which covered a period of some twenty-three years. His centre of active ministration was in the Worcester districts and his principal Mass-centres were Harvington Hall, Rushock Court, near Bromsgrove and Purshall Hall hard by. His missionary excursions took Father

John Wall further afield into the regions of Birmingham:

"Not very long, indeed, before his capture, he happened to be at King's Norton, near Birmingham. Here he had a very narrow escape of being arrested, and was only saved by a Protestant gentleman who took pity on him, and, at his own peril, concealed him in his own house. The good Franciscan could not find words to express his gratitude, but before leaving his benefactor, he said to him: 'If it please God that I have to die for the Faith, I will offer my life's blood for your soul.' The gentleman's name was Thomas Milward. The martyr's holocaust was accepted by God, and five years after the tragedy at Worcester we find recorded in Father Leo Randolph's register, among those reconciled to the Faith: 'A.D. 1684. *Thomas Millward, of King's Norton, County of Worcester, 19th January.*'" Father Leo Randolph was Father John Wall's Franciscan missionary colleague. (Cf. *Forgotten Shrines*, p. 264, Dom Bede Camm, O.S.B.)

It was through an accident that Father John Wall was arrested when staying in the house of his friend, a Mr. Finch of Rushock Court. At midnight a raid was made on the house by a party in search of a gentleman who was in debt. Breaking down the doors, they entered a bedroom, in which they found Father Wall in bed. They soon guessed who he was and they carried him off in triumph. A certain individual named Rogers, who had betrayed Father Wall as a priest and had secured the priest's commitment to prison, on leaving the court immediately after taking a false oath, met suddenly with a strange but grave accident: while crossing a bridge he was knocked down by an ox and seriously injured. "His two companions, who had taken a like oath against the said priest, both of them died in a boiling cauldron, where one was trying to help the other who had fallen in; and the mistress of these two servants, who had advised them to commit the crime, had her own brother imprisoned in Newgate, and before the priest was put to death, this man was executed for having killed his own illegitimate child." (*Foley's Records, S.J.*, Vol. 5, p. 867, Footnote.)

Father John Wall was imprisoned at Worcester in the early December of 1678. During his term of incarceration, he was taken to London to be examined by Titus Oates and Bedloe, who, failing to fabricate any plausible connection of the martyr with the Plot, endeavoured to induce him with fair promises to take the forbidden oath of supremacy. Without betraying the fact that he was a priest, for the sake of the many notable Catholics and friends who had been giving him shelter, the Blessed John Wall firmly repudiated the unlawful oath and evaded the snares of his iniquitous examiners. The date of Father Wall's trial at Worcester before Judge Atkins was 25th April, 1679. The martyr said very little at his trial and the four witnesses against him were, with the exception of one, coerced to give their evidence. Nevertheless the jury after their retirement returned and brought in a verdict of high treason. The judge himself appears to have been disappointed, but was bound to pronounce the death sentence; for he was not immune from the epidemic of terror raging all over the country at that time and deliberately propagated by Shaftesbury's iniquitous and blackmailing agents. He frankly admired the prisoner before him, who was so palpably immune from it. After the passing of the death sentence, the Blessed John Wall made a bow and said in a loud voice: " Thanks be to God; and I beseech God to bless your lordship, and all this honourable bench." The judge replied: " You have spoken very well; I do not intend you shall die, at least for the present, until I know the King's further pleasure." The King had no delusions about those who were actually a menace to his royal life, and for the time being the royal wishes had very slender chances of being either communicated to the judge in question or to the man whose life he wished to save.

The place appointed for the execution was at Red Hill, near Worcester, a spot already blessed with the blood of two Jesuit martyrs: a priest, the Blessed Edward Oldcorne, and a Jesuit lay-brother, the Blessed Ralph Ashley, who were both hanged, drawn and quartered for the Faith at Red Hill on 7th April, 1606.

On 22nd August, 1679, the Blessed John Wall was taken to the same place and hanged, drawn and quartered for his priesthood.

During his last days in prison, the Blessed John Wall was attended in all his spiritual needs by the good priest, Father William Levison, whose brother, the Franciscan, the Venerable Francis Levison who had been arrested for the Plot, died of his sufferings in Worcester gaol, 11th February, 1680.

CHAPTER 18

NO DEFEAT

JOHN PENKETH, a Liverpool man, barely escaped execution for his priesthood and devoted apostolate during this period. He was born in 1630 at Penketh of Catholic parents whose noble lineage gave the locality its name. The family had become impoverished because of recusancy and loyalty to the ancient Faith. In his early years he had received a good preliminary education as he himself states: " I have made my studies under private tutors and at private schools. I was always a Catholic, and left England on the 13th of August, 1651, to proceed to Rome where in the family of Christ I shall be more sure to avoid the vanities of the world and its dangers, being moved also to this by an ardent desire of gaining souls, if found worthy of the priesthood."

For a time he studied at St. Omer's, and in spite of his strong desire to become a priest, he generously offered to go into service in some nobleman's household to relieve the family expenses. Instead of this, he went to the Low Countries, where he served as a soldier in the wars of the time. There was no faltering in his vocation and soon he was able to resume his studies.

He was ordained priest at Rome on 17th December, 1657, and for a period was the Spiritual Father and Confessor of the English Benedictine nuns at Brussels. In April, 1662, he left to become a Jesuit, and after his profession in the year 1666 he went on to the English mission. For a time he was an itinerant missioner, residing at the Stonyhurst mansion of the Shireburns, to whom he was chaplain with liberty to minister to Catholics in the neighbouring villages. Of these Chipping was the more thickly populated. " This ancient manor was held by Richard de Chepin soon after the Conquest. It subsequently passed to the Knowles family and afterwards to the Shireburns. Leagram Hall, now the seat of John Weld, Esq. (i.e. in the nineteenth century), with the manor was granted by Queen Elizabeth Tudor to Dudley, Earl of Leicester, of whom Sir Richard Shireburn purchased it. This mission was served from a very early period by the Fathers of the district, most probably from the mansion of Stonyhurst, the seat of the Shireburns. According to tradition, Father John Penketh was a missioner there. The mission ceased to be served by the Jesuits in 1857." (*Foley's Records, S.J.,* Vol. 5, p. 339.)

After this Father John Penketh served in other parts of Lancashire, for example, at Bedford, Leigh and at Culcheth, a township in the region of West Derby, and it is thought that as early as 1670 he was serving Leigh from Culcheth. However, during the period 1678-1679 when the storm of persecution broke forth like a sudden whirlwind, although he had received timely warning to go into some safe place of concealment, the priest ignored it and remained with his flock. Beset by stratagems and perils, he took fresh courage and fervour. Word was brought to him that a number of persons in a remote village desired his ministrations. The Father rose in the dead of night, taking with him a man who was trusty and well acquainted with the road. They had gone one or two miles only when they unexpectedly met a Justice of the Peace, named Risley, who was well known to the priest from whom the same Risley had received many favours and acts of kindness. This man civilly accosted Father Penketh as an intimate friend, invited him into his house, and insisted on the guide entrusting him to his care.

The Father, not suspecting any deceit, committed himself to Risley's care accordingly.

He detained the priest, however, that night as his prisoner. The next day Father Penketh was taken under arrest to Lancaster gaol to be tried at the assizes. Risley collected witnesses and, although most had taken flight, so as not to be forced to give evidence against their wishes, he captured four of them and used his authority to compel them to perform the unwelcome task.

Father Penketh was arrested and imprisoned at the same time as another missionary priest, Father Richard Barton. Both were tried at Lancaster and condemned to death for the Faith and the priesthood, but the sentence was not carried out and they were detained in prison, until their release at the accession of James II. (*C.R.S.*, Vol. 48, p. 426. n. 471.)

The chief accuser of John Penketh was formerly a penitent of his, who had fallen in love with the daughter of a Justice of Peace, a stiff Protestant, and was persuaded by her, under a promise to marry him, to accuse Penketh. As this witness was coming back from the court after having accused the priest, he was taken ill and in the space of ten days died with much contrition, confessing to all that visited him his grievous sin. " The person who told me this," says the narrator of the incident, " was present when the disconsolate father of the young woman, with her mother and sister, came to the prison some eight days after his death and, kneeling at Father Penketh's feet, with many tears begged his pardon in the dead man's name . . ." (Cf. *Foley's Records, S.J.*, Vol. 5, pp. 334-335, Footnote.)

A third priest, who was tried and condemned to death with Penketh and Barton, but reprieved with them, died of his sufferings in Lancaster gaol. He was the Rev. Richard Birket. The year of his death is given as 1680. It appears that he had lived at Brindle or in the neighbourhood; that he had an entire estate of his own, and gave £400 to be invested, the interest of which was to be devoted to the help of the Catholics of Brindle. In the reign of James II, by the assistance of the congregation, a chapel at Brindle or Slatedelf, now called South Hill, was built but, in consequence of the Revolution breaking out soon after the arrival of William of Orange, and the no-Popery disorders, little use could be made of it. After the Jacobite Rising of 1715, the Commissioners then sitting in Preston seized upon it as forfeited by reason of " superstitious uses." It appears that it could easily have been bought back by local Catholics of means, but the bitter reactions after the short-lived period of optimism during the reign of James II had broken the spirit if not the hearts of many Catholics. No one in the locality was willing to make the purchase, although a trifle would have redeemed it. Thus the chapel remained until 1734, when it was converted into a workhouse. The bell, after lying buried for many years, was dug up and sold to Eccleston chapel and the old altar rails went to the same chapel. The proceeds were apparently spent afterwards on the house and chapel at Slatedelf.

A steady and fair-minded survey of the horrors suffered by loyal Catholics, for well over a century before the reign of the last Stuart, will enable anyone to realise the extent of the relief, joy and optimism of Papists when James II became King. It ought not to be difficult to gauge the dreadful chagrin and hopeless disappointment, when after so short a respite the nightmare of persecution like a black pall enshrouded again the lives of the faithful.

As in the case of many other devoted priests, so in that of Father John Penketh, it was a broken heart that killed him. The no-Popery riots brought this valiant soldier of Christ to his knees: " Broken down with apostolic labours, succumbed. He was very old and scarcely able to stand when, being called to the bedside of a sick man, he hastened thither, consoled him, administered the Sacraments, and with great difficulty returned home. He was immediately seized with his last illness and, fortified with the Last Sacraments, John Penketh, alias Rivers, died on 1st August, 1701, at the age of seventy-one.

In Jesuit archives at Rome it is stated of him that "what is required to render a man an apostolical labourer and a perfect Jesuit, all this was found in Father John Penketh."

The following extracts from *Foley's Records, S.J.*, Vol. 7, page 800, in reference to the large farm called Haighton Hall mentioned *ut supra* in chapter 10, page 132, will be of great local interest, and all the more so, because of the built-up priests' hiding place in the cellar under the main living-room. Only a part of the original Hall remains at the present time.

"The Wadsworth family originally came from Yorkshire into Lancashire. John Wadsworth, grandson of James Wadsworth, of Halifax, county York, settled in Lancashire, and his son Hugh married first the daughter of William Farrington, Esq., who, however, died without issue. By a second wife there were born to him two sons, Robert and Nicholas, the latter of whom married the daughter of Robert Albin of Whittingham, Lancashire, who brought him lands in Haighton, Whittingham and elsewhere. The issue of this marriage was Hugh, the eldest son; Robert, who went overseas to study in 1655; and a daughter, Elizabeth, who married successively John Singleton and Thomas Carter, and is described as Mrs. Cosey in 1704.

"Hugh Wadsworth of Haighton Hall, gentleman, the eldest son, returned a pedigree at the visitation of Dugdale in 1664, and was living in 1671. He married Margaret, daughter of Christopher Towneley, second son of John Towneley of Towneley, and his wife Margaret, daughter and heiress of Sir Richard Towneley, Kt., and had issue Nicholas, Robert of Preston, gentleman, in 1703, and Christopher. Nicholas, the eldest son, of Haighton Hall, Lord of the Manors of Fulwood, Great and Little Caddeley, was aged nine at the visitation of 1664, and died 23rd October, 1702, leaving by his wife, Judith, a large family as follows: Hugh Wadsworth of Haighton Hall, gentleman in 1704; Robert Wadsworth, who after studying for some years at a school kept by the Jesuits at Scarisbrick Hall, Lancashire, was sent to Douay in 1700, and was afterwards living at Clock House, Fulwood; Nicholas, living in 1709; Joseph Wadsworth of Catterall, Lancashire, gentleman, who took an active part in the Stuart rising of 1715, for which he was executed at Garstang, 14th February, 1716; William, living in 1709; Thomas Wadsworth, S.J., Scholastic, born December, 1693, entered the Society of Jesus, 7th September, 1712, and died at Liege, aged twenty-six, on 16th July, 1719; Anne, unmarried in 1722; and Dorothy, wife of Richard Shuttleworth, of Brockside, Lancashire, gentleman."

The Nicholas Wadsworth, head of this large family, was one of the number of the local Catholic gentry who secured the lease of the land, including Ladywell and the old chapel at Fernyhalgh. The present chapel is about a quarter of a mile away from the site of the old chapel at Ladywell, and was built along with the presbytery by the Rev. Anthony Lund in 1795, who also laid out the cemetery. The heroic courage and apostolic energy needed and expended on this undertaking at that time will, it is hoped, appear in the subsequent chapter.

CHAPTER 19

THE DARKEST HOUR

IN the seventeen-thirties, Father Cornelius Morphy, a Jesuit, served the mission at Brindle and Slatedelf, a man beloved of his flock and neighbours. "Regarding him it is recorded that a gang of priest-catchers came to take him off, when several of the neighbours, who heard of the matter, went and hid themselves behind a hedge leading to the chapel, being determined if the gang succeeded in bringing him off, to rescue him or lose their lives. The gang, however, did not take him, though he was at home, his mild language having softened their hearts; and as the pursuivants returned, his friends, concealed quietly behind the hedge, heard the fellows laying the blame on each other for not bringing him away with them; and so they remained till the priest-catchers had gone by." (*Foley's Records, S.J.*, Vol. 5, pp. 338-9.)

In this adventure, Father Cornelius Morphy was more fortunate than many other priests in the Lancashire mission field at the time. From the year 1688, throughout the eighteenth century until the year of the Catholic Emancipation, 1829, was a period of obscure heroism of hunted priests and their scattered flocks. The Catholic nobility were driven from their rightful place in English society, and in the majority of cases had been robbed of their homes and estates. So the missionary priests of those days possessed less than hitherto the advantages of comparatively secure homes and safe harbourage.

The Titus Oates persecution and the Orange Revolution had everywhere in the country seriously depleted the number of priests, through deaths and banishment, so that the remaining scattered clergy were in truth chosen soldiers of Christ, fighting a last stand in the trenches, the ditches, the holes and the garrets.

The Catholic Record Society has already stored in its volumes a gold mine of heroic apostolic labours and incidents along with those preserved in the *Records of the English Jesuits,* compiled by Brother Henry Foley, S.J., formerly an eminent townsman and lawyer of Worcester. If, therefore, the complete story of this dark period were brought out in a single volume, Catholics and all interested readers would be astonished and edified by the glory of the struggle and the ultimate victory of what has been too readily accepted as an inglorious period.

It is beyond the scope of this little book to attempt the whole tale, as it was lived out in Catholic Lancashire, and there is only space available in this concluding chapter to make reference to a few of the incidents by way of example. There were some well-marked crises which excited local and anti-Catholic animosity to spates of cruel mob-persecution: The landing of William of Orange in 1688, the Jacobite Rising of 1715, the second Jacobite Rising of 1745, and the " Gordon Riots " during which almost by a miracle of providence the saintly Bishop Challoner escaped from cruel murder. All these crises were interspersed with localised anti-Papist mob-raids up and down the country which inflicted intense sufferings on priests and people.

" When James II came to the throne, local Catholics of Fernyhalgh and district courageously set about building a new chapel on the old site by the well (Ladye Well). In 1685, half an acre of the Chapel tenement was bought from Hugh Charnley, yeoman, who for a certain sum of money, and for other causes and considerations, granted a lease thereof for a thousand years to George Leyburne of Nateby, Nicholas Wadsworth of Haighton, Cuthbert Hesketh of Whitehill, Goosnargh, and Robert Shepherd of Broughton, gentleman . . . The building was designed to look like the larger houses of the district . . . the ground floor was the priest's house, and a big upper room served for the chapel. The whole cost £225 7s. 2½d., and was finished by the end of 1686. Catholics flocked to it, so that in September, 1687, Bishop Leyburne could confirm 1,099 people there . . . but dark days soon again descended. William of Orange had driven James across the sea and the Jacobite rebellions did not make matters easier for the faithful of Lancashire. The incumbent of Ladye Well, the Rev. Christopher Tuttell, had to flee in 1700, 1714, and 1718 . . . In 1718, a determined raid carried off vestments and plate from neighbouring houses in which they had been hidden and, in 1718, soldiers secured booty to the value of £100, while the Rev. C. Tuttell and his nephew, who was assisting him, the Rev. Edward Melling, barely escaped with their lives." (*C.R.S.*, Vol. 31, pp. 1-2.)

In connection with Fernyhalgh, mention should be made of Alice Harrison, called also Dame Alice. She was born at Fulwood Row, near Preston, was well educated and brought up a member of the State church. She was converted by reading Catholic books. She remained firm, was severely persecuted, corporally chastised, and when this would not reclaim her, turned adrift by her father. She was encouraged by the priest at Fernyhalgh, probably the Rev. Edward Melling, to open a school near Fernyhalgh, on the top of the hill near the chapel at Ladywell.

She had a numerous school, and children flocked to her not only from the neighbourhood of Preston and the Fylde, but also from Liverpool, Manchester, London and all parts of England. She admitted scholars of all religions to the number of between 100 and 200. She had one other assistant called Mary Backhouse. The scholars boarded, some with the Dame and others in the cottages and farm-houses of the neighbourhood. They paid 1/6d. per quarter to the Dame for schooling, and £5 per annum for board and lodging and all, on their way to and from the school, always stopped to say a Pater, Ave and Credo at Our Lady's Well. The Rosary, Litanies, etc., were said every day, but those pupils and children who were not Catholics were at liberty to absent themselves from these devotions if they pleased.

All the people in the district of Fernyhalgh were Catholics at the time, and not only encouraged but protected the little Dame. Dame Alice lived to a great age, and in her decline was indebted for a comfortable retreat to the Catholic family of the Gerards. When she died she was buried in the Catholic portion of the cemetery at Windleshaw, near St. Helens. Dame Alice had retired from her labours in 1760, so that the period of her fruitful school-work would have been from 1727 to 1760, and during that time she not only founded an efficient Catholic school but maintained it throughout a period of persecution. What is still more creditable is the fact that her school became a nursery of many vocations to the priesthood and the religious life. The names of some of her pupils, all distinguished priests, are given here: the Rev. Richard Kendal, President of the college at Standon Lordship, and his younger brother, the Rev. Hugh Kendal, President of the college at Sedgeley Park. Both of them were born at Fulwood, Preston; the Rev. James Willacy, President of Old Hall Green College, born at Catforth; the four brothers, priests, Richard, Ralph, Thomas and William Southworth, direct descendants of Sir John Southworth of Samlesbury Hall. The Rev. Thomas Southworth succeeded the Rev. Hugh Kendal in the year 1781 as President of Sedgeley Park, a post he held for some ten years. He died in 1816.

Fuller information is contained in *Biographies of English Catholics,* by the Rev. Dr. John Kirk, D.D., pages 111-112 and page 215. John Kirk was born on 13th April, 1760, and died on 21st December, 1851. According to his account, Dame Alice's school after her retirement in 1760, was carried on by one of her pupils, Mr. Peter Newby, who communicated many details to a Mr. Gradwell, from whom Dr. Kirk obtained information. Interesting details were also supplied by a Miss Singleton of Preston, an old lady who had been one of Dame Alice's scholars and who for many years afterwards had boarded several of her pupils.

The locality of Fernyhalgh was not the only district to suffer from cruel mob-persecution in more or less the same neighbourhood. " After the Popish Plot, Catholicism revived with the accession of James II, and in the short-lived optimism of that period, the same Cuthbert Hesketh of White Hill (Goosnargh), who had proved a benefactor to Fernyhalgh, planned even more generously for his own locality. He gave a plot of land at White Hill to the English Province of the Franciscans in 1687 whereon they established ' the residence of the Holy Cross,' described shortly after Dutch William's landing as a ' chapel and a little dwelling at one end.' Cuthbert Hesketh had given £200 (yielding £10 a year) for a missioner who was bound to say two Masses per week for the said Cuthbert and his wife, to serve the poor Catholics of Goosnargh and ' Chipping,' and, if so permitted, to live permanently at the chapel of White Hill (the locality is known now as Whitechapel). In answer to this pious wish, the mob tore the roof off the chapel, the walls were ordered to be levelled, and the materials were either sold or laid up safely. At this time the Reverend John Appleton was serving the mission." It seems certain that the name is Father Henry Appleton, O.F.M., who was serving the Goosnargh mission,

1710-1738. (Cf. *The Franciscans in England*, 1600-1850, by Father Thaddeus, O.F.M., p. 187.)

But there was worse to follow: " Shortly after 1715, when the attainder of the Heskeths led to the closing of their domestic chapel, another chapel was opened in the building near the old Hall at White Hill, and the Franciscans placed a member of the local family of the Holmes, Father Germain Holmes, O.F.M., in charge of it. Here he worked unobtrusively among his own people, until the Jacobite rising of 1745 stirred up a revival of persecution, when Father Germain was seized and carried off to Lancaster. He died in the Castle gaol there, a confessor for the Faith, in 1746." (*C.R.S.*, Vol. 31, pp. 166-167.)

The lists of recusant Catholics from Chipping, Leagram, Bowland and Thornley-cum-Wheatley during the years 1715-1716 contain surprising numbers of devoted people, when compared with the small congregations of Catholics in those rural regions at the present time. Like their co-religionists in other parts of Lancashire, large numbers of them had been reduced to penury by sequestrations, fines and other invidious kinds of economic and social persecution for their Faith. Driven from their homelands and homesteads, they were compelled to crowd into the neighbouring towns like Blackburn and Preston to find a livelihood in the growing industries of cotton-mills, mines and iron works. In numerous cases their very names denote kinship with the erstwhile noble families of the county.

In the north of Lancashire, the manor house of a great and steadfast Catholic, Sir Thomas Preston, at Dalton in Furness, was served as a Catholic centre by many notable priests, among whom was Nicholas Grimshaw. " The Rev. Nicholas Grimshaw, the other Catholic chaplain at the manor, baptised 9th December, 1630, was the second son of John Grimshaw, of Clayton Hall, county Lancaster, Esq., by Anne, daughter and co-heiress of Abraham Colthurst of Burnley, Esq., a family now represented by the Trappes-Lomax, of Clayton Hall. According to Dugdale's visitation of Lancashire in 1664, Nicholas Grimshaw was a student at Douay in Flanders, though he does not appear under his own name in the printed diaries of the college. When he became a chaplain to Sir Thomas Preston is unrecorded, but he was one of them at the time of the raid on the manor in 1678. Upon his flight he seems for a time to have sought refuge with his brother at Clayton Hall, but the latter and his wife, Elizabeth, daughter of Stephen Tempest of Broughton Hall, county York, Esq., were both arrested, convicted of recusancy and heavily fined in 1679, in which year it is probable that Nicholas Grimshaw himself was apprehended and possibly died in prison, as he totally disappears from sight . . . This raid appears to have completely broken up the chaplaincy at the manor, and it was never revived so far as is known. The estate was soon afterwards seized by the Crown, and Mass ceased to be said at Furness Abbey." (*C.R.S.*, Vol. 20, p. 6.)

Previously, another apostolic Lancashire priest had served the Catholics at the Manor, Dom John Dionysius Huddleston, O.S.B., born on 15th April, 1608, at Farington Hall, Leyland . . . he it was who, when stationed at Somerset House, the palace of the Queen-Dowager, reconciled Charles II to the Church on his death-bed, 5th February, 1683.

The mission of St. Andrew's, Cottam, always a stronghold of the Faith, suffered atrociously during the eighteenth century: " Rev. Gilbert Haydock, a younger son of the Squire of Cottam, William Haydock, the elder, and his wife, Jane, the daughter of Hugh Anderton, of Euxton Hall, Lancashire, was born at Cottam Hall in 1682, and was sent to Douay, where he took the oath of the alumni, 8th September, 1703 . . . he went to Cambrai to receive the two major orders in 1706, and was ordained priest there in 1708, leaving Douay for the mission in his native country in April, 1709. On the mission it is reported that his apostolic zeal and labours were attended with the happiest effects in the conversion and care of souls. Following upon the defeat of the Jacobite Rising at Preston in 1715, a raid was made on Cottam Hall, and Gilbert Haydock was discovered hiding in a great oak tree in what was formerly the park at Cottam, the site of which is known to this day as ' Catch-field.' He was seized and committed to Lancaster Castle, where he endured several months' incarceration on account of his sacred calling. While still a prisoner, he received the appointment of confessor to the English Augustinian nuns of the convent of St. Monica, Louvain, where, having obtained his release, he arrived on 1st August, 1716 . . ." (Cf. *C.R.S.*, Vol. 15, p. 109.)

A more serious onslaught on the Catholic congregation at Cottam is given as follows: " The Rev. John Harrison, born 21st September, 1714, son of John Harrison of Lea, adjoining Cottam, yeoman, and his wife Elizabeth, daughter of Christopher Walmesley, of Preston, was the priest at the time, who served Cottam. He was sent to Douay College, where he arrived in September, 1729, and there was ordained subdeacon 2nd April, 1739, deacon 1st April, 1741, and priest at Arras on the following 23rd December, after which he left the college to take charge of the mission at Cottam. The retreat of Prince Charles in 1745 was followed by a wave of persecution, and ' No-Popery' mobs roamed about the country, destroying Catholic chapels and other property. After wrecking St. Mary's in Friargate, Preston, the ruffians marched to Cottam, and attacked Mr. Harrison's house and chapel and, though he resisted with intrepidity, both were burnt down, after which for two years no Mass was said at Cottam. The Rev. John Harrison then removed to Towneley Hall, the seat of the Towneleys, which he served for thirty-three years, until his infirmities obliged him to retire from missionary labour in 1779, and he withdrew to the house of his brother Lawrence, in Friargate, Preston, where he died on or about 16th January, 1780, aged sixty-five. Until the chapel either was restored or a new one erected at Cottam, the Catholics of the district had to attend the neighbouring missions at Preston, Ladywell, Salwick Hall, Mowbreck Hall, and Newhouse, Newsham." (*C.R.S.*, ibid., p. 110.)

This was not the end of trouble at Cottam: " In 1768, during the anti-Jacobite and Non-Popery ferment in Preston, an infuriated mob, after destroying St. Mary's Chapel in Friargate, and burning that at Cottam, moved in the direction of Newhouse with the intention of demolishing the chapel there. Mr. Hankinson, a neighbouring Protestant, met the rioters near Hollowforth Mill and persuaded them not to molest the Rev. John Carter, probably a son of Robert Carter, a yeoman of Thistleton. Mr. Hankinson highly praised the priest, and then appeased them by giving them something to eat and drink, after which the mob marched back to Preston." (Ibid., p. 320.) In those troublous times the priests held on to their missionary posts, in many cases sleeping in their chairs at night-time so as to be at the ready for sick-calls and on the alert for raids.

The Rev. James Smith of Lea Town completely broke down under the strain of superintending the building of the new chapel at Lea. He was " born 25th December, 1775, son of James Smith, formerly of Hazleheads, but latterly of Ward's House, Salwick, and was sent to the English College at Valladolid in Spain, where he was ordained priest and came to reside with his father at Ward's House, and superintend the erection of the new chapel . . . dedicated to St. Mary . . . and priest's house at Lea Town, to which he was appointed by the Bishop. Here he remained till his health broke down and he exchanged missions with the Rev. James Haydock, chaplain to the Traffords of Trafford House, near

Manchester. His health, however, grew worse, and in the following year he had to retire from missionary duty, and eventually died in the hospital at Manchester, 26th January, 1827." (Ibid., p. 156.)

The Catholic Trafford family, with the exception of the lapse of a kinsman in the reign of Elizabeth Tudor, retained throughout the penal days not only a strong faith but a certain measure of prosperity, which by Divine providence and the generosity of the family was largely utilised in providing for the needs of isolated and scattered groups of Catholics in the districts adjacent to Manchester. The chaplain from Trafford House had a large and extensive mission, including Barton, Eccles, Pendleton, Pendlebury, Patricroft, Stretford, Sale-Moor and Altrincham. In 1792, the energetic Father James Haydock, a kinsman of a martyr, with all the help Mr. John Trafford of Trafford House could give him, strove with successful results to save from the wreckage much of the fruit of the Blessed Ambrose Barlow's apostolic labours. In the districts outlined there were at the time no more than about 300 Catholics and the chapel at Trafford House, although not very large, was sufficient for the time being. The harvest was not long in coming, for in 1856 Sir Humphrey Trafford gave a new and larger school at Trafford to replace the old one, and in 1868, the same Catholic gentleman built the present fine church at Trafford at a cost of some £24,000. (Cf. *Haydock Papers,* pp. 205-7.)

After the Reformation and all through the penal period, St. Mary's, Friargate, was the mother-chapel of Preston. The locality was formerly the site of a much larger religious establishment consisting of the conventual buildings of the Franciscans, until the suppression of the monasteries and religious houses. The name " Friargate," however, has remained and it is apparently more than a mere coincidence that the locality contained a spot that was reserved for the little chapel, from which in course of time the other Catholic parishes in Preston have either directly or indirectly originated.

Although twice destroyed by anti-Papist rioters even after Catholic Emancipation in 1829, an anti-Catholic and riotous mob for a third time set upon and destroyed St. Mary's, Friargate, in the year 1852. Undaunted by any of these heart-breaking reverses, the Jesuit missioners built the present-day chapel in 1856, and shortly after, in luminous white rose, St. Walburge's with the great spire; a landmark for miles around, denoting the triumph of the ancient Faith and the victory of those who died and suffered for it in the county.

"Father Alexander Leigh, S.J., a native of Lancashire, born 1681, became a Jesuit at Watten, 4th December, 1700, under the alias of John Layton, junior, and was professed of the four vows, 2nd February, 1718 . . . In 1712-1719, he was a missioner in Worcester and throughout that district. In 1728-1729, he was serving in the Suffolk district, and in 1730 at Preston, his address being, ' To be left at the White Bull in Preston.' He purchased a house in Friargate, Preston, in 1733, which was then used as the only Catholic chapel in the town. The old chapel of St. Mary was built in 1761." (*Foley's Records, S.J.*, Vol. 7, p. 448.) A more detailed account follows.

"In the reign of James II the Catholics of Preston had been accustomed to attend divine service in a barn at Fishwick, a township adjoining Preston, and it was probably there that Bishop Leyburn gave Confirmation when he visited Preston in 1687. A tenement at the lower end of Friargate was subsequently used. This house is supposed to be the same which in 1733 was purchased by Father Alexander Leigh and was called ' Grey-stocks.' It now forms part of the site of St. Mary's, Friargate. The house was used as a chapel until the year 1761, when a bold step was taken and the old chapel of St. Mary was built by Father Patrick Barnewall. The greatest caution was used; the chapel was built behind the front houses in Friargate so as to be quite shut out from view. The mysterious building was carried on in the name of Mr. Clifton of Lytham, and passed by the name of the ' new building ' . . . The chapel was dedicated in honour of our Blessed Lady. Father Barnewall did not live to see the results of his courageous step; he died the next year, 1762, soon after the opening. In 1763, a ' No-Popery ' cry was raised, the new chapel was forcibly entered and gutted by the mob, and Father John Smith, the missioner, had to fly for his life, which he only saved by crossing the Ribble on horseback.

" From the earliest ascertainable period, the mission in Preston was entirely under the charge of the Jesuits, until the erection of the beautiful and commodious church of St. Augustine in 1838-1840 . . .

" Until the year 1774 Father John Jenison was the only priest supplying the mission; but owing to the increase of the congregation, he was allowed an assistant in the person of Father Nicholas Sewell, who was left in sole charge in 1775 Father Sewell the next year wrote to invite his old confrère Father Joseph Dunn, then serving at Callaly Hall, near Alnwick. In his letter, he says: ' I don't know which is the best road. There is no fly across the country, and you must either come by a post-chaise or a horseback, as you are become so good a jockey. When you come, ask for Friargate, and then inquire where I live, or where the old priest lives.' " (Cf. *Foley's Records, S.J.*, Vol. 5, pp. 394-396.) Thus " Daddy Dunn " came to Preston, and St. Wilfrid's was built in 1783.

" The heroic clergy of the dark period, whether secular or regular, wrote little or nothing of their own sufferings during those days of heart-breaking persecution by the somewhat hidden hand of opposition and frustration; a powerful hand that at any moment could seize and grip its victim. There are plenty of instances, and one may be selected under the head of ' Scholes,' near Prescot, Lancashire, a mission founded in 1728 by a member of the Catholic Sefton family, the Rev. William Viscount Molyneux. It is stated that long before that date there had been two Catholic chapels, each about two miles from Prescot, one of which to the north-east, at Wolfall Hall. This mission had been served by a Dominican Father from Bornheim; but the last priest there was the Rev. John Green . . . From the records of the Leeds Sessions held in 1745, the following extract relating to the same priest . . . shows that the flame of persecution was not extinct at that date, nor yet the constancy of the faithful clergy to their holy religion.

" ' Whereas a person who calls himself John Green, of Sunderland Hall, near Ribchester, in the county of Lancaster, gentleman, was lately apprehended at Halifax . . . and brought before this court upon suspicion of being a Papist, and a person disaffected to His Majesty's person and Government, whereupon the oaths of allegiance and supremacy appointed to be made . . . were tendered and read over to the said John Green here in open court, and the said John Green refusing to make repeal and subscribe the said oaths and declaration pursuant to the statutes in that behalf; and upon his examination here in the said open sessions, confessing himself to be a Papist, and that he was travelling from place to place, and not making it appear that he hath any certain and fixed habitation or place of residence, nor giving a sufficient reason for his travelling in the manner aforesaid; and this court having a good cause for suspecting him to be a Popish priest, and of carrying on a treasonable correspondence with Papists and persons disaffected to His Majesty,

King George, and the Government of these kingdoms; and the said John Green appearing to this court to be a very dangerous person, it is therefore ordered that the said John Green be committed to His Majesty's gaol, the Castle of York, kept for the county of York, there to be detained in safe custody until he shall be discharged by due course of law.' " (*Foley's Records, S.J.,* Vol. 6, p. 694.) This good priest, like his colleagues at the time, had to make long and arduous journeys in obedience to a summons from afar for the ministrations of a priest, and he rightly did not think the Halifax pursuivants and the gentlemen of the assizes at Leeds the proper authorities to whom he had to give an account of his stewardship. Such proceedings and events explain the incident in connection with another notable Catholic Lancashire man of those days: " William Massey of Puddington, Esq., the eldest son of Edward Massey, and his wife, Alice, daughter of Richard Braithwait (sic), of Barnside, county Westmoreland, born 15th May, 1658. He was a zealous Catholic and warmly attached to the Stuart family while upon the throne, and after the Revolution (1688), having given his allegiance to James II, he did not conceive that anyone but the Prince who had received it could release him from the obligation thereby contracted. In 1715 he joined the Stuart Rising and is traditionally said to have fled home after the Battle of Preston, and to have effected his escape to the Wirral by a desperate adventure of swimming his horse over the Mersey below Hooton. He was seized at Puddington Hall, imprisoned in Chester Castle and died shortly after. He was buried at Burton, 15th February, 1718." (*Foley's Records, S.J.,* Vol. 7, p. 735, Footnote.)

In the meantime, the adventure of the priest who was serving the mission at Westby in the Fylde proves more than ever that in the eighteenth century the penal laws and statutes were not dead letters. This priest was Father Edward

Barrow, a Jesuit, who was born at Westby in 1660 and was most probably the son of John Barrow, yeoman, who appears as a recusant in Westby-cum-Plumpton, 1667. Edward Barrow became a Jesuit at Watten on 7th September, 1683, and was admitted to his final vows on 2nd February, 1693. He was sent on to the English mission in Lancashire and was appointed chaplain to the Cliftons at Westby Hall. It is very probable that he was related to the Jesuit martyr, the Blessed William Barrow, a victim of the Titus Oates Plot persecution, who himself was born at Weeton, a district in the Fylde adjoining Westby.

After the defeat of the Jacobites in 1715, one of the two High Constables for the Amoundness Hundred, a certain John Smith, made out his report and returns in reference to the township of Westby-cum-Plumpton, and delivered them to the " Hon. Commissioners for Forfeited Estates given over to Superstitious uses." John Smith handed his returns in to these authorities in October, 1716, and among them is the report that " About a year ago, one Mr. Barrow, a Popish priest, was convicted at the Lancaster sessions, 15th January, 1716-1717, as a Popish recusant under the description of Edward Barrow, reputed Romish priest . . . he was outlawed." (Cf. *C.R.S.*, Vol. 15, pp. 3-4.)

The constable in question had not been able to capture this priest and so the accountant-general to the Forfeited Estates Commission, Mr. Chambers Slaughter, " was very anxious to catch Father Barrow, and the description he gives of his proceedings in his correspondence with the Commissioners reads like a romance, or a thrilling narrative of a priest-hunt in the days of Elizabeth Tudor. Father Barrow took refuge at Lytham Hall, but paid repeated visits to Westby Hall." (Cf. *Haydock Papers*, pp. 232 seq.)

From the same sources it is reported that Slaughter himself discovered various hiding-places in the chapel, and obtained from them "a large quantity of folio books, among which were several MSS., a large gilt head of St. Ignatius, some altar linen and a crucifix, also priest's vestments, some household linen, and a large picture of the Virgin Mary, which I suppose by the size covered the wall at the altar."

"As these goods were being conveyed away," the report of Slaughter continues, "the date being 9th March, 1716, the people of Kirkham came out and, unharnessing the horses, put them back in the stables from whence they had been hired, in order to convey Father Barrow's books, etc., to Preston." Mr. Chambers Slaughter, whose object was to apprehend Father Barrow at all costs, continues his report: "But by the help of a constable and some other assistance, I secured the horses and brought away the goods." (Ibid., *C.R.S.*, loco citato.) Father Barrow, however, was never captured and in spite of all Mr. Chamber Slaughter's efforts, remained at Westby Hall until his death in August, 1721, aged sixty-one.

Westby Hall is no longer in existence, having been incorporated into farm-buildings, but the usual " upper-room " chapel over a lower-storey farm dwelling was built, to which access was provided by an outside flight of rough stone steps. The last Jesuit priest serving the mission at Westby Hall was Father Joseph Postlewhite, S.J., born 7th April, 1784, son of William and Elizabeth Postlewhite of Westby. This old " step-up " chapel was eventually dismantled and the new church of St. Anne's, Westby, was solemnly opened on 26th August, 1860.

A typical example of a " step-up " chapel provided for Catholics in the days of persecution may be seen to this day in Alston Lane, Grimsargh, with the farm dwelling on the lower storey, which was provided from a part of the estate of the Catholic recusant family of the Hothersalls. When the Reverend Henry Sharples came to Alston Lane in 1849, he built the present church from the designs of Mr. Hansom in 1854. For many years the old room of the " step-up " chapel was used as a school, until 1927 when the new schools were built and opened. The old chapel is now a dwelling house.

Most of the country chapels built in nearly every part of Lancashire during the eighteenth century and elsewhere by the dauntless industry and persevering Faith of the persecuted Catholics still bear the unmistakable style of the dwelling-house with the large upper room. Whether it is the chapel at Gillmoss, or at Fernyhalgh, Cottam, Newhouse, Lea, Claughton, or even at the renovated church of St. Mary's Friargate, the style is that of the first Apostolic chapel, the Coenaculum, with its " upper room "—the style of the Church in persecution.

The Catholics of Wigan suffered no less than their brethren in Preston and elsewhere. In both towns, at the accession of James II, " there was a great and joyful harvest." On 14th and 15th September, 1687, the good Bishop Leyburn had confirmed as many as 1,331 persons at Wigan. The harvest may be truly said to have been great and joyful. " This may be truly said of Wigan, where the foundations of a handsome College had been laid. Some of the Jesuits resided there and taught classes numbering more than a hundred scholars. The old chapel was so small as hardly to contain half the numbers that flocked to it. There were constant sermons which the Mayor or chief magistrate of the town and his suite were accustomed to attend. The materials for building a new church were already prepared, and a site for the College fixed upon, when the Revolution broke out. A furious and excited mob then destroyed to the foundations all that had been raised, and scattered it to the winds." (Cf. *Foley's Records, S.J.*, Vol. 5, p. 319 and p. 403.)

Other than the martyrs and itinerant missionaries of earlier days, the earliest stationary Jesuit missioner at Wigan " was

Father James Canell, who was probably there during the time of the destruction of the foundations of a new mission and college. He is named in a document signed by Miss Clare Gerard, dated 3rd April, 1696, by which she directed the four executors named in her will, viz., William Gerard of Garswood, Esq., John Gillibrand of Chorley, Richard Worthington and Thomas Worthington of Wigan, Esquires, to pay the interest of a small legacy towards the maintenance of a priest in or about Wigan." (Ibid., p. 405.)

Father Canell died at Wigan in 1722 at the age of seventy-three. Other Jesuit missioners at Wigan were Father Piers Mostyn and Father Charles Brockholes. Father Mostyn became third baronet on the death of his father on 15th November, 1720, but apparently did not use the title. He died among his devout parishioners at Wigan, being only forty-five years of age on 29th August, 1735. He was succeeded by Father Charles Brockholes who served the mission from nearby Blackrod until 1740, when he came to Wigan permanently. He died there on 20th February, 1759, at the age of seventy-five. He is generally considered to have been the greatest promoter of the Wigan mission in those times: he built a house and a chapel out of his own patrimony, which he was permitted to use for the purpose.

Within the vicinity of Wigan and St. Helens, a district which had been blessed with so many Lancashire martyrs and confessors, the old Collegiate church at Upholland in the Middle Ages appears to have resurrected itself in the college of St. Joseph's, Upholland, nobly renovated and rebuilt. The college of St. Bede's, Manchester, has a strong bond of faith with the ancient Collegiate church, whose warden died in prison for his priesthood and the Faith. To the Catholic people who pay their visits in large parties each year, Stonyhurst is not only a monument of past history, nor just a great Catholic public school; it is a tangible expression of the unbreakable continuity of the ancient Faith and is irrevocably interwoven into the Catholic life of England.

In conclusion, the martyrs and confessors who have been presented in a gruesome pageantry were very English. All of them had a strong appreciation of the good things of life upon which they deliberately turned their backs, for the sake of their Faith and for the salvation of souls. The modern mind will find it difficult to capture the true significance of the brave stand they made, but the defect cannot be laid at their door. Their secret is summed up in the beautiful words of the priest-poet, Gerard Manley Hopkins, S.J.:

> " *O feel of primrose hands, O feet,*
> *That want the yield of plushy sward;*
> *But thou shalt walk the golden street,*
> *And house and unhouse the Lord.*"

INDEX OF MARTYRS AND CONFESSORS